Microsoft Word 2003 for Seniors

Addo Stuur

Microsoft Word 2003 for Seniors

Getting Familiar with Word Processing

www.visualsteps.com

This book has been written using the Visual Steps™ method.
Cover design by Studio Willemien Haagsma bNO
Copyright 2006 by Visual Steps B.V.

Translated by Grayson Morris and Marleen Vermeij
Edited by Ria Beentjes and Marleen Vermeij
Proofread by Chris Hollingsworth

First printing: April 2006
ISBN 90 5905 184 X

Would you like more information?
www.visualsteps.com

Do you have questions or suggestions?
E-mail: info@visualsteps.com

Website for this book:
www.visualsteps.com/word2003
Here you can register your book.

Register your book
We will keep you aware of any important changes that are necessary to you as a user of the book. You can also take advantage of our periodic newsletter informing you of our product releases, company news, tips & tricks, special offers, etc.
www.visualsteps.com/word2003

Table of Contents

Foreword

Word processing is without a doubt one of the computer applications that has helped to make the Personal Computer (PC) so popular.
I first made use of it when writing my thesis during my college years. For a sloppy typist like me, even a primitive computer was a fantastic invention: no more fiddling with correction fluid or having to type pages over and over again. Though the programs back then were very limited and hard to use, I never touched another typewriter. The program *Word 2003* that you will work with in this book is a marvel of technology compared to those early programs. It has a wealth of features and is not hard to use.

I hope you enjoy this book.

Addo Stuur

P.S. Your comments and suggestions are most welcome. My e-mail address is: addo@visualsteps.com

Introduction to Visual Steps™

The Visual Steps manuals and handbooks offer the best instructions on the computer expressway. Nowhere else in the world will you find better support while getting to know the computer, the Internet, *Windows*, and other computer programs.

The Visual Steps method, which makes all of our books for seniors so special, features the following:

- **Content:** The special needs and requirements of the beginning user with little or no technical background have been taken into account.
- **Structure:** Self-paced, learn as you go. Proceed step by step with easy-to-follow instructions. What's more, the chapters are organized so that you can skip one or repeat another as desired.
- **Illustrations:** Plentiful use of screen illustrations to show you whether you're on the right track.
- **Format:** Full-sized book and large print make it easy to read.

In short, these are manuals that I believe will be excellent guides.

Dr. H. van der Meij

Faculty of Applied Education, Department of Instruction Technology, University of Twente, the Netherlands

What You'll Need

In order to work through this book, you'll need to have a few things on your computer.

 The most important requirement for using this book is that you have the US version of **Microsoft Word 2003** installed on your computer.

 Your computer should also have the US version of **Windows XP**.

 You'll need a working **Internet connection** if you want to visit the website for this book. Among other things, the website contains extra practice material and tips.

 We recommend a printer for some of the exercises. If you don't have a printer, you can just skip the printing sections.

Prior Computer Experience

This book assumes a minimum of prior computer experience. Nonetheless, there are a few basic techniques you should know in order to use this book. You need to be able to:

- click, double-click, and drag with the mouse
- start and stop programs
- type and edit text
- start up and shut down *Windows*

⇨ Please note:

If you don't have a basic knowledge of word processing, read through **Appendix B** first.

If you don't know how to do these things yet, you can read the book ***Windows XP for Seniors*** first:

ISBN 90 5905 044 4

Paperback

US $19.95
Canada $26.95

Windows XP for Seniors has been specifically written for people who are taking their first computer steps at a later age. It's a real "how to" book. By working through it at your computer, you can learn all the information and techniques you need to enjoy working with your computer. The step by step method ensures that you're continually learning how to get the most out of your computer.

What You'll Learn
When you finish this book, you'll have the skills to:
- work independently with your computer
- write a letter using your computer
- create illustrations
- adjust your computer settings so you can work with it most comfortably

For more information, visit
www.visualsteps.com/winxp

How to Use This Book

This book has been written using the Visual Steps™ method. It's important that you work through each chapter **step by step**. If you follow all the steps, you won't encounter any surprises. In this way, you'll quickly learn how to use *Word 2003* without any problems.

In this Visual Steps™ book, you'll see various icons. This is what they mean:

Techniques
These icons indicate which technique you should use:

⊂⊃	The mouse icon means you should do something with the mouse.
▦	The keyboard icon means you should type something on the keyboard.
☞	The hand icon means you should do something else, for example turn on the computer.

Sometimes we give you a little extra help in order to work through the book successfully.

Help
You can get extra help from these icons:

⇨	The arrow icon warns you about something.
✖	The bandage icon can help you if something's gone wrong.
✓	The check mark icon appears in the exercises. These exercises help you to reinforce the techniques you've learned.
👣1	Have you forgotten how to do something? The number next to the footsteps icon tells you where you can find it in the appendix *How Do I Do That Again?*

This book also contains general information and tips about computers and *Microsoft Word 2003*. This information is in separate boxes.

Extra Information
Information boxes are denoted by these icons:

	The book icon gives you extra background information that you can read at your convenience. This extra information is not necessary for working through the book.
	The light bulb icon indicates an extra tip for using *Word 2003*.

The Website for This Book

This book has its own website, where you can find practice texts and current information. Any changes or errata that are important for working through the book will also be announced on this website.

You can visit the website at this address:

www.visualsteps.com/word2003

Practice Files

Chapters 1, 2, 3, 4, 5, and 6 in this book make use of practice texts and photos. You can find these files on the website.

You can download the files on the page *Practice files*:

You can read how to download these files in **Appendix A** in the back of this book.

1. Changing Your Word Settings

Word 2003 is a word processor with many features. In addition to the many options for processing and editing text, it allows you to adjust the program settings to suit your own needs.

When you start *Word 2003* for the first time, you'll be using the manufacturer's default settings. You may be satisfied with these at first. Once you have a little more experience, you can change these settings to optimize *Word 2003* to your way of working.

To get the screen shots in this book to match what you see on your own screen, you will sometimes need to change certain settings in *Word 2003*. We will discuss these changes in the chapters where they are needed.

In this chapter, you'll learn how to:

- start *Word 2003*
- change smart menu settings
- change toolbar settings
- change ruler settings
- open a practice text
- change the way *Word 2003* displays documents
- display hidden formatting marks
- turn off the Assistant
- close *Word 2003*

➡ Please note:

To work through this chapter, you'll first need to download the files
Internet Connections.doc and Ben Franklin.doc from the website and save them in the
 My Documents folder.

You can read how to do this in Appendix A at the back of this book.

Starting Word 2003

You can start *Word 2003* using the *Start button*:

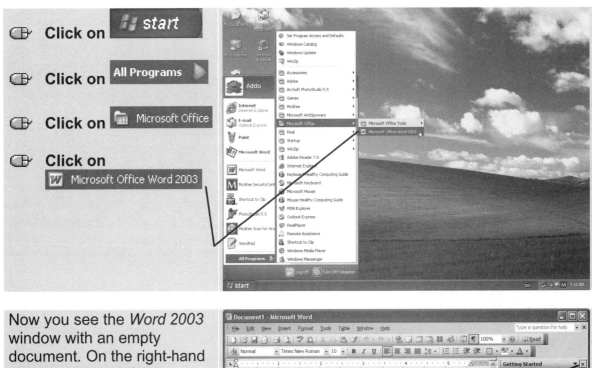

Click on [start]

Click on [All Programs]

Click on [Microsoft Office]

Click on [Microsoft Office Word 2003]

Now you see the *Word 2003* window with an empty document. On the right-hand side you see the *Getting Started* Task Pane. You won't need this window in this book.

Click on ☒ to close the *Getting Started* Task Pane

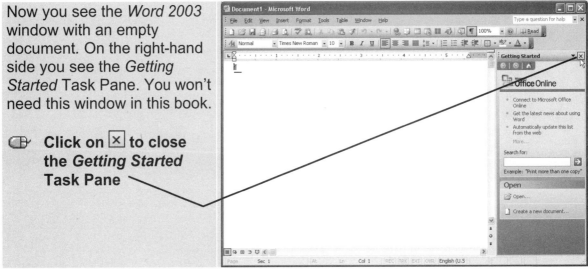

You can adjust many different *Word 2003* settings to your preferences. To have the screen shots in this book match what you see on your screen, you can change your *Word 2003* settings to match the examples in this book.

Smart Menus

Word 2003 features collapsible/expandable menus or so-called "smart" menus. Some people question the value of this setting, however, and it is especially confusing for beginning users. You can see what a smart menu is if you click on one of the menus.

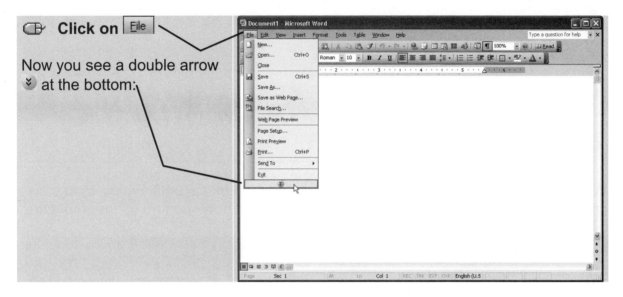

Click on File

Now you see a double arrow ✹ at the bottom:

➡ **Please note:**

The list of commands may look different on your screen.
Word 2003 always shows the most recently used commands first.

✖ **HELP! I don't see any arrows.**

Then smart menus are turned off in your *Word 2003*.
☞ **Just skip this section**

Click on ✹

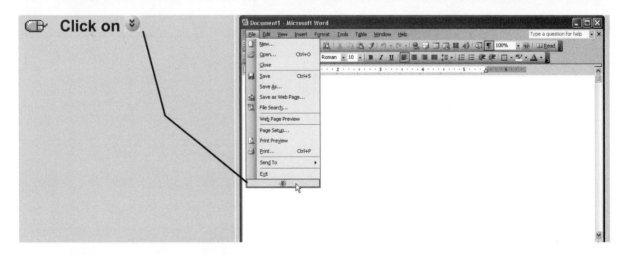

Now you see that the list has expanded to include more commands:

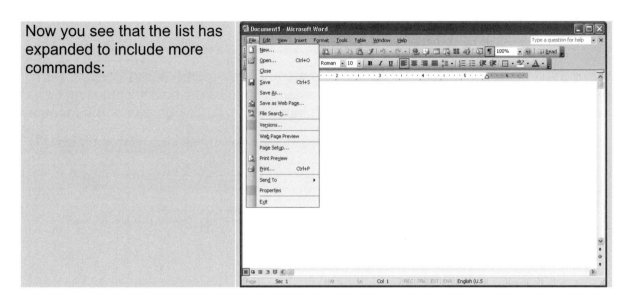

We'll turn off the smart menus so that the screen shots in this book match what you see on your screen. Most users like that better. Here's how you turn off smart menus:

Click on View

Click on Toolbars

Click on Customize...

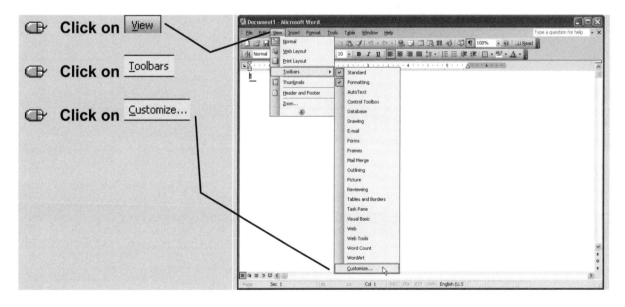

Now you see the *Customize* dialog box:

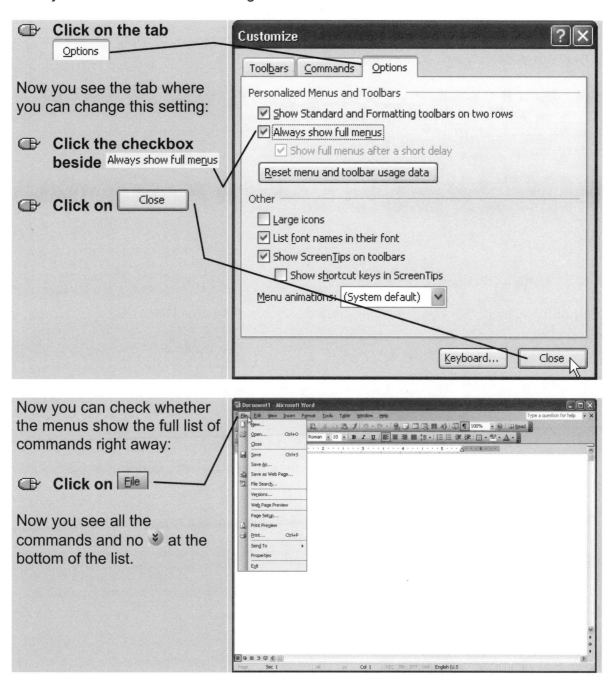

☞ **Click on the tab**
Options

Now you see the tab where you can change this setting:

☞ **Click the checkbox beside** Always show full menus

☞ **Click on** Close

Now you can check whether the menus show the full list of commands right away:

☞ **Click on** File

Now you see all the commands and no ⏷ at the bottom of the list.

The *Word 2003* settings have now been changed. When you click on a menu, you will see all the commands.

Changing the Toolbar Settings

You're going to set up *Word 2003* so that you see two toolbars. A toolbar consists of a bar with buttons. Each button has a particular function.

You see at least one toolbar at the top of the *Word 2003* window: ──────

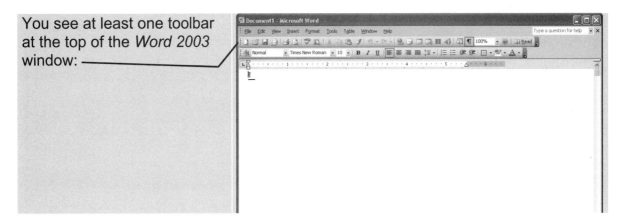

The number of toolbars you see depends on your settings for *Word 2003.*

By default, *Word 2003* shows this toolbar: The *Standard* toolbar.

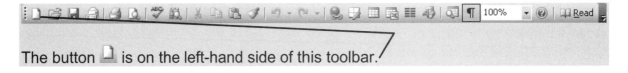

The button ⬜ is on the left-hand side of this toolbar.

These kinds of toolbars are separate elements that you can put in different places in the window.

First, you're going to check which toolbars are active. Here's how you do that:

☞ **Click on** `View`

☞ **Click on** `Toolbars`

Now you see a list of toolbar names:──────

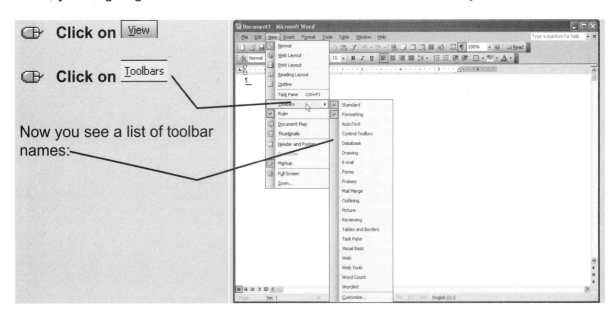

Right now, you only need the *Standard* toolbar.

☞ **Make sure there is only a check mark beside** ✔ Standard 👣7

☞ **Make sure there is <u>no</u> check mark beside the other toolbars** 👣5

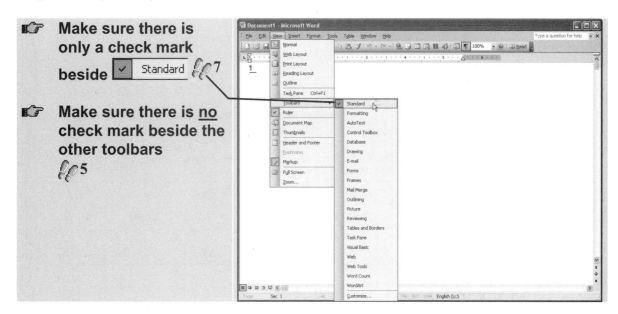

You can drag a toolbar with the mouse to another place in the window.

A toolbar has a kind of handle ⋮ for this on the far left-hand side:

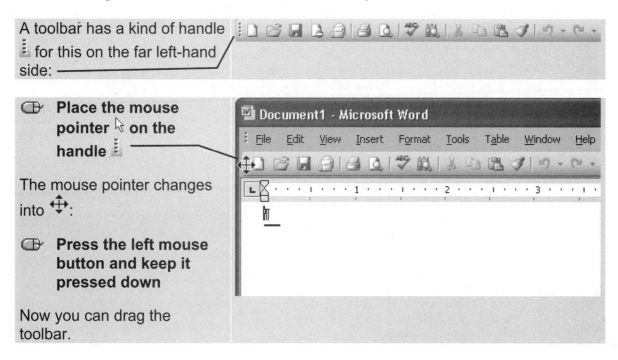

☞ **Place the mouse pointer** ↖ **on the handle** ⋮

The mouse pointer changes into ✛:

☞ **Press the left mouse button and keep it pressed down**

Now you can drag the toolbar.

Drag the arrow to the center

You see that the toolbar changes into a floating toolbar:

Release the mouse button

The floating toolbar is now in the center of your screen.

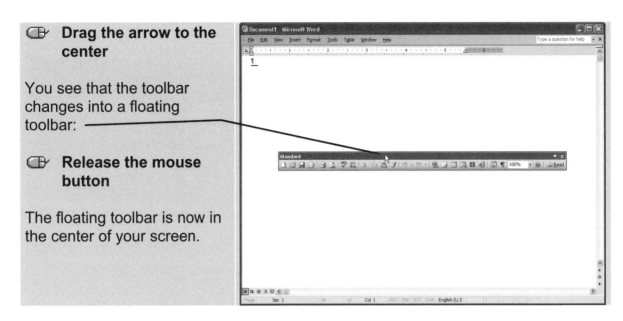

You can drag the toolbar to the top of the main window this way.

Place the mouse pointer on the dark blue portion of the toolbar

Press the mouse button and keep it pressed down

Drag the toolbar upward

You see that the toolbar no longer floats and snaps back into place:

Release the mouse button

The toolbar is back in its regular spot.

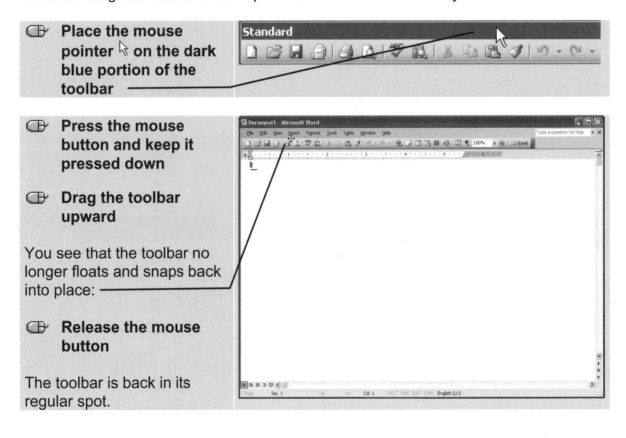

You can also drag the toolbar to the side or the bottom of the window. You can try that yourself.

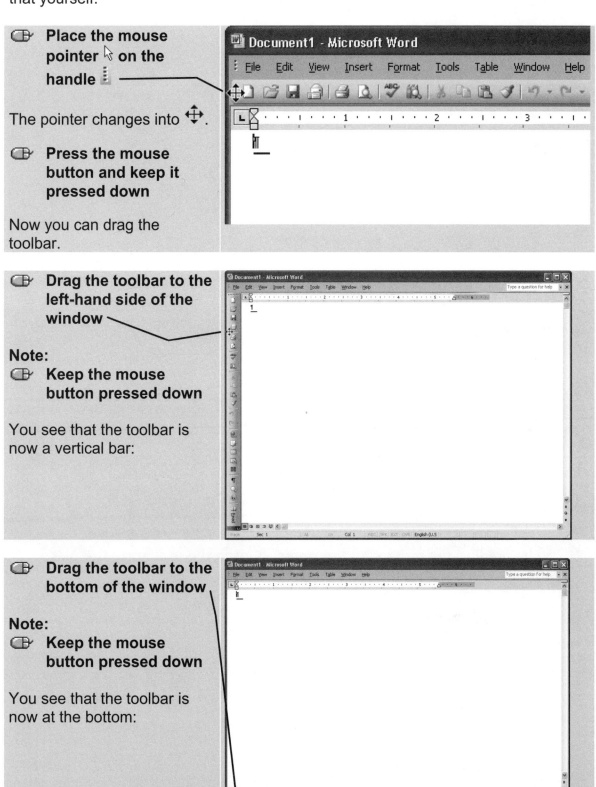

☞ **Place the mouse pointer on the handle** ──────

The pointer changes into ✛.

☞ **Press the mouse button and keep it pressed down**

Now you can drag the toolbar.

☞ **Drag the toolbar to the left-hand side of the window**

Note:
☞ **Keep the mouse button pressed down**

You see that the toolbar is now a vertical bar:

☞ **Drag the toolbar to the bottom of the window**

Note:
☞ **Keep the mouse button pressed down**

You see that the toolbar is now at the bottom:

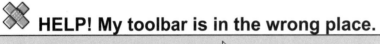

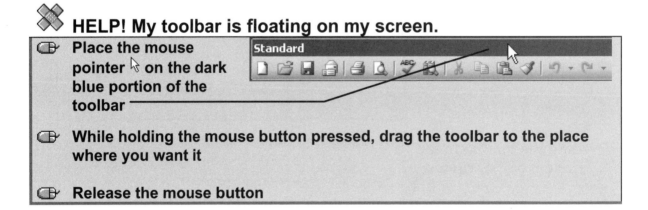

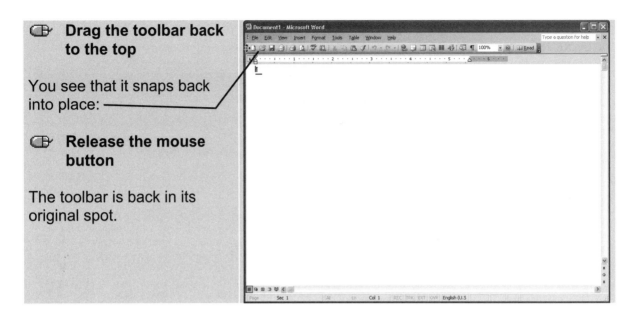 **Drag the toolbar back to the top**

You see that it snaps back into place: —————

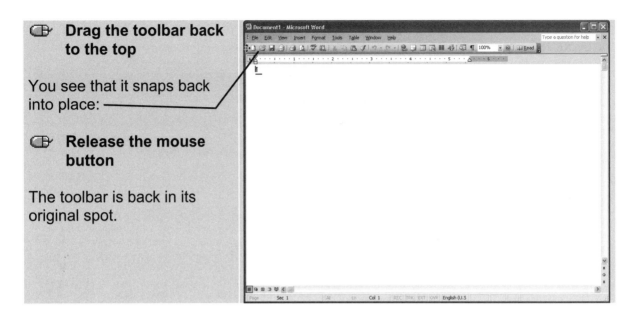 **Release the mouse button**

The toolbar is back in its original spot.

HELP! My toolbar is in the wrong place.

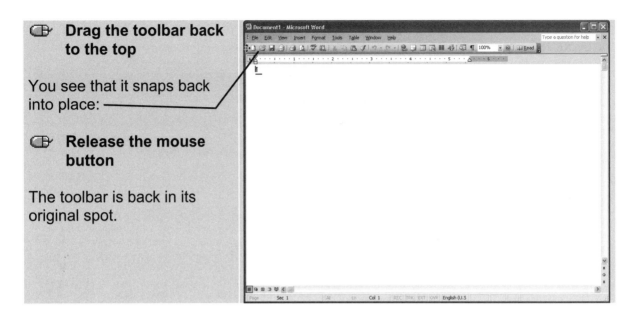 **Place the mouse pointer ▷ on the toolbar's handle ⋮. The mouse pointer turns into ✥**

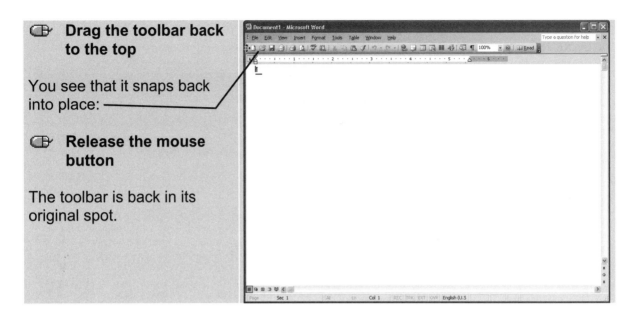 **Drag the toolbar to the right place**

HELP! My toolbar is floating on my screen.

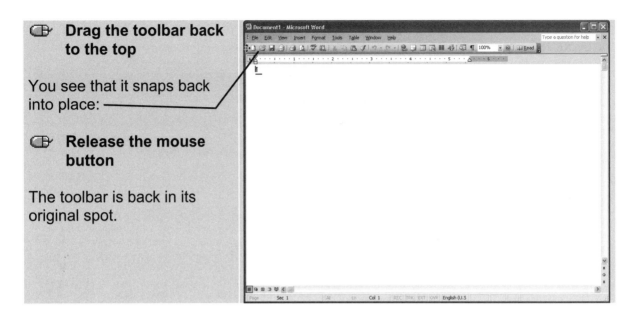 **Place the mouse pointer ▷ on the dark blue portion of the toolbar** ——————

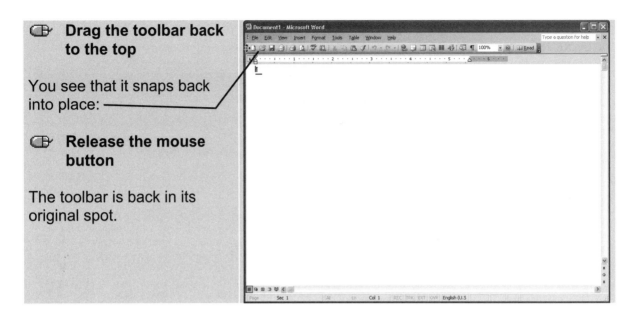 **While holding the mouse button pressed, drag the toolbar to the place where you want it**

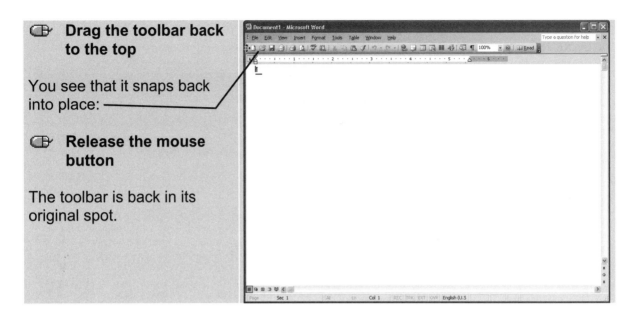 **Release the mouse button**

The Formatting Toolbar

Another handy toolbar to have open while working through this book, is the *Formatting* toolbar.

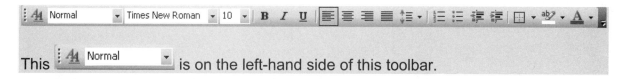

This 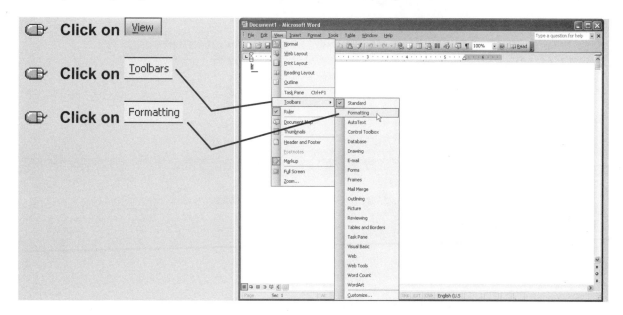 is on the left-hand side of this toolbar.

First, you're going to activate this toolbar. Here's how you do that:

👆 **Click on** View

👆 **Click on** Toolbars

👆 **Click on** Formatting

You can put the *Formatting* toolbar in different places in the window.

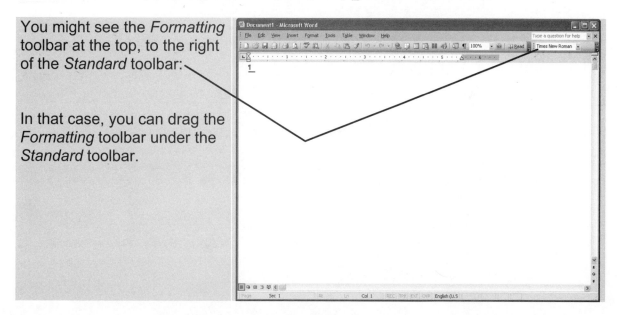

You might see the *Formatting* toolbar at the top, to the right of the *Standard* toolbar:

In that case, you can drag the *Formatting* toolbar under the *Standard* toolbar.

You might see the *Formatting* toolbar under the *Standard* toolbar:

In that case, the toolbar is already in the right place.

You might see the *Formatting* toolbar floating:

☞ **See where your *Formatting* toolbar is**

🖱 **If necessary, drag it under the *Standard* toolbar**

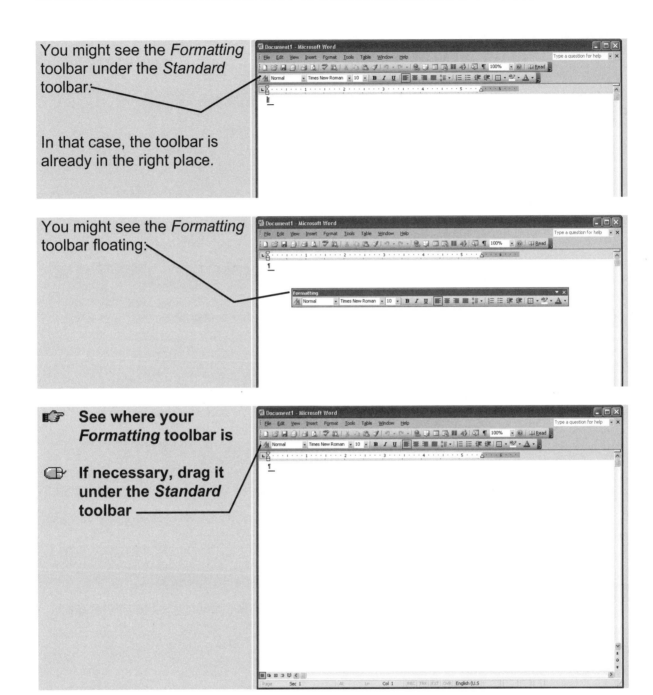

Word 2003 now shows two toolbars: the *Standard* toolbar, and underneath it, the *Formatting* toolbar:

The Ruler

It's convenient when you're formatting text if you can see the ruler at the top of the window:

If you don't see the ruler, you can activate it like this:

Click on View

Click to place a check mark beside Ruler

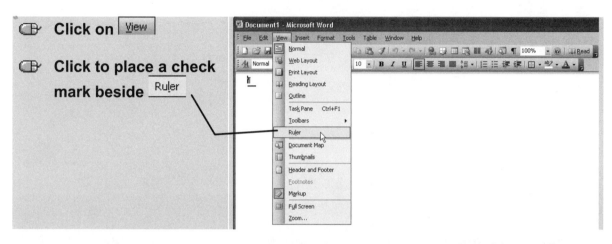

The ruler should now be visible under the toolbars:

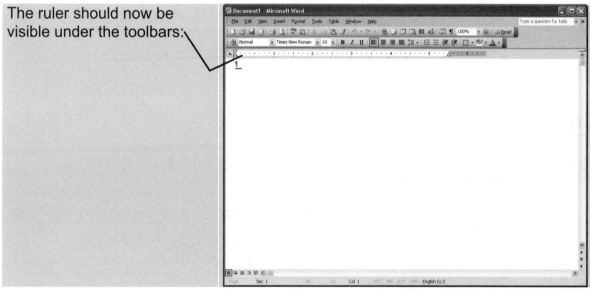

Closing a Document

You can close this window with an empty text now.

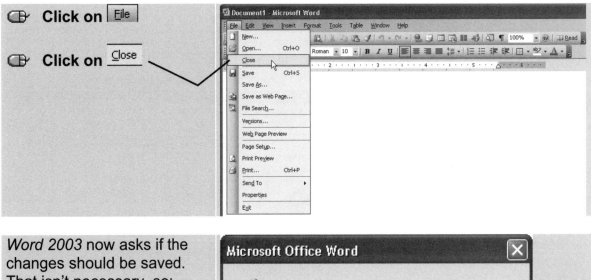

👆 **Click on** File

👆 **Click on** Close

Word 2003 now asks if the changes should be saved. That isn't necessary, so:

👆 **Click on** No

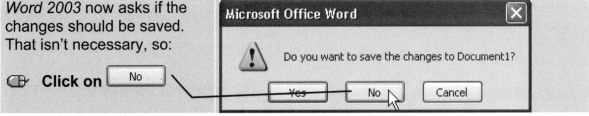

The empty document has now been closed.

Opening a Practice Text

You'll need to open a downloaded practice text to work through the rest of this chapter. Here's how you do that:

👆 **Click on** File

👆 **Click on** 📂 Open...

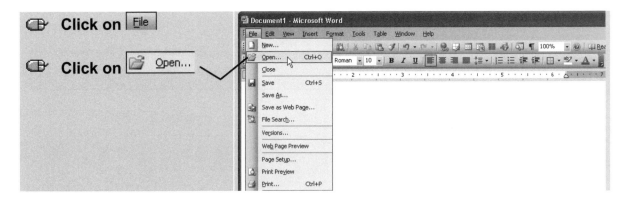

When you downloaded the practice files from the website, you saved them in the
📁 My Documents folder.

You see the *Open* dialog box:

☞ **Click on**
   [Internet Connections.doc]

☞ **Click on** [Open]

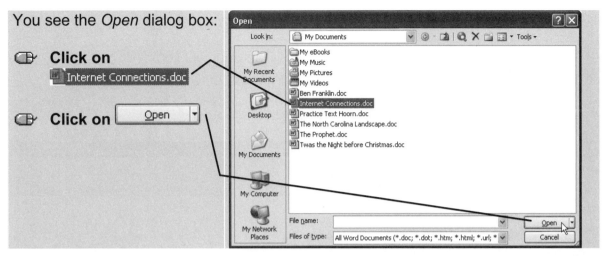

Now you see this text:

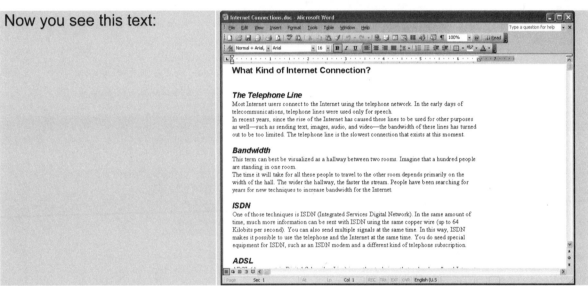

Viewing Your Documents

Word 2003 can display text in different ways.

☞ **Click on** [View]

At the top of the menu, you see various ways to display a document:

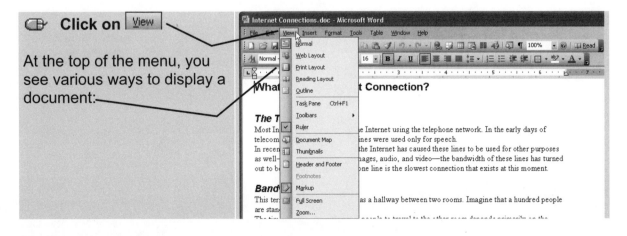

These are the two most important:

- the *Print Layout* view: this shows you what the page will look like on paper
- the *Normal* view: this is the best view for entering text

You can see the difference between the two like this:

Click on

    Print Layout

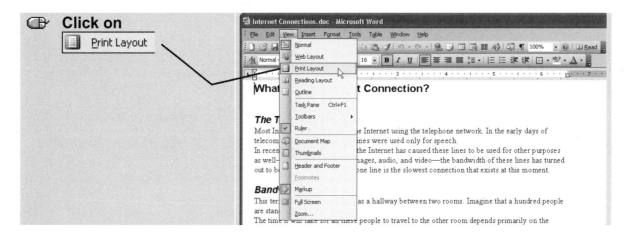

Now you see the sheet of paper the way it will look when it is printed:

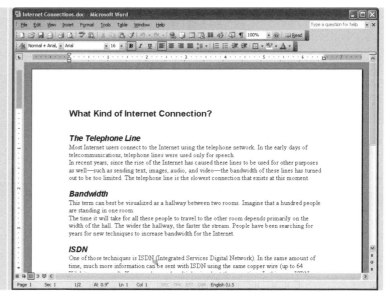

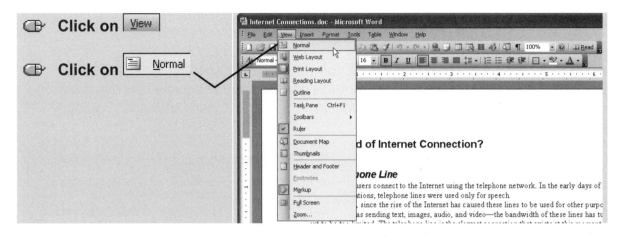

Now you just see a white work area where you can edit the text:

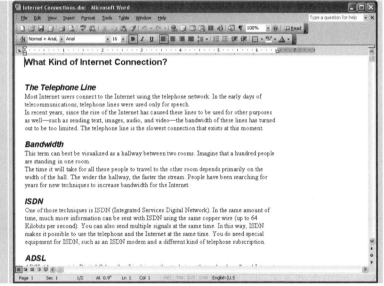

The setting you like best is a matter of preference. We will mostly use the *Print Layout* in this book.

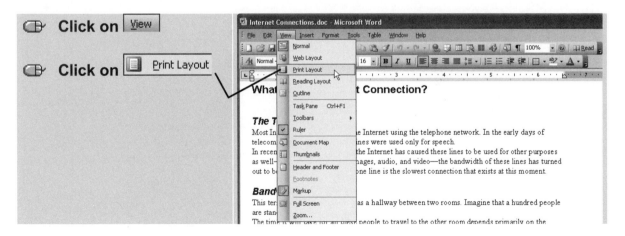

Hidden Formatting Marks

Word 2003 uses a number of symbols you usually don't see and that don't get printed. These include symbols to mark the end of a paragraph and for a tab. When you format text, it can be useful to know how to display these hidden formatting marks. Here's how you do that:

Click on Tools

Click on Options...

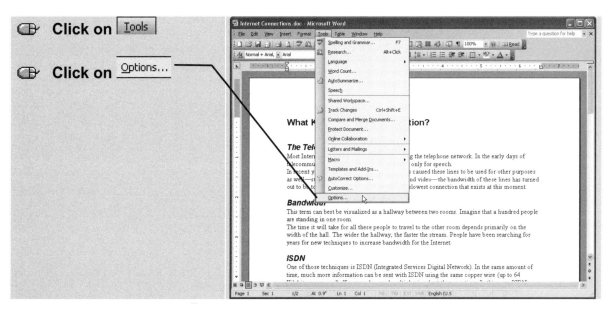

You see the *Options* dialog box:

Click on the tab View

You select the display for formatting marks here:

Click on the checkbox beside All

Click on OK

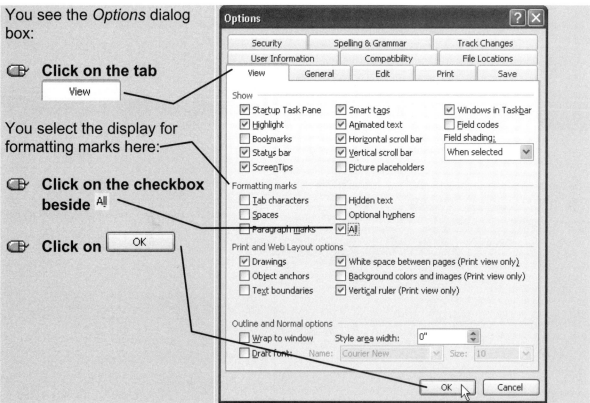

Now you will be able to see all the hidden formatting marks.

Now you see various strange symbols in the text: These symbols only show up on your screen. They won't be printed on paper.	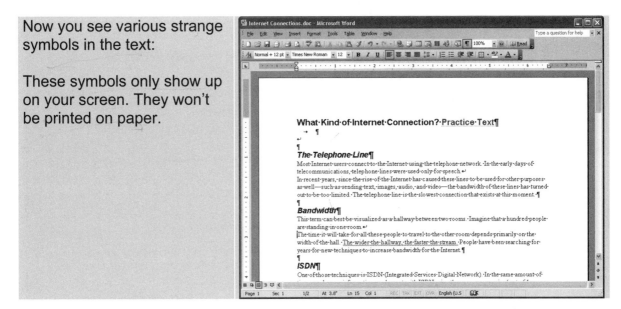

The most important symbols used in this book are:

A space (a dot ·)	**of·Internet**
An end-of-paragraph mark	¶
An end-of-line mark	↵
A tab symbol	→

There are other symbols which aren't used in this book.

An optional hyphen	¬
Hidden text	**Practice·Text**

You can turn the hidden formatting marks back off.

☞ **Click on** Tools	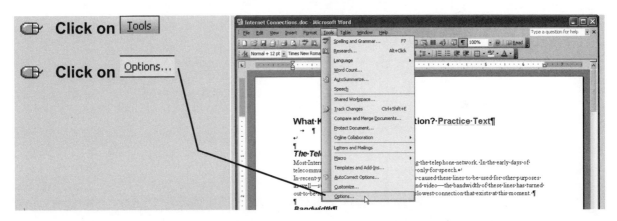
☞ **Click on** Options...	

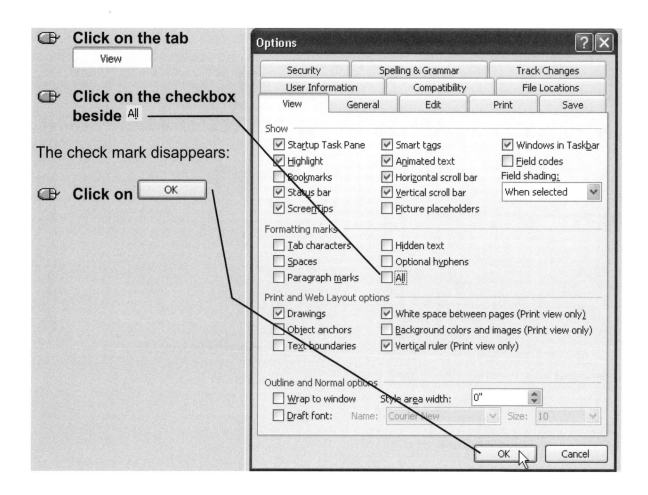

☞ **Click on the tab** View

☞ **Click on the checkbox beside** All

The check mark disappears:

☞ **Click on** OK

Turning the Assistant Off

You might see the *Office Assistant* somewhere on your screen.

The *Office Assistant* can take on many different forms:

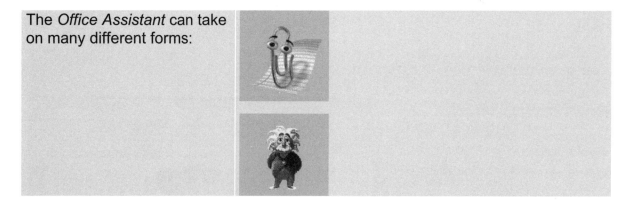

Turn off the *Office Assistant* while you're working through this book. Otherwise the Assistant may interfere with your work. Here's how you turn it off:

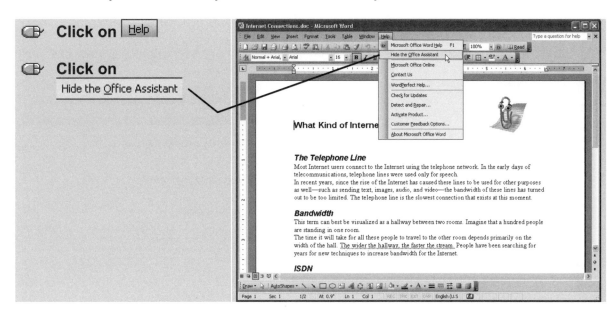

Click on Help

Click on
Hide the Office Assistant

The Assistant will no longer be visible.

Tip

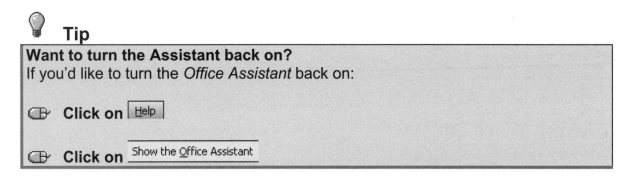

Want to turn the Assistant back on?
If you'd like to turn the *Office Assistant* back on:

Click on Help

Click on Show the Office Assistant

Closing the Practice Document

You don't need to save the practice text, so you can close the window now.

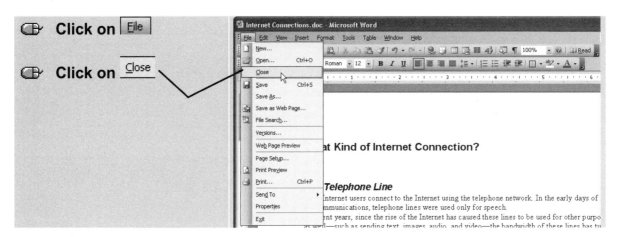

HELP! Should I save my changes?

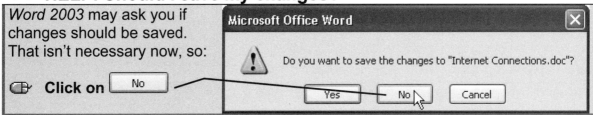

Word 2003 may ask you if changes should be saved. That isn't necessary now, so:

Click on [No]

Closing Word 2003

You can close *Word 2003* now. Here's how you do that:

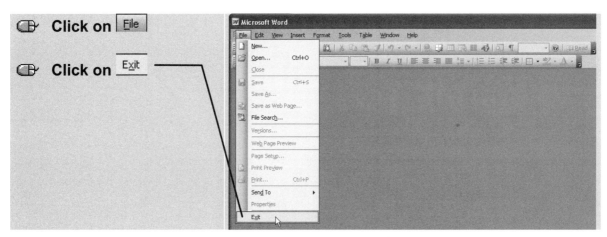

Click on [File]

Click on [Exit]

You can practice what you've learned in the following exercises.

Exercises

Have you forgotten how to perform a particular action? Use the number beside the footsteps to look it up in the appendix *How Do I Do That Again?*

Exercise: Toolbar

In this exercise, you'll practice activating and moving a toolbar.

✔ Start *Word 2003.* [6]

✔ Turn off the *Standard* toolbar. [7]

✔ Turn on the *Standard* toolbar. [7]

✔ Move the *Standard* toolbar to the bottom of the window. [8]

✔ Move the *Standard* toolbar back to the top of the window. [8]

Exercise: Viewing Documents

In this exercise, you'll practice displaying text in different ways.

✔ Open the document Ben Franklin.doc in the My Documents folder. [9]

✔ Select *Print Layout* view to display the text. [10]

✔ Display the hidden formatting marks. [11]

✔ Turn the hidden formatting marks back off. [11]

✔ Select *Normal* view to display the text. [12]

✔ Close *Word 2003* without saving anything. [13]

Background Information

The History of Word Processing

You probably remember a time when word processing didn't exist. In the day of the mechanical typewriter, word processing meant the entire text had to be typed in again, but this time without the mistakes. There was no way to remove mistakes or move whole sections of text to another part of the document with a few simple keystrokes, as you can today. And special effects, such as printing text in boldface, were barely possible.

When the electric typewriter came on the market, that changed a little. These typewriters could justify a text, for example. You could also correct errors, as long as they weren't too far back in the text. This was possible because these typewriters had a small memory, in which small sections of text could be temporarily stored.

This was already progress; but the great leap forward toward real word processing came with the computer. Computers have a much larger memory than electronic typewriters. Moreover, they can save the text onto diskettes and read it back in later. That means you can edit much larger texts.

There were two kinds of computer word processors. The first kind was a special computer, fully dedicated to word processing. These sometimes had a separate screen the size of a regular piece of paper. The other kind was the general computer, which could be used for all kinds of other tasks in addition to word processing: tasks like bookkeeping, inventory control, and games.

In the beginning, the special word processing computers were better suited for word processing than the general computer. The first word processing programs for the Personal Computer weren't very easy to use. You had to specify special effects with all kinds of codes, and you could only see the result after you'd printed out the document. *WordPerfect* and *WordStar* were the most widely used programs in the early years.

Word processing software kept on developing, and eventually the *WYSIWYG* programs came on the market. *WYSIWYG* stands for *What You See Is What You Get*. In other words: what you see on the screen is what will be printed on paper. They still use all kinds of codes, but the user no longer sees them.

The rise of the graphical operating system *Windows*, which replaced the text-based *DOS*, made *WYSIWYG* word processors the norm. At the same time, the special word processing computers disappeared, and the word processor *Word* came along. This program and the *Office* package, of which it was a part, became increasingly popular. So popular, in fact, that *Word 2003* is now by far the most widely used word processing program.

Tips

 Tip

Want a different Assistant?
Does a talking paper clip seem silly to you? Then you can choose a different
Assistant:

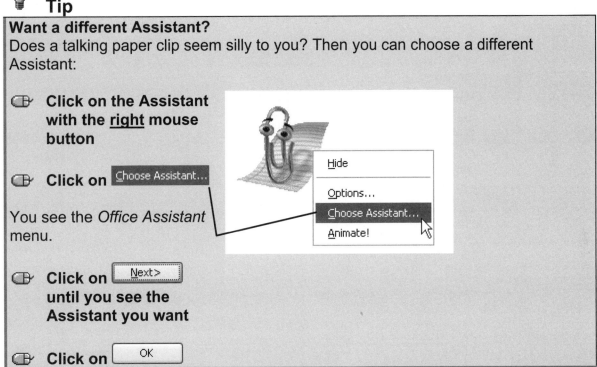

☞ **Click on the Assistant
with the <u>right</u> mouse
button**

☞ **Click on** `Choose Assistant...`

You see the *Office Assistant*
menu.

☞ **Click on** `Next>`
**until you see the
Assistant you want**

☞ **Click on** `OK`

Tip

Shortcut Keys

You can access frequently performed commands or operations by using the following keys or combinations of keys.

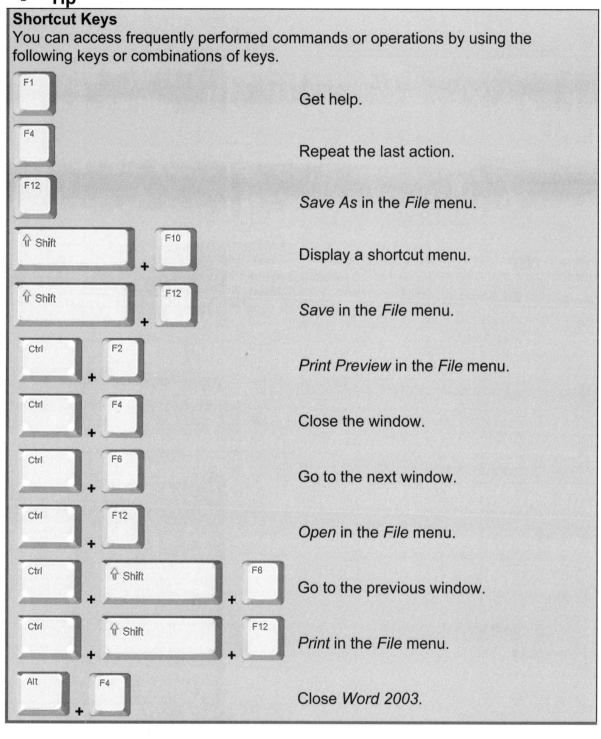

F1	Get help.
F4	Repeat the last action.
F12	*Save As* in the *File* menu.
Shift + F10	Display a shortcut menu.
Shift + F12	*Save* in the *File* menu.
Ctrl + F2	*Print Preview* in the *File* menu.
Ctrl + F4	Close the window.
Ctrl + F6	Go to the next window.
Ctrl + F12	*Open* in the *File* menu.
Ctrl + Shift + F6	Go to the previous window.
Ctrl + Shift + F12	*Print* in the *File* menu.
Alt + F4	Close *Word 2003*.

2. Entering Text

When you first start typing text into *Word 2003*, you run the risk of being confronted with all kinds of strange phenomena. Weird zigzag lines appear under some words, and "1st" automatically turns into "1st". What's happening?
Well, *Word 2003* is trying to help you out by checking the text that you type for mistakes and automatically correcting them. These spelling and grammar tools can be very useful once you know how to set them up and use them. And if you don't like them, you can always turn them off. After all, you're the boss in *Word 2003*.

In this chapter, you'll learn how to:

- type text
- use the automatic spelling checker
- use *AutoText*
- use synonyms
- use *AutoCorrect*
- set up automatic text functions
- type international characters
- insert symbols
- change spelling
- use hyphens
- insert nonbreaking spaces

⇨ Please note:

To work through this chapter, you'll first need to download the files 📄Ben Franklin.doc and 📄smokies.jpg from the website and save them in the 📁 My Documents folder (if you haven't already).

You can read how to do this in Appendix A at the back of this book.

Typing Text

In this book, we assume that you're already somewhat familiar with the keyboard, and that you can do the following things:

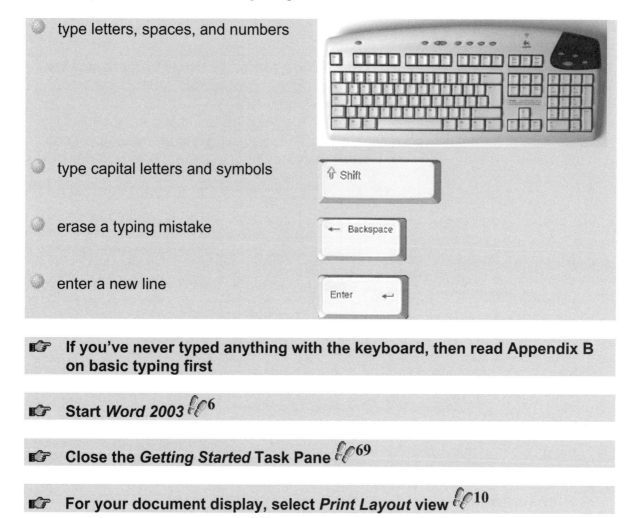

- type letters, spaces, and numbers

- type capital letters and symbols

- erase a typing mistake

- enter a new line

☞ **If you've never typed anything with the keyboard, then read Appendix B on basic typing first**

☞ **Start *Word 2003* 𝓁𝓁⁶**

☞ **Close the *Getting Started* Task Pane 𝓁𝓁⁶⁹**

☞ **For your document display, select *Print Layout* view 𝓁𝓁¹⁰**

To improve readability, you're going to choose a new font first. Here's how you do that:

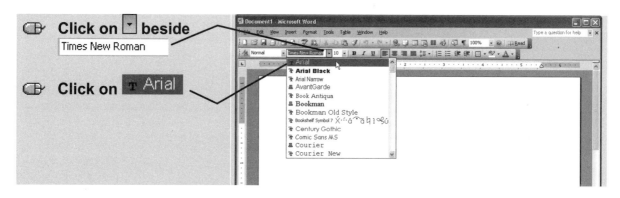

☞ **Click on** ▾ **beside**
Times New Roman

☞ **Click on** T **Arial**

Automatic Spelling Checker

Word 2003 has various built-in tools that can help you as you type. Take a look:

 Type: when you type in some text,

You see that *Word 2003* replaces the first letter with a capital letter:

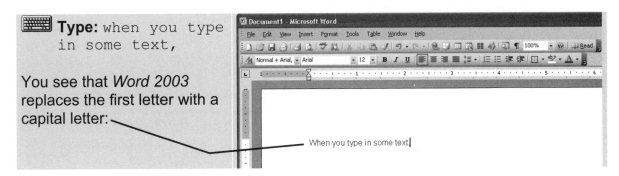

HELP! I don't see a capital letter.

Is there no capital letter on your screen? Then automatic correction is turned off. You can turn it on like this:

☞ **Click on** Tools , 🗲 AutoCorrect Options...

☞ **Click on the tab** AutoCorrect

☞ **Click in the checkbox beside** ☐ Capitalize first letter of sentences

☞ **Click on** OK

Now the text you type is immediately checked for spelling errors by *Word 2003*. Give it a try:

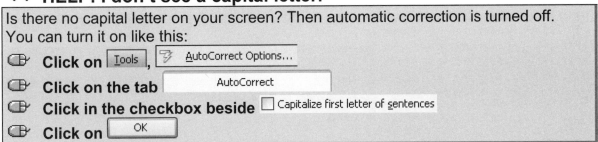 **Type:** it will bee checked immidiatly

Press Enter ⏎

You see that the incorrectly spelled word *immidiatly* is underlined with a red zigzag line 〰〰〰〰 :

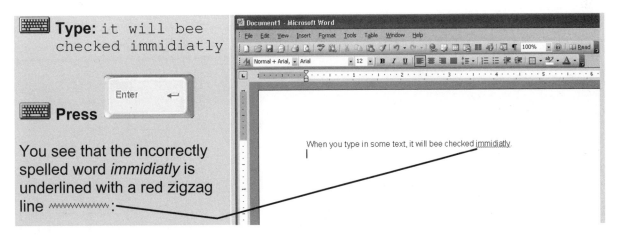

Note that *Word 2003* won't recognize all mistakes. It doesn't recognize the mistake *bee* (instead of *be*), for example. That's because the word *bee* is a correct English word.

HELP! It isn't checking my spelling.

Is there no zigzag line under *immidiatly* on your screen?
Then AutoCorrect is turned off. That's okay; just keep going.

 Tip

Don't want a capital letter at the beginning of your text?
If you want the first word to begin with a lowercase letter instead of a capital letter,
you can simply delete the capital letter and type in a lowercase letter.

AutoText

Word 2003 has a tool for quickly entering frequently used words without having to
type them yourself. There are various phrases you can use.

Click on Insert

Click on AutoText

Click on Salutation

You see a list with opening
phrases for a letter:

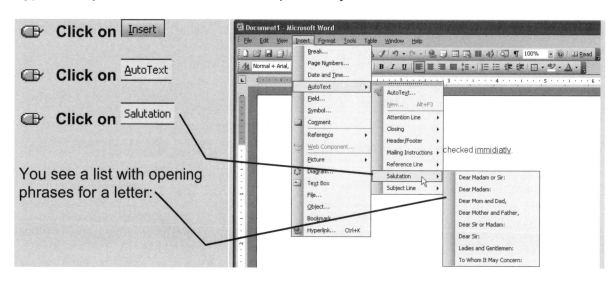

You can insert one of these phrases.

Click on Dear Sir or Madam:

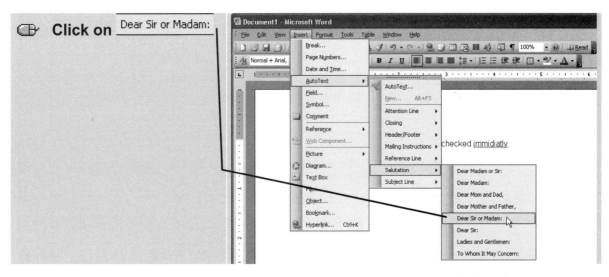

The text is inserted:

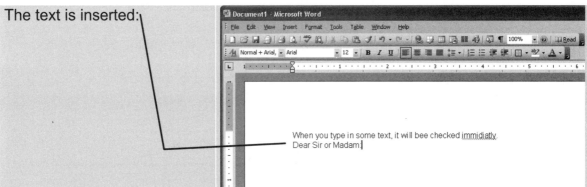

You can add frequently used words, such as the name of your town, to the list yourself. Here's how you do that:

Click on Insert

Click on AutoText

Click on AutoText...

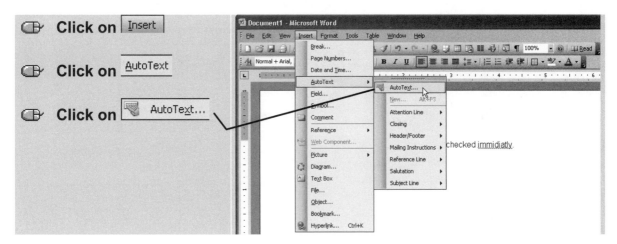

Now you see the *AutoCorrect* dialog box with a list of entries:

⌨ **Type:** Sarasota

🖱 **Click on** Add

The word has now been added to the list of AutoText phrases.

🖱 **Click on** OK

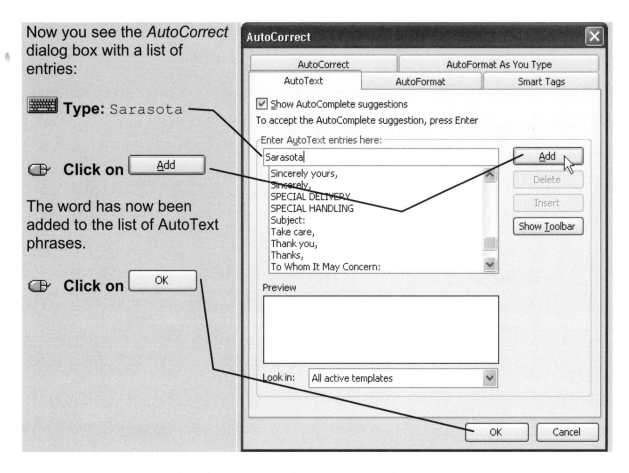

When you type in the first four letters of the word, you'll see that *Word 2003* now recognizes this word.

⌨ **Type:** Sara

You see a box

Sarasota (Press ENTER to Insert)

above the text:

You can accept this text like this:

⌨ **Press** Enter ←

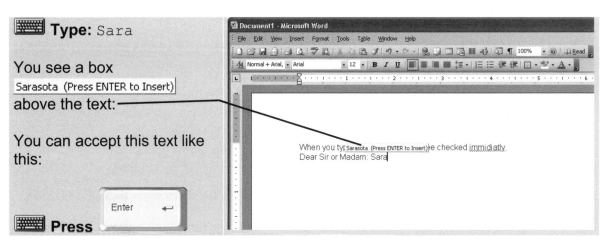

The word *Sarasota* is filled in.

Synonyms

Word 2003 can also help you formulate your text. *Word 2003* has a list of synonyms that can be helpful for finding the right words.

⌨ **Type:** is a
prominent

🖱 **Click with the <u>right</u> mouse button on the word *prominent***

🖱 **Click on** Synonyms

You see various synonyms for the word *prominent:*

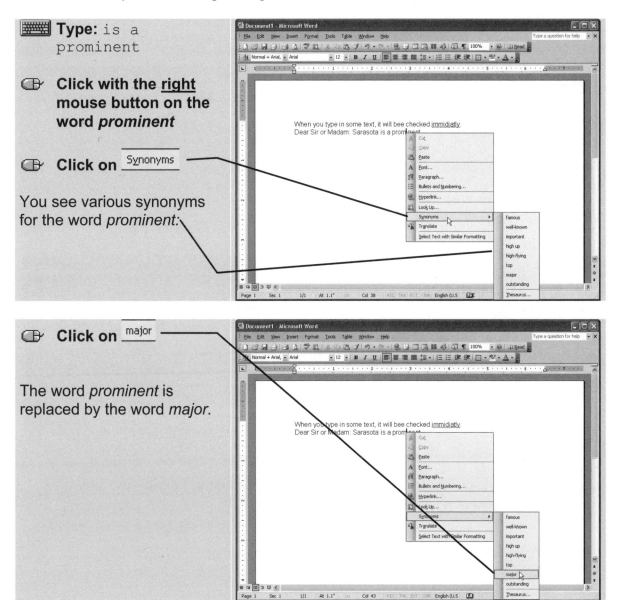

🖱 **Click on** major

The word *prominent* is replaced by the word *major*.

AutoCorrect

Word 2003 also has a tool that tries to correct any mistakes you make. Give it a try:

Type: `city`

Now type a mistake:

Type: `ont he`

Type a space

You see that *ont he* is corrected to *on the*:

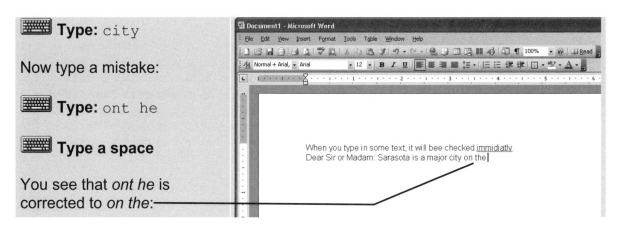

Word 2003 will also automatically format text sometimes. Give it a try:

Type: `1/2`

Type a space

You see that *1/2* is replaced with the symbol ½:

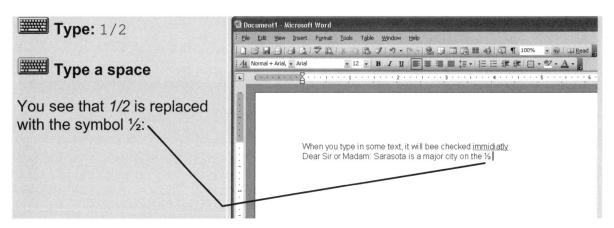

Not every user will be happy with these automatic functions. Sometimes they give you the feeling you don't have any control over the text.

Changing the Automatic Function Settings

You can set up the automatic functions to suit your own preferences. It's a good idea to take a look first at all the automatic functions *Word 2003* has to offer. That will help prevent frustration if you get the feeling that *Word 2003* isn't doing what you want it to do.

Click on Tools

Click on
AutoCorrect Options...

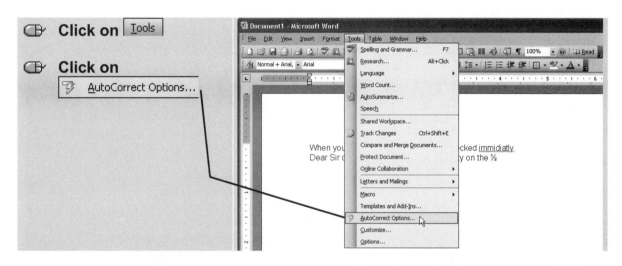

Now you see the *AutoCorrect* dialog box:

Click on the tab
AutoCorrect

Correct two initial capitals: the second letter will become a lowercase letter: ─────

Capitalize first letter of sentences: the first letter of every sentence is automatically turned into a capital letter:─────

Replace certain words by others in the list:─────

☞ **View the list of combinations**

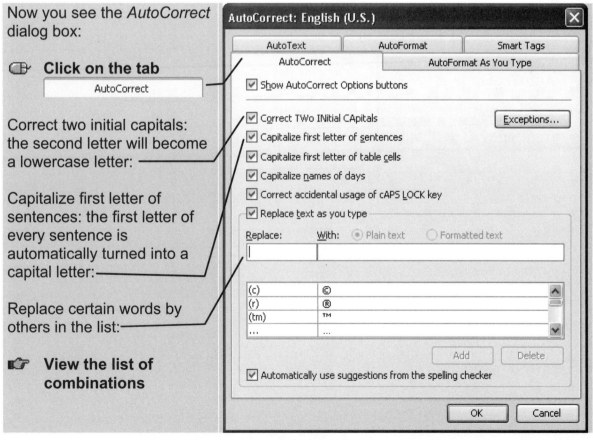

Tip

Check Your Spelling As You Type

On the tab ⎸ AutoText ⎹, you see the option
☑ Automatically use suggestions from the spelling checker at the bottom. This automatically replaces misspelled words with words from the spelling checker list. If you don't like this function, you can turn it off.

In this window, you see the text that can automatically be entered with the *AutoText* option.

Click on the tab
⎸ AutoText ⎹

Word 2003 will suggest a word or phrase when you type in the first few letters (if that word is in the *AutoText* entries list):

You can add your own entry here:

☞ **View the list of AutoText entries**

☞ **Add a text you use frequently, if you'd like**

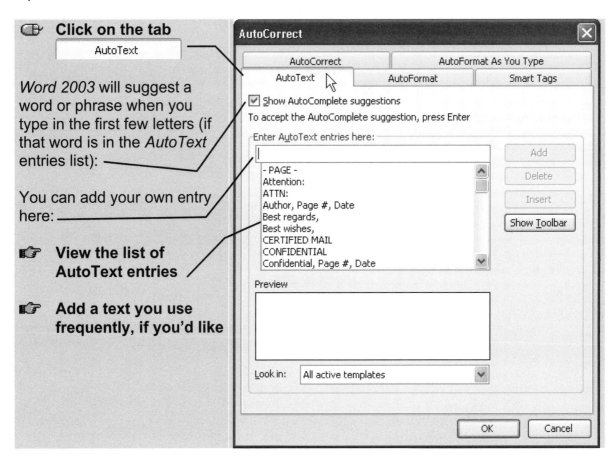

You can also set up automatic formatting in this window.

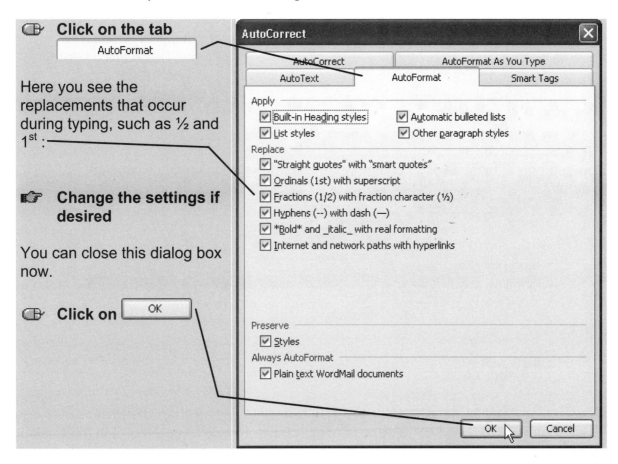

☞ **Click on the tab**

> AutoFormat

Here you see the replacements that occur during typing, such as ½ and 1st :

 Change the settings if desired

You can close this dialog box now.

☞ **Click on** OK

The dialog box shows:

AutoCorrect

Tabs: AutoCorrect | AutoFormat As You Type | AutoText | AutoFormat | Smart Tags

Apply
- ☑ Built-in Heading styles
- ☑ Automatic bulleted lists
- ☑ List styles
- ☑ Other paragraph styles

Replace
- ☑ "Straight quotes" with "smart quotes"
- ☑ Ordinals (1st) with superscript
- ☑ Fractions (1/2) with fraction character (½)
- ☑ Hyphens (--) with dash (—)
- ☑ *Bold* and _italic_ with real formatting
- ☑ Internet and network paths with hyperlinks

Preserve
- ☑ Styles

Always AutoFormat
- ☑ Plain text WordMail documents

OK | Cancel

💡 **Tip**

One snazzy formatting change is to replace regular "quotation marks" with curly (or smart) "quotes":

☑ "Straight quotes" with "smart quotes"

Typing International Characters

If you look at the keyboard, you'll notice there are no letter keys with umlauts or accents such as ë, é, or è. Nonetheless, they are easy to type. There are different ways to do this. The most convenient way is to use the so-called "dead" keys.

These three keys are the dead keys:	

You use one of these keys in combination with the letter you want to accent. For example:

ë	" and then e
ö	" and then o
é	' and then e
è	` and then e
ê	^ and then e
ç	' and then c

⇨ **Please note:**

Does it not work as described when you type  **and then the letter** e?
Then your keyboard isn't set up to use "dead" keys. Consult Appendix C in the back of this book. It describes how you can change your keyboard settings.

Try typing the word café:

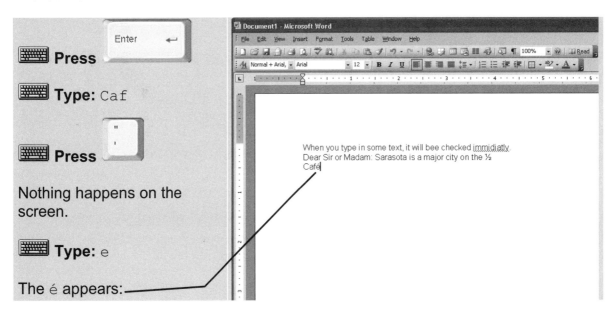

Press [Enter]

Type: Caf

Press ["]

Nothing happens on the screen.

Type: e

The é appears: ——

These keys are called "dead" because nothing happens when you press them. The symbol only appears after you press another key. Try another letter, such as the ö. This one is a little more complicated, because you also have to use the Shift key. Otherwise you can't type the quote mark ".

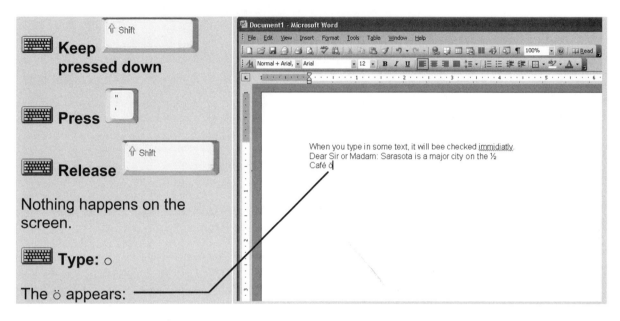

You can use this method to type all possible letters of this type, such as é, è, ë, ê, ñ, or ç.

Typing Quotation Marks

If the quotation mark key is "dead," then how do you type a quotation mark? You use the key with the space bar. Give it a try:

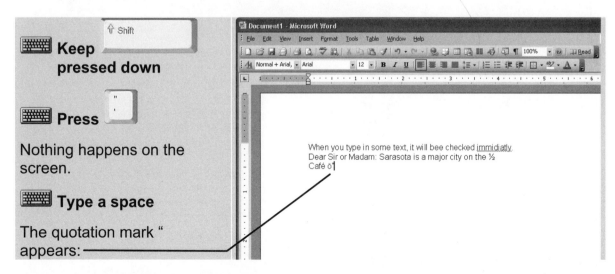

Note that you will have to press the space bar again in order to type a real space.

Inserting Symbols

There is another way to enter various symbols. Here's how you do it:

☞ **Click on** Insert

☞ **Click on** Symbol...

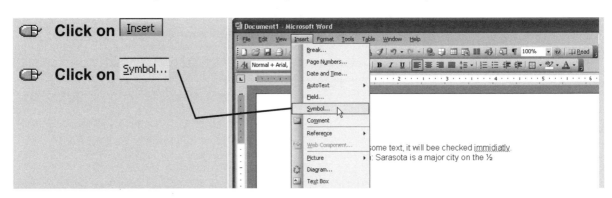

Now you see the Symbol dialog box:

☞ **Click on the tab** Symbols

Is Font: not on (normal text)?

Then:

☞ **Click on** ⌄ **in the list** Font:

☞ **Click on** (normal text)

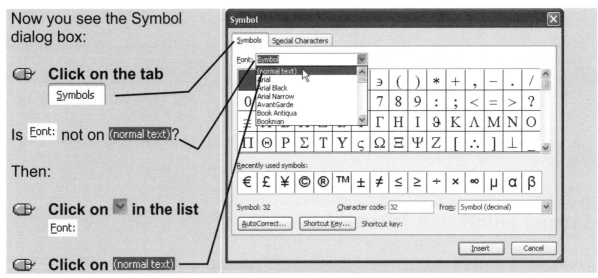

You see various symbols that you can insert into your text:

☞ **Click on** @ **for example**

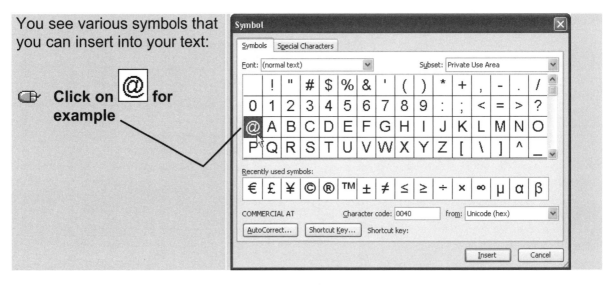

Now you can add the symbol into your text.

Click on Insert

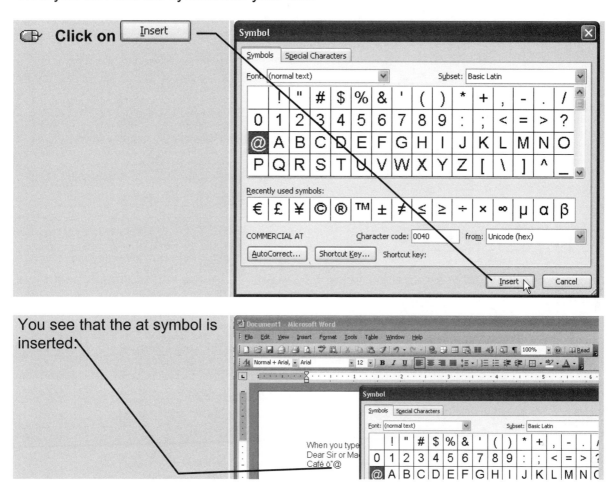

You see that the at symbol is inserted:

You can insert multiple symbols one after another in this window, such as items in the list of special characters.

Click on the tab Special Characters

Click on § Section

Click on Insert

Click on Close

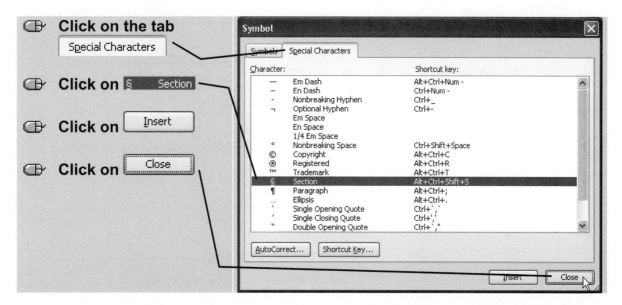

Both the at symbol and the
section symbol have now
been inserted:

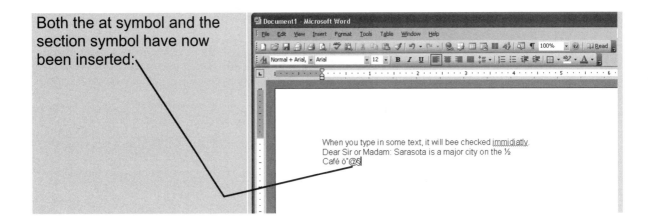

Capital Letter Usage

There's one last tool you can use to change lowercase letters into capital letters. Give
it a try:

⌨ **Type a space**

⌨ **Type:** amsterdam

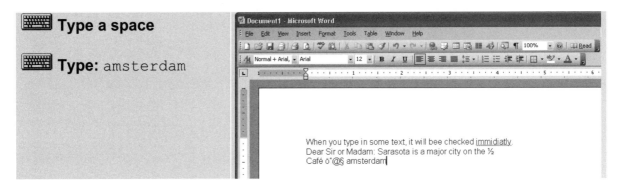

You can make this word start with a capital letter this way:

🖱 **Click on** Format

🖱 **Click on** Change Case...

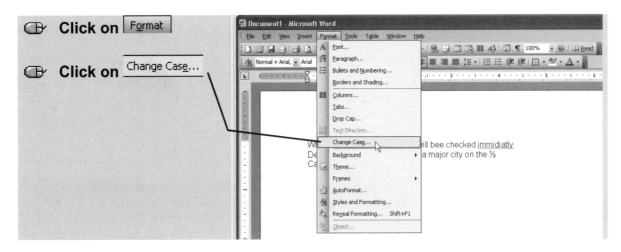

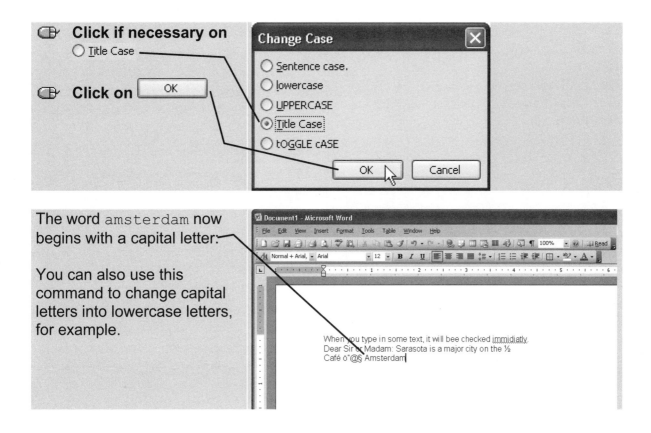

Click if necessary on ○ Title Case

Click on OK

The word amsterdam now begins with a capital letter.

You can also use this command to change capital letters into lowercase letters, for example.

Changing the Spelling

Before you close this document, you can fix the spelling mistake in the word *immidiatly*. Here's how you do that:

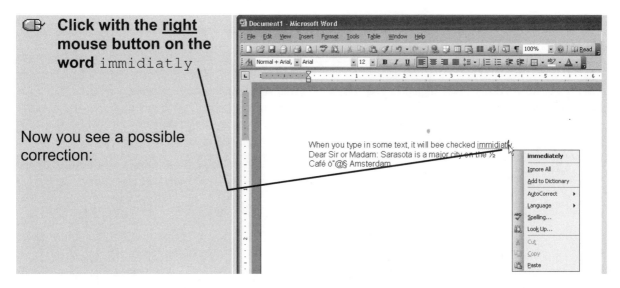

Click with the right mouse button on the word immidiatly

Now you see a possible correction:

Click on immediately

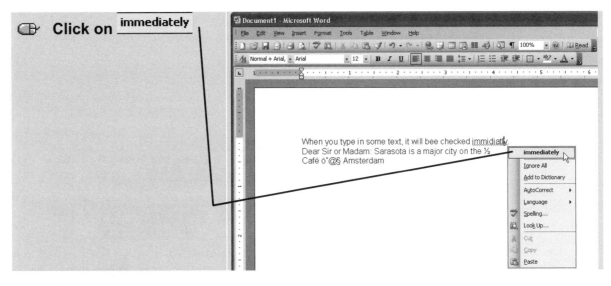

The word *immidiatly* is replaced by *immediately*.

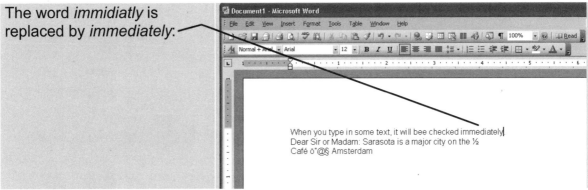

☞ **Close this document and don't save the changes** 𝄞14

Hyphens

After you've typed in some text, you can use the hyphenation feature of *Word 2003* to hyphenate the words at the end of a line. This helps to fill out the lines nicely. You can best try this out on a practice text.

Click on File

Click on 📂 Open...

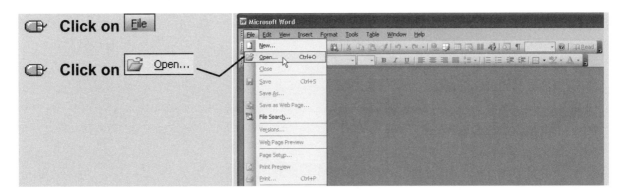

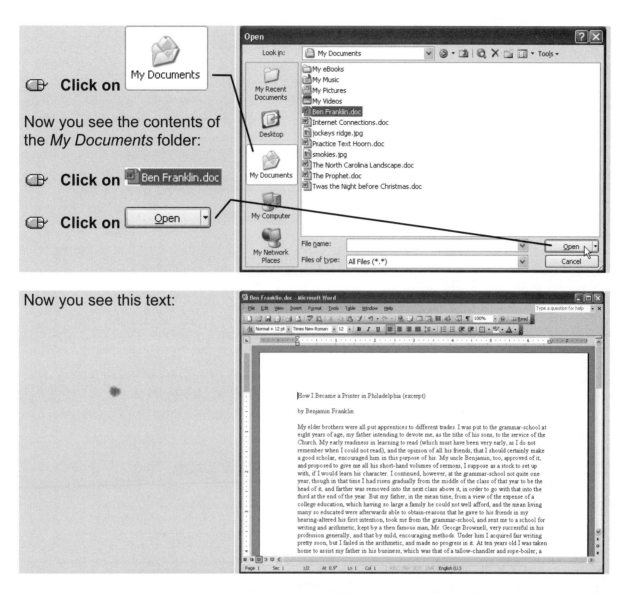

Click on My Documents

Now you see the contents of the *My Documents* folder:

Click on Ben Franklin.doc

Click on Open

Now you see this text:

Now you can hyphenate the words in the text. Here's how you do that:

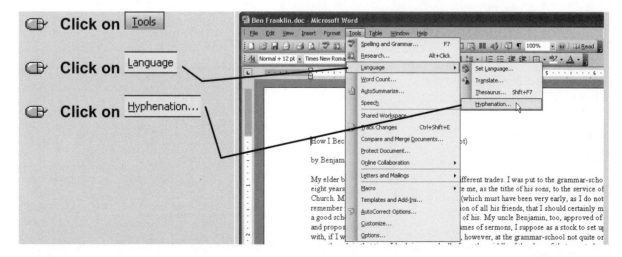

Click on Tools

Click on Language

Click on Hyphenation...

Now you see the
Hyphenation dialog box:

You can best see what's
happening if you choose
manual hyphenation:

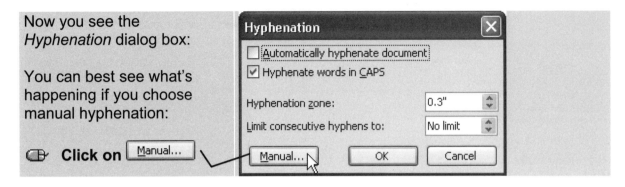

☞ **Click on** Manual...

Word 2003 searches for words in the text that can be hyphenated.

The first word it finds is
remember:

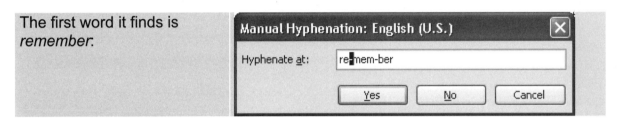

The black stripe is on the first hyphen. That's the preferred place for hyphenating this
word. But you can select a different place by clicking on it. *Word 2003*'s hyphenation
isn't perfect for all words, but in this way you can specify where the hyphenation
should occur.

☞ **Click for example at
the beginning of** -ber

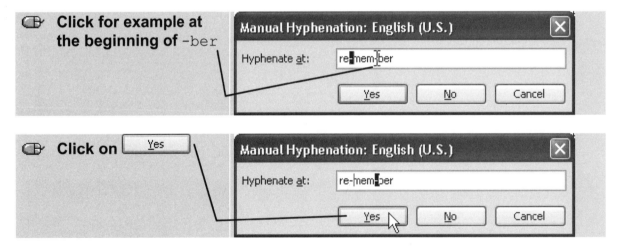

☞ **Click on** Yes

The next suggestion isn't so attractive: *col-lege*:

So tell *Word 2003* not to
hyphenate this word:

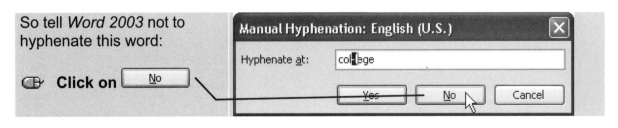

☞ **Click on** No

You don't have to go through the whole document.

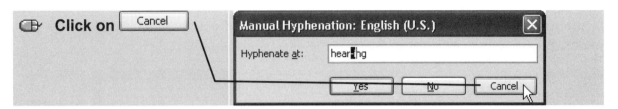

 Tip

Optional Hyphens
By default, *Word 2003* uses so-called **optional hyphens**. If you edit a text and a word now fits in its entirety onto a line, this hyphen will automatically disappear.

That's not what happens when you enter a hyphen with the ▭ key.
This is a so-called **nonbreaking hyphen** that remains in the text even if the word fits on one line.

 Tip

Placing Optional Hyphens Yourself
You can also add in optional hyphens yourself.

You do that by pressing [Ctrl] [–] .

 Tip

Nonbreaking Hyphens
Word 2003 has a second kind of hyphen, the **nonbreaking hyphen**. This is a dash that isn't considered to be a hyphen.
An example is the dash in the word *e-mail*. By using a nonbreaking hyphen, you make sure the word won't be hyphenated after the *e-* in *e-mail*. You can enter a nonbreaking hyphen by pressing:

 .

 Tip

Deleting Hyphens

You can delete optional or nonbreaking hyphens using the key.

Nonbreaking Spaces

A nonbreaking space is a special symbol you can use if you want to make sure two words stay together. An example is a name like General Motors.

Click after one ─────

Delete the space there:

Press

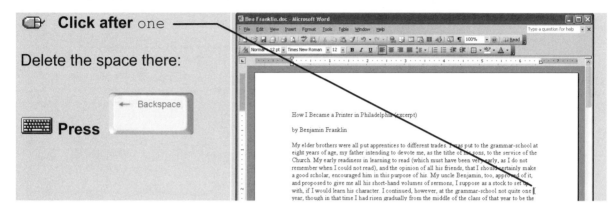

Now the two words *one* and *year* are right beside each other: ─────

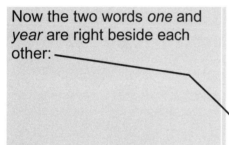

Now you can insert the nonbreaking space:

Keep Ctrl **and**

Shift **pressed down**

Press the space bar

Release the keys

The two words are beside each other on one line now:─────

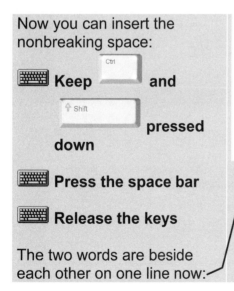

You can use this technique to keep two or more words together on the same line.

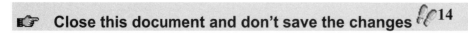

Close this document and don't save the changes 14

You can practice what you've learned in the following exercises.

Exercises

Have you forgotten how to perform a particular action? Use the number beside the footsteps to look it up in the appendix *How Do I Do That Again?*

Exercise: Inserting Symbols

In this exercise, you'll practice inserting symbols.

✓   Open the document 📄 The North Carolina Landscape.doc in the 📁 My Documents folder. 👣9

✓   Insert the ® symbol after the title. 👣15

Exercise: Hyphenation

In this exercise, you'll practice hyphenating words.

✓   Start manual hyphenation. 👣16

✓   Add a hyphen after *Moun* in *Mountains*. 👣17

✓   Stop hyphenating. 👣19

✓   Close *Word 2003* without saving anything. 👣13

Background Information

Entering Text without Typing

If you have a text on paper that you'd like to have on your computer, you could type it in letter by letter. But you can also call on a **scanner** for help.

A scanner is a device with which you can transform paper photos and texts into digital information. That's the kind of information programs use. You can add a scanned photo to your text in *Word 2003*, for example. You can have an *OCR program* edit and translate scanned text. *OCR* stands for *Optical Character Recognition*.

OCR means the program reads the text off the paper and turns it into a text that can be read by programs like *Word*. These programs can even recognize handwritten text, but it has to be very legible. It goes without saying that a printed text is much easier for an *OCR program* to recognize.

Once the *OCR program* has converted the text, you can save it as a regular document. Then you can import it into *Word 2003*. Since the conversion process is never perfect, you'll need to check the text and fix any errors first. But that's still a lot less work than having to type in the whole text yourself.

Tips

 Tip

Want to see the hyphens and nonbreaking spaces?

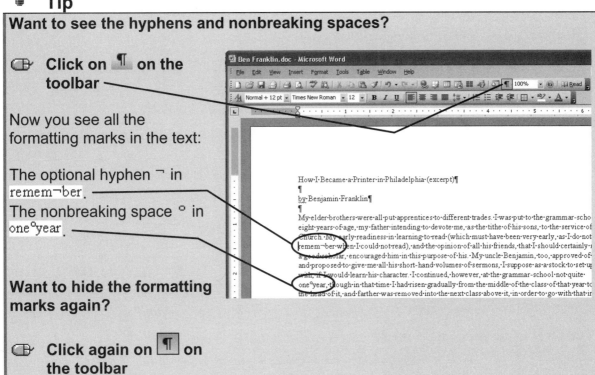

☞ **Click on ¶ on the toolbar**

Now you see all the formatting marks in the text:

The optional hyphen ¬ in remem¬ber.

The nonbreaking space ° in one°year.

Want to hide the formatting marks again?

☞ **Click again on ¶ on the toolbar**

 Tip

Other Special Symbols

On the tab 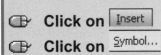 in the *Symbol* dialog box, you see a list of additional special characters.
You can insert, for example, the © symbol into the text, or a nonbreaking space.

You open the *Symbol* dialog like this:

☞ **Click on Insert**

☞ **Click on Symbol...**

Tip

An Alternate Way to Type International Characters

In addition to using the dead keys and the *Symbol* dialog box, you can also use the [Ctrl] key to type letters like é and à.

First press the key for ' (or '), release it, and then press the desired letter, pressing [Shift] at the same time if you want a capital letter.

[Ctrl] [~] then: [A], [E], [I], [O] or [U]   à, è, ì, ò, ù

[Ctrl] ["] then: [A], [E], [I], [O], [U] or [Y]   á, é, í, ó, ú, ý

[Ctrl] [Shift] [:] then: [A], [E], [I], [O], [U] or [Y]   ä, ë, ï, ö, ü, ÿ

[Ctrl] [Shift] [^ 6] then: [A], [E], [I], [O] or [U]   â, ê, î, ô, û

[Ctrl] [Shift] [~] then: [A], [N] or [O]   ã, ñ, õ

[Ctrl] [Shift] [& 7] then: [A], [O] or [S]   æ, œ, ß

[Ctrl] [Shift] [@ 2] then: [A]   å

[Ctrl] [<] then: [C] or the right-hand [Alt] [<] then: [C]   ç

[Ctrl] [? /] then: [O]   ø

3. Formatting Characters and Words

The overwhelming popularity of word processing programs has affected the way text is handled in the production of books and magazines. In the old days, an author wrote text by hand or typed it out first and later delivered it to the publisher. Then the layout person or typesetter took care of the appearance of the text, and the printer performed the task of printing. Nowadays, word processing programs and printers are so advanced that an author, himself can be in charge of his text layout and printing. You, too can format your documents in many various ways. You can experiment with fonts, font-size and features such as boldface and italics to give your text a whole new look.

You can apply formatting to your text when you are done typing or set up your desired formatting beforehand.

In this chapter, you'll learn how to:

- select characters and words
- make words italic, underlined, bold, and colored
- apply multiple kinds of formatting
- format beforehand or afterward
- select a different font
- increase or decrease the size of the letters
- print the text

⇨ Please note:

To work through this chapter, you'll first need to download the files
Practice Text Hoorn.doc and The Prophet.doc from the website and save them in the
My Documents folder (if you haven't already).

You can read how to do this in Appendix A at the back of this book.

Opening a Practice Text

You'll need to open a practice text to work through this chapter. Here's how you do that:

☞ **Start** *Word 2003* $\ell\ell^6$

☞ **Close the** *Getting Started* **Task Pane** $\ell\ell^{69}$

☞ **For your document display, select** *Normal* **view** $\ell\ell^{12}$

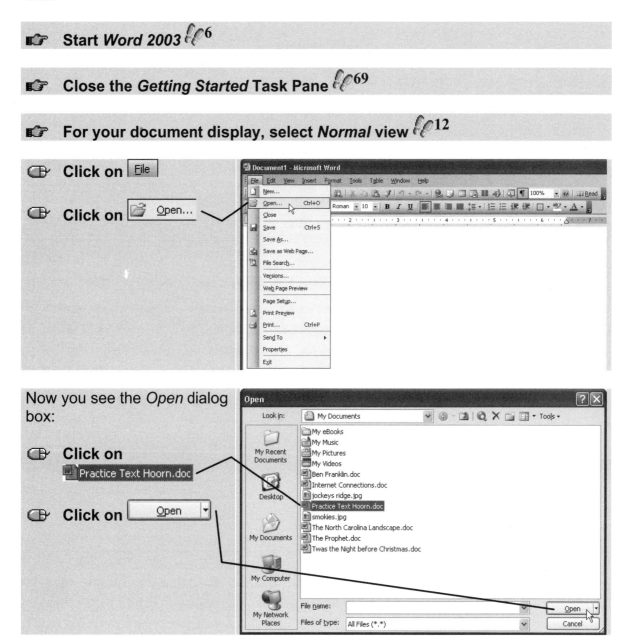

Now you see this text:

You're going to format this text.

Text Formatting

The goal of text formatting is to make the text clearer and more attractive.
A description for tourists might look like this as a plain text:

Hoorn
In the province of North Holland, not too far from Amsterdam, lies the beautiful old harbor town of Hoorn. The town acquired city rights in 1357 and reached the peak of its glory in the seventeenth century, when the Dutch East India Company took up residence there.
The Old Dutch character of the town has been well preserved, as can be seen from the Hoofdtoren (Main Tower) at the old harbor, a landmark for many people entering Hoorn from the water.

The text layout is pretty bland. With a few simple formatting effects, such as boldface, italics, and underlined letters and here and there a different font, the text will look a lot more lively.

That same text can look like this:

Hoorn

In the province of North Holland, *not too far from Amsterdam*, lies the beautiful old harbor town of **Hoorn**. The town acquired city rights in 1357 and reached the peak of its glory in the seventeenth century, when the **Dutch East India Company** took up residence there.

Historic Harbor
The Old Dutch character of the town has been well preserved, as can be seen from the **Hoofdtoren** (Main Tower) at the old harbor, a landmark for many people entering Hoorn from the water.

This chapter will show you step by step how to apply the above formatting yourself.

Selecting Text

You must always select the text first before you can apply formatting. By selecting text, you specify what part of the document you want to change. Then you specify what should be done with that text. In other words:

First select ... then act.

There are many ways to select text. The next sections will cover the most important selection methods. Sometimes there are multiple ways to select a block of text. In that case, you can use your favorite method.

Bold Text

You can make words **bold** if you want to emphasize something in the text, for example. First you have to select the word or words:

First select ... then act.

The simplest way to select text is to drag the mouse pointer over that text. You keep the left mouse button pressed down while you're dragging. Give it a try by making the words **Dutch East India Company** bold.

Click with the mouse pointer in front of Dutch

Drag the mouse pointer along Dutch East India Company

Release the mouse button

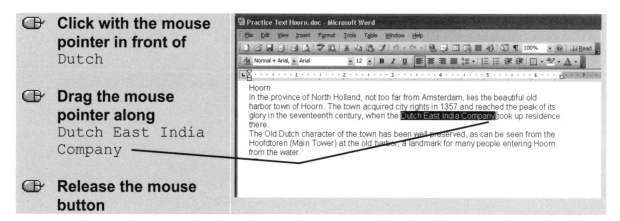

The selected text has a black background.

HELP! A different block of text has been selected.

If you drag a little too far up or down, the previous or next line will also be selected. Undo that selection.

Here's how you do that:

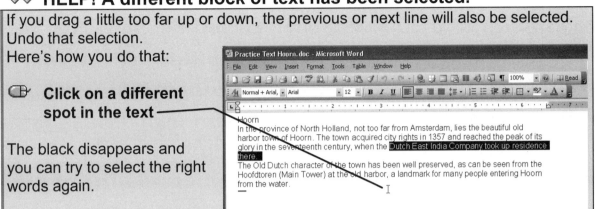

 Click on a different spot in the text

The black disappears and you can try to select the right words again.

Once you've selected the text, you can make it bold.

 Click on **B**

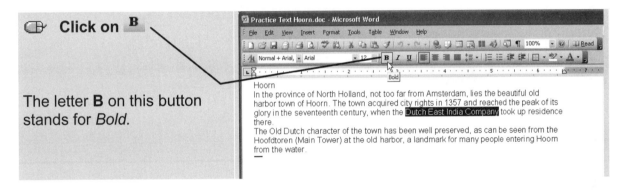

The letter **B** on this button stands for *Bold.*

 ## Please note:

The button **B** has now changed color and shows a border. That indicates that the button is active.

You can't really see that the text is bold until you undo the selection.

 Click on a different spot in the text

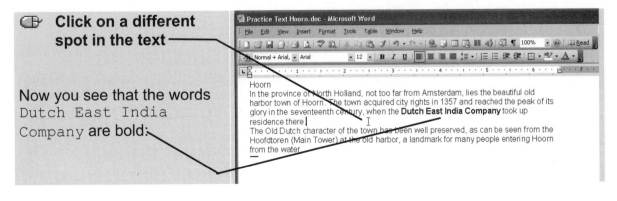

Now you see that the words Dutch East India Company **are bold:**

Selecting a Word

You can select a single word by double-clicking on it with the mouse.

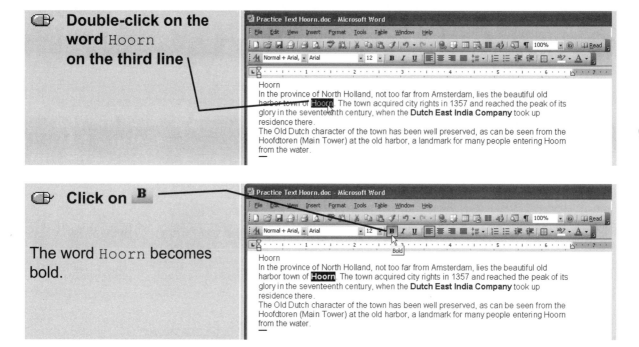

☞ **Double-click on the word** Hoorn **on the third line**

☞ **Click on B**

The word Hoorn becomes bold.

You can change the formatting for a single word even more easily. When the cursor is somewhere in the word and you click on the B button, the word becomes bold. So you don't have to select the word first. Give it a try:

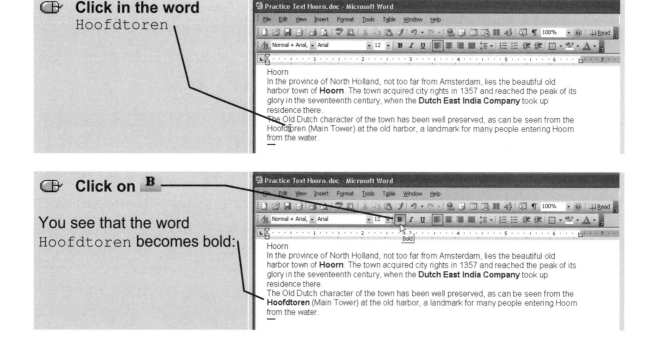

☞ **Click in the word** Hoofdtoren

☞ **Click on B**

You see that the word Hoofdtoren **becomes bold:**

⇨ Help! The word doesn't become bold.

If the word doesn't become bold, you will have to change a setting:

☞ **Click on** Tools **/** Options...

☞ **Click on the tab** Edit

☞ **Click a checkmark in the box in front of** When selecting, automatically select entire word

Italic Text

Italic text is often used to separate titles, names, or sayings from the rest of the text. You can apply this kind of formatting the same way you make text bold. Keep in mind:

First select ... then act.

☞ **Select the text**
not too far from Amsterdam

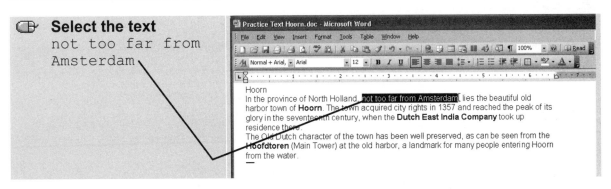

☞ **Click on** *I*

The letter *I* on the button stands for *Italic*.

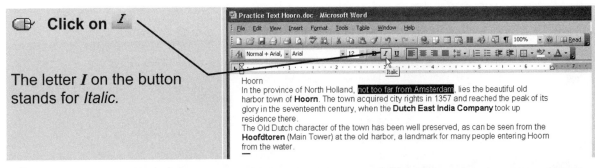

☞ **Click somewhere in the text**

You see that the words are now in italics:

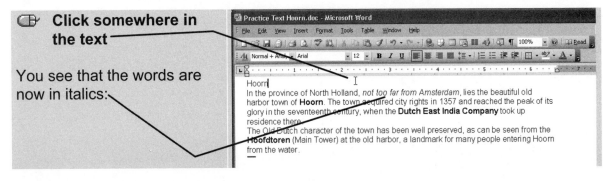

Underlined Text

Underlined text is sometimes also used to emphasize words or make a heading in the text stand out better. You can underline text the same way you make it bold or italic.

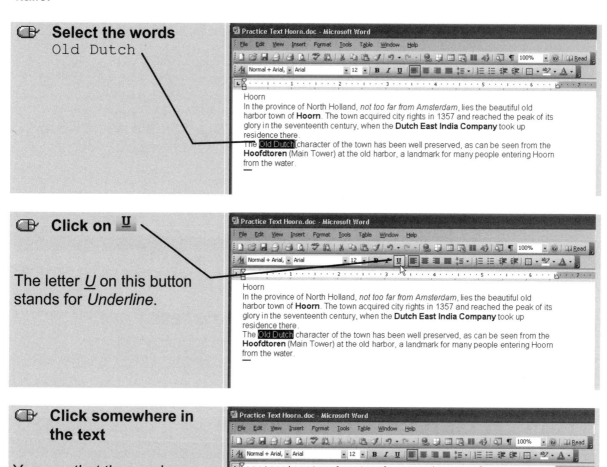

☞ **Select the words**
`Old Dutch`

☞ **Click on** U

The letter *U* on this button stands for *Underline*.

☞ **Click somewhere in the text**

You see that the words are now underlined:

Combining Formatting Types

You can also combine multiple formatting types. For example, you can make text:

- **bold and underlined**
- ***bold and italic***
- *italic and underlined*
- ***bold, italic, and underlined***

By combining these formatting functions, you can specify degrees of importance: bold and underlined stands out more than just bold, for example.
The next sections will show you how to combine the different formatting functions.

Set Up Formatting Beforehand

If you know beforehand how you want to format a particular block of text, you can specify that before you start typing. Then you don't have to select the text later in order to format it. You're going to add a heading to the text now. The heading will be bold and underlined.

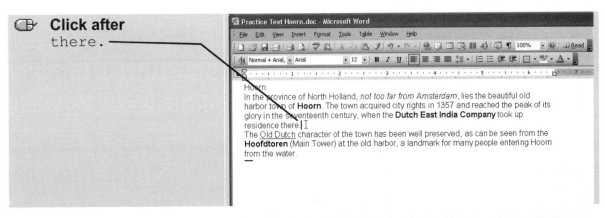

Click after there.

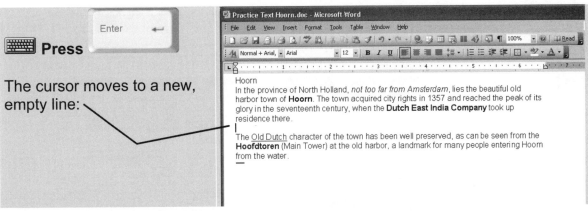

Press Enter

The cursor moves to a new, empty line:

⌨ **Press again**

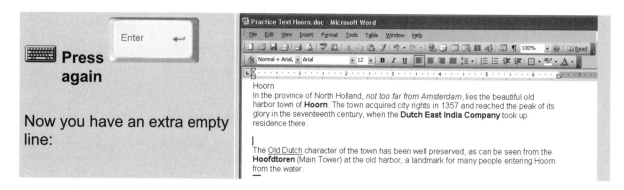

Now you have an extra empty line:

Now you have two empty lines under the line containing the word "there." You can set up the desired formatting and type in the text now.

🖱 **Click on B**

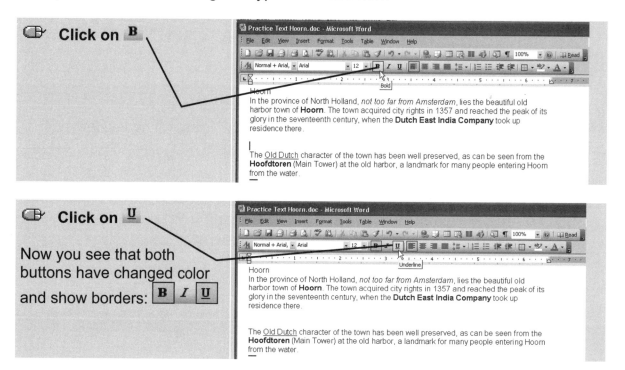

🖱 **Click on U**

Now you see that both buttons have changed color and show borders: **B** *I* **U**

 Tip

It doesn't matter whether you click on bold **B** first and then on underlined **U** or the other way around.

⌨ **Type:**
    Historic Harbor

You see that the text is immediately bold and underlined:

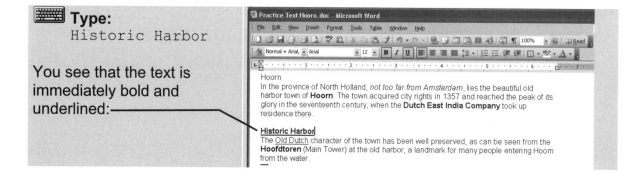

Colored Text

You can use a color other than black for your letters. You'll see the selected color on your screen, and if you have a color printer you can print your text in color. You can apply color in the same way as other kinds of formatting.

First select ... then act.

Double-click on the word `landmark`

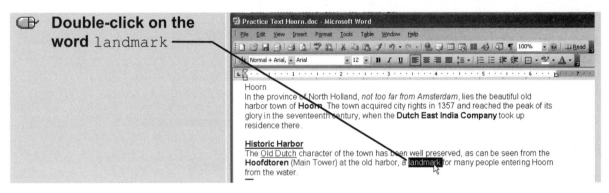

Click on **A**

Click somewhere in the text

Now the word is the same color as the bar under the letter **A** :

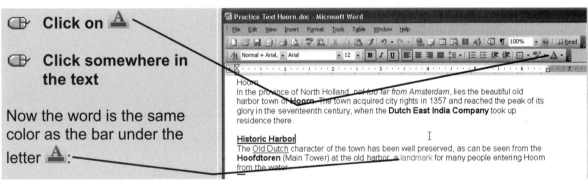

Of course, you can select a different color. To do that, don't click on the **A**, but on the little triangle ⁻ beside it.

Double-click on the word `landmark`

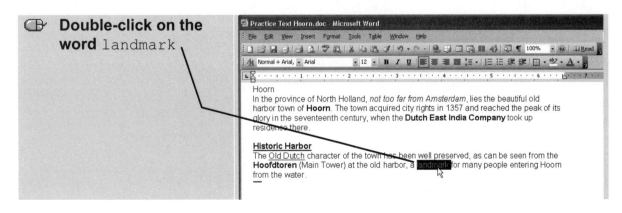

☞ **Click next to ▲ ˅ on ˅**

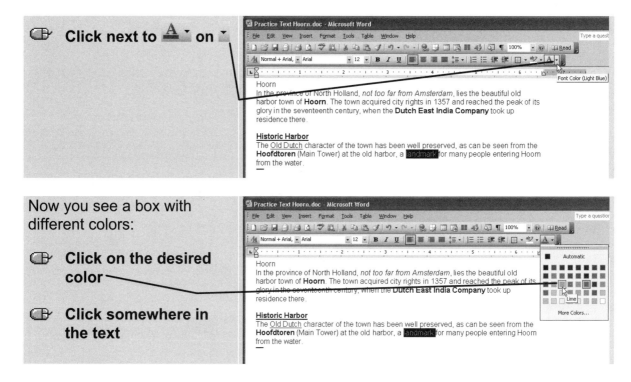

Now you see a box with different colors:

☞ **Click on the desired color**

☞ **Click somewhere in the text**

The selected text appears now in the chosen color.

Removing Formatting

You can also remove formatting. The formatting buttons are on and off switches. So italics can be *on* or *off*. You can see that from the button: if it's on, it's a reddish color and has a blue border. If it's off, there is no border and the button is blue.

All buttons are off:	**B** *I* <u>U</u>
Italics are on:	**B** *I* <u>U</u>

☞ **Select the words** Old Dutch

You see that the <u>U</u> button is activated:

☞ **Click on** <u>U</u>

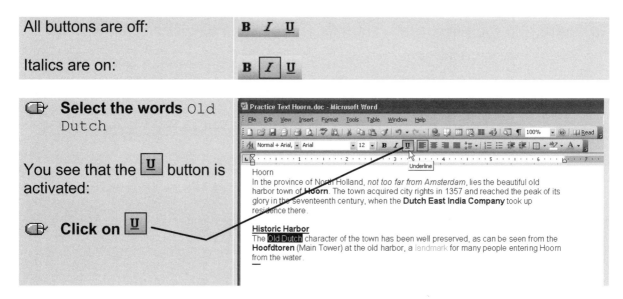

You see that the <u>U</u> button is no longer activated:

☞ **Click somewhere in the text**

The words *Old Dutch* are no longer underlined:

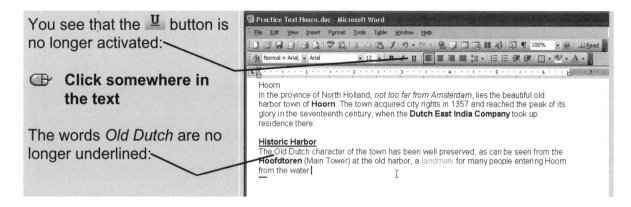

You can always change the formatting this way.

Changing the Font

There are all kinds of typefaces (fonts), from sleek modern fonts to classic newspaper fonts. *Word 2003* usually uses two fonts by default:

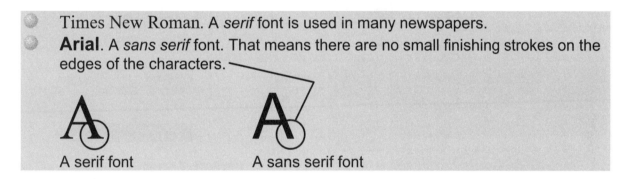

- Times New Roman. A *serif* font is used in many newspapers.
- **Arial**. A *sans serif* font. That means there are no small finishing strokes on the edges of the characters.

A serif font   A sans serif font

When you start a new document in *Word 2003, Times New Roman* is usually the default font. In the practice text you're going to use now, the font is set to *Arial*, a modern, sleek, and easy to read font.

You can see the selected font here in the formatting toolbar:

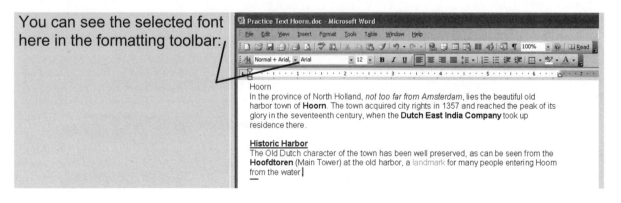

You can also change the whole text or part of the text from one font to a different font. As always, you have to select the text first. Here's how you can select all the text at once:

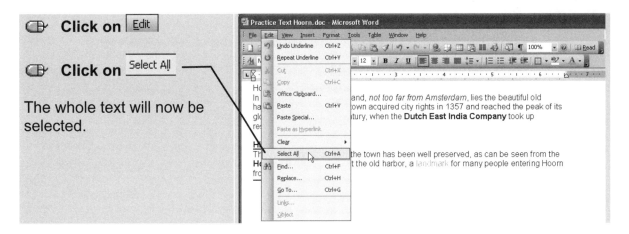

Click on Edit

Click on Select All

The whole text will now be selected.

Now you can change the font. Here's how you do that:

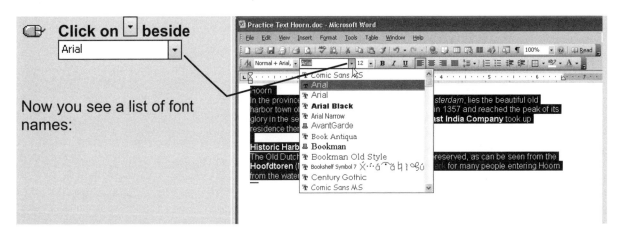

Click on ⏷ **beside**

Arial

Now you see a list of font names:

➡ **Please note:**

The fonts shown in the list will vary from computer to computer.

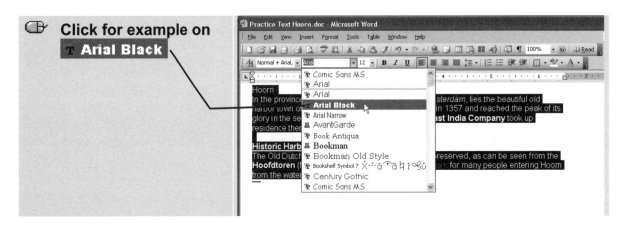

Click for example on

Arial Black

⬚→ Click somewhere in the text

You see that the font is now different:

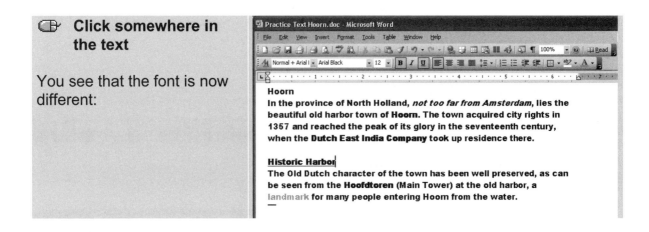

Undo

It isn't a very pretty sight, so you'll probably want to change it back to its original state using the *Undo* command. You do that with the ⬚ button.

⬚→ Click on ⬚

⬚→ Click somewhere in the text

The font is changed back to *Arial*:

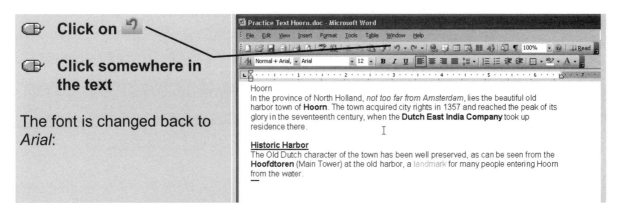

Of course, you can also change the font for parts of the text. Again, remember:

First select ... then act.

☞ Select the text
`Historic Harbor`

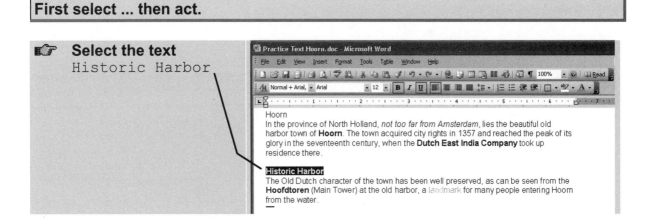

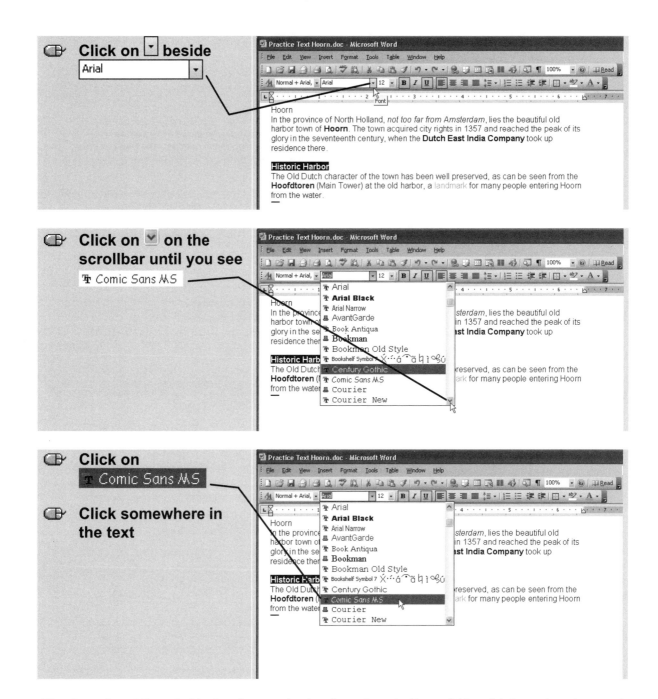

The heading *Historic Harbor* is now in the font *Comic Sans MS*, which makes it stand out better.

Tip

Not Too Many Fonts

If you look at the list, you'll see that there are an enormous number of fonts:

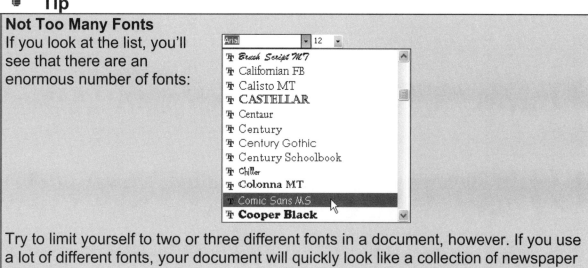

Try to limit yourself to two or three different fonts in a document, however. If you use a lot of different fonts, your document will quickly look like a collection of newspaper clippings.

Changing the Font Size

You can use fonts in different sizes, from very small to very large. You can display the title in a larger font, for example. First you need to select the text whose size you want to change.

Double-click on the heading Hoorn

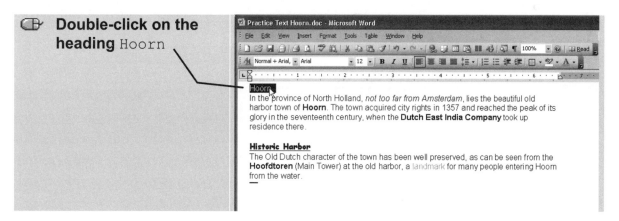

Now you can select the font size. The font size is always expressed as a number. That number stands for the number of points that make up the letter. The larger the number, the larger the letters.

Click beside 12 on

You see a list of numbers:

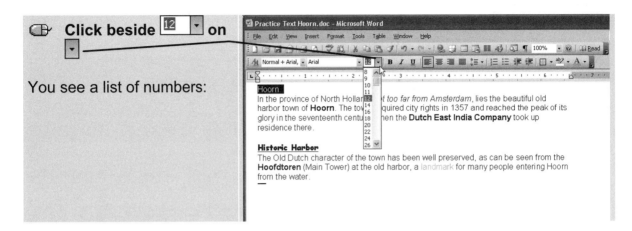

By default, *Word 2003* uses a 12-point font. You can select a larger font from the list.

Click on 20

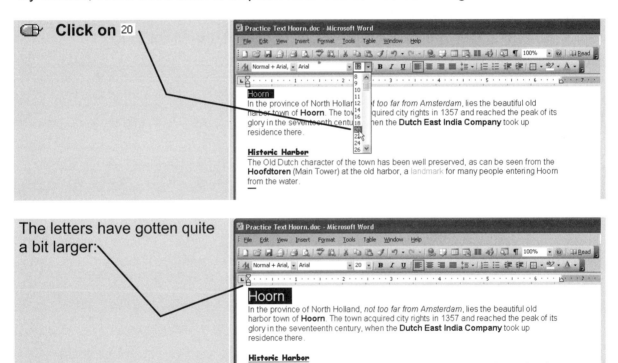

The letters have gotten quite a bit larger:

If the word is still selected, you can go on to change the font to *Comic Sans MS*. You don't have to select it again first.

 HELP! The text is no longer selected.

If you already clicked somewhere else by accident, then the selection has been canceled. The word `Hoorn` will no longer have a black background.

☞ **Select the word again before continuing**

Click beside

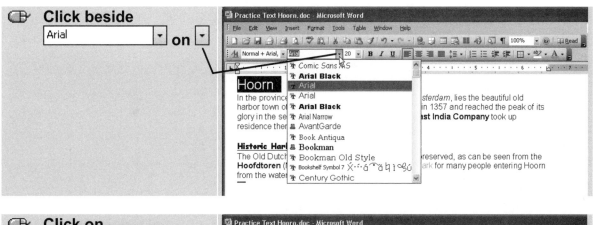

Click on

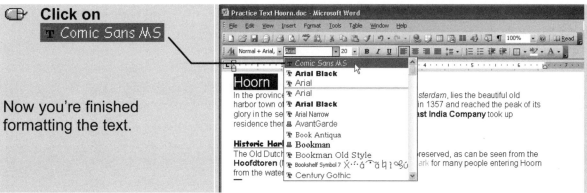

Now you're finished formatting the text.

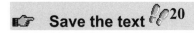

Printing Text

You can print a text on paper.

You print a text using a printer:

If You Don't Have a Printer

You can still do the exercise; you just won't be able to give the actual command to print the text.

Before you print the text, it's a good idea to see exactly what it's going to look like on paper. *Word 2003* has a special command for this.

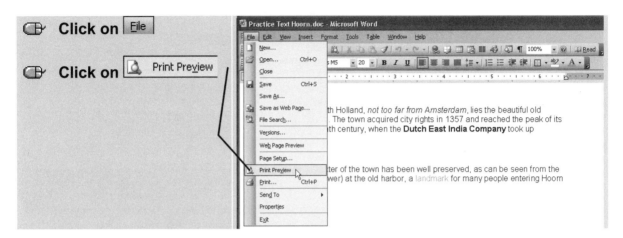

Click on File

Click on Print Preview

Now you see this window containing a miniature version of the page the way it will look when it is printed:

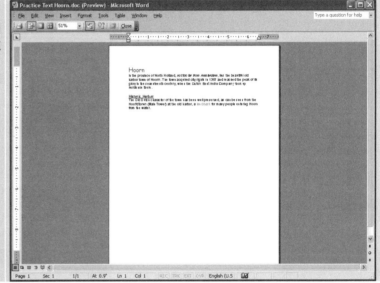

You can see how the text is positioned on the paper.

Click on Close

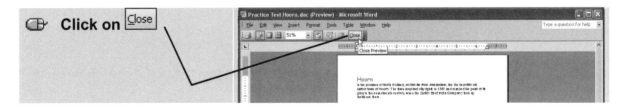

For now, you can print this text the way it is.

 Please note:

It's important that you always check first whether your printer is ready to print before you give the print command.

☞ **Check whether the printer is on**

☞ **Check whether the printer has paper**

Is everything ready? Then you can give the command to print.

👉 **Click on** File

👉 **Click on** 🖨 Print...

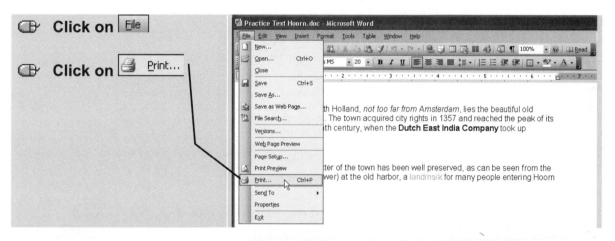

Now you see the *Print* dialog box where you can adjust the print settings:

👉 **Click on** OK

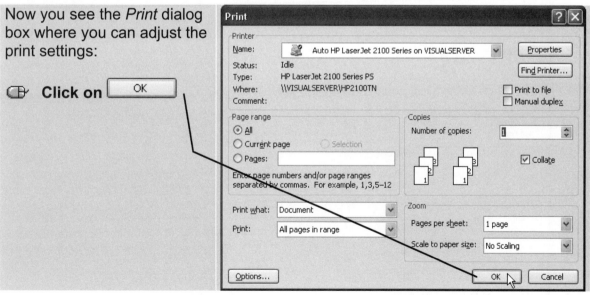

Your letter will be printed. Now you can practice what you've learned in the following exercises.

Exercises

Have you forgotten how to perform a particular action? Use the number beside the footsteps to look it up in the appendix *How Do I Do That Again?*

✔ Open the practice text 📄 The Prophet.doc in the 📁 My Documents folder. ᐟᐟ⁹

✔ Change the words `The Prophet` to the font *Arial*. ᐟᐟ²¹

✔ Change the words `The Prophet` to font size 26. ᐟᐟ²²

✔ Make the words `The Prophet` bold. ᐟᐟ²³

✔ Make the name `Kahlil Gibran` italic and bold. ᐟᐟ²⁴ ᐟᐟ²³

✔ Make the text `On Children` bold and underlined. ᐟᐟ²³ ᐟᐟ²⁵

✔ The text should look like this now:

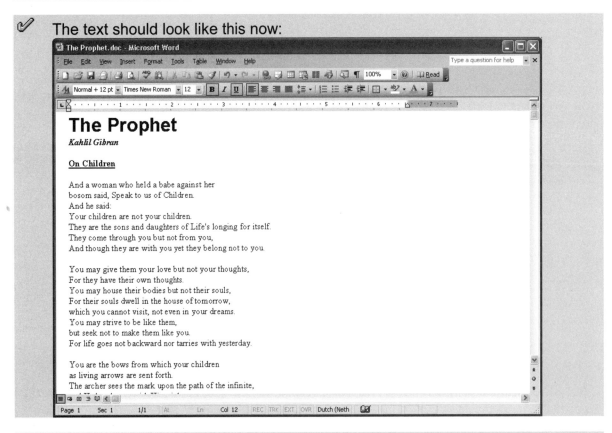

✔ Close the text and don't save the changes. ᐟᐟ¹⁴

Background Information

Desktop Publishing

A text is just a text. You set it down on paper, and that's that. It may be rather unattractive, and you might have several blank spaces dotted around the page. Presenting texts in an attractive way and preventing blank spaces is a task that occupies **DTPers**. **DTP** stands for **desktop publishing**. A desktop publisher is concerned with page formatting: both the presentation and the structure.

Before the computer age, page formatting often went hand in hand with a lot of measuring, calculating, and adjusting. Today, DTP software takes care of a lot of that work for the DTPer. Using this software, you can format pages professionally with headings, columns, photos, and more using just a few clicks and drags of the mouse.

Many of today's word processing programs such as *Word 2003* offer DTP features. For example, you can add photos and illustrations wherever you like, you can divide the text into columns, and you can format the text with various fonts. Nonetheless, real DTP programs offer a much wider range of features. Well-known DTP programs include *Adobe PageMaker* and *Microsoft Publisher*.

Fonts

There are countless fonts for the PC. You can see which fonts are installed on your computer by looking at the fonts list in *Word 2003*.

Most fonts can be used at every desired size. Usually you can choose any size between 8 points and 72 points:

a b c (8 points)   a b c (72 points)

But you can also enter a larger point size yourself by clicking in the font size box and typing in the desired number. You can type in any desired size, even a font with letters as large as an 8.5" x 11" sheet of paper. You can use a huge font like this to make a sign, for example.

Tips

 Tip

Shortcut Keys for Formatting Commands
Instead of giving commands using the mouse, you can use the following key combinations:

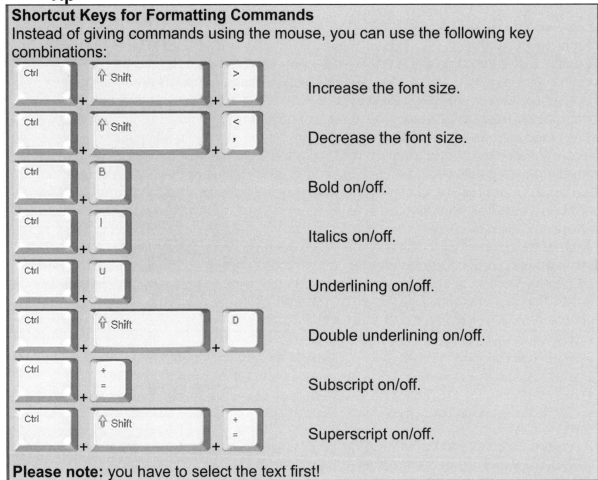

Increase the font size.

Decrease the font size.

Bold on/off.

Italics on/off.

Underlining on/off.

Double underlining on/off.

Subscript on/off.

Superscript on/off.

Please note: you have to select the text first!

Tip

Superscript and Subscript

If you're working with formulas, the ability to display text as a superscript or a subscript may come in handy. Using superscript, you can display text higher and smaller than the regular text on a line. For example, consider mathematical formulas such as $a^2 + b^2 = c^2$. Using subscript, the text is placed a little lower than the regular text. Very convenient if you want to write CO_2 for example.

You can put a text in superscript or subscript like this:

👉 **Click on the** Format **menu**

👉 **Click on** A Font...

👉 **Click on the tab** Font

👉 **Click to check** ☐ Superscript **or** ☐ Subscript

👉 **Click on** OK

Now you can type in your text in superscript or subscript. When you're ready to continue with regular text, turn the superscript or subscript back off.

You can also select the desired text and then turn on superscript or subscript.

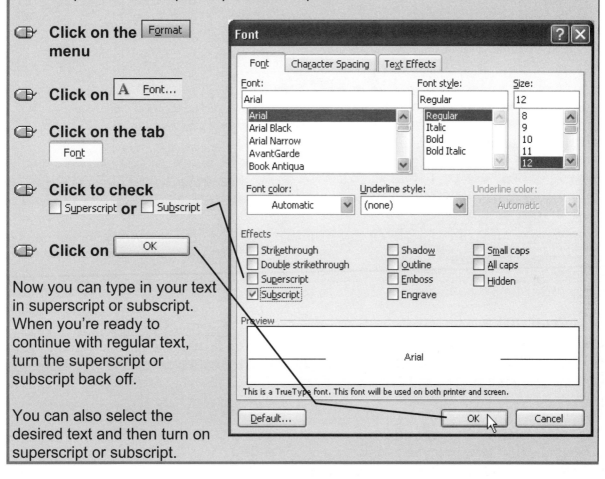

Tip

The Print Dialog Box
In this dialog box, you can make various adjustments that will affect the way your documents are printed.
If your document is large, you do not have to print the entire document each time. You can select just one page to be printed by activating

◯ Curr**e**nt page :

Or print several pages by activating

◯ Pa**g**es:

and typing the page numbers in the box. For example: 1,2,4,7.

You can also choose to print only the even or the odd pages:

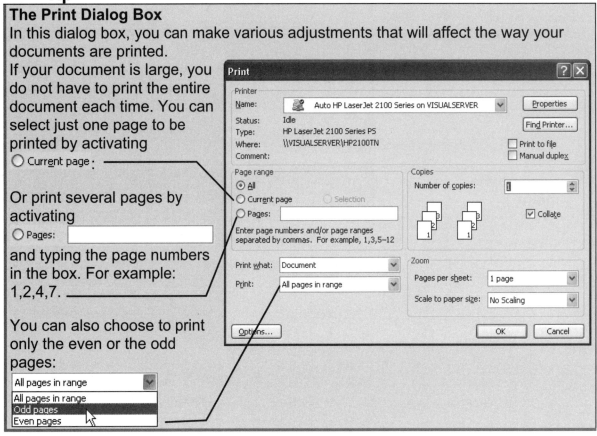

 Tip

The Print Dialog Box
You can also print multiple pages on one sheet of paper. The pages will then be shrunk and printed. This is one way to save paper.

Pages per s**h**eet: 1 page

You can select how many pages should be printed on one sheet of paper here.

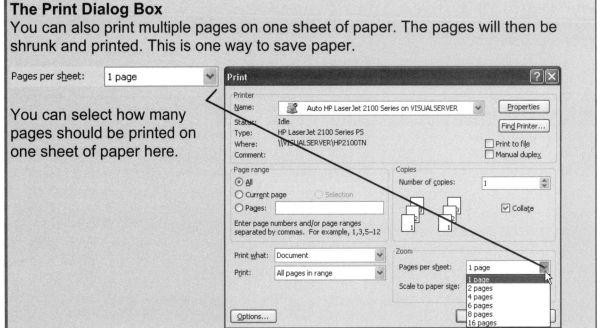

4. Formatting Paragraphs

All word processing programs work in more or less the same way. In the previous chapter we looked at how you can format characters and words, and you saw how to make text bold, italic, and underlined.

In this chapter you're going to go a step further and see how you can format paragraphs. In word processing programs, a character (a letter, symbol, or number) is the smallest unit you can format. A sentence is a larger unit of text: it begins with a capital letter and ends with a period, a question mark, or an exclamation point. A sentence can contain multiple lines. The paragraph is a whole block of text consisting of one or more sentences and closed by pressing the Enter key. In this chapter you'll learn how to format sentences, lines, and paragraphs.

In this chapter, you'll learn how to:

- recognize paragraphs
- select paragraphs, sentences, and lines
- select the entire text
- select multiple lines
- left align, right align, and justify a paragraph
- center a paragraph
- use formatting styles
- copy formatting

⇨ Please note:

To work through this chapter, you'll first need to download the files
📄 Practice Text Hoorn.doc and 📄 Twas the Night before Christmas.doc from the website and save them in the 📁 My Documents folder (if you haven't already).

You can read how to do this in Appendix A at the back of this book.

Selecting a Paragraph

A word processing program recognizes the following building blocks for a text:

- symbols and letters
- words
- sentences
- lines
- paragraphs
- pages
- the entire text

In the previous chapter, you formatted characters and words. You can also format lines, sentences, and paragraphs in various ways. Before you do that, it's important to understand exactly what a sentence or a paragraph is.

A **sentence** is a block of text that begins with a capital letter and ends with a period, a question mark, or an exclamation point. A sentence can contain multiple **lines**.

A **paragraph** is a block of text that consists of one or more **sentences**. It may take up one or more **lines** on paper. The next paragraph always begins at the left margin. To begin a new paragraph, you press the Enter key.

Word 2003 can automatically select lines, sentences, and paragraphs for you.

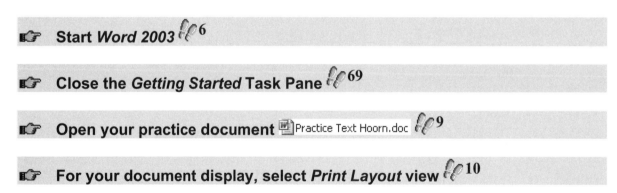

☞ **Start** *Word 2003* 6

☞ **Close the** *Getting Started* **Task Pane** 69

☞ **Open your practice document** [W] Practice Text Hoorn.doc 9

☞ **For your document display, select** *Print Layout* **view** 10

You can select a paragraph by clicking somewhere in the paragraph three times in quick succession.

Click three times quickly in this part of the text ⎯⎯⎯⎯⎯

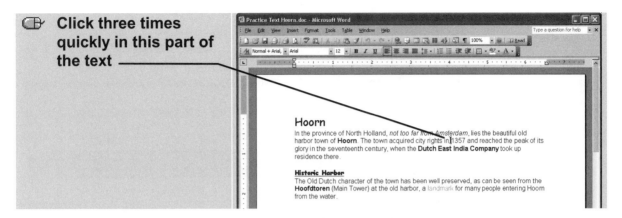

The paragraph is now selected. It runs from the first capital letter to the first time the Enter key was pressed after that:

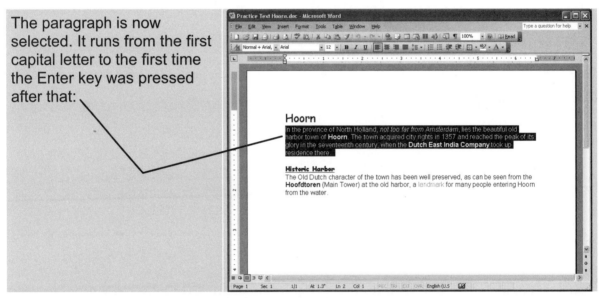

It doesn't matter where in the paragraph you click. You can click at the beginning, at the end, or somewhere in the middle. It is important, however, that you:

- click evenly, don't click click, then wait and click again
- click in the same place: don't move the mouse while you're clicking

After you've selected the paragraph, you can change the formatting just the way you did in the previous chapter. For example, you can underline the text.

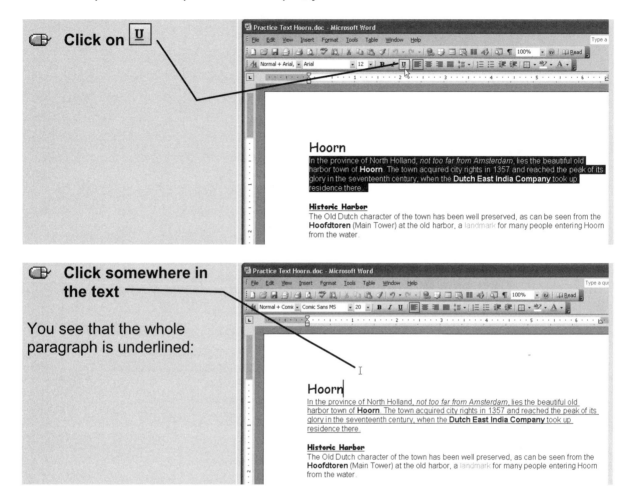

Click on U̲

Click somewhere in the text

You see that the whole paragraph is underlined:

You'll discover in this chapter that the paragraph is an important concept in *Word 2003*. Some types of formatting can only be applied at the paragraph level.

Selecting a Line

You can also select a single line. Here's how you do that:

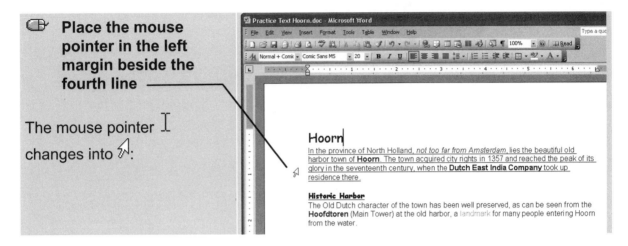

☞ **Place the mouse pointer in the left margin beside the fourth line** ───

The mouse pointer I

changes into :

💡 **Tip**

Sometimes you have to gently move the mouse pointer I to the left or to the right before it changes into 🖑.

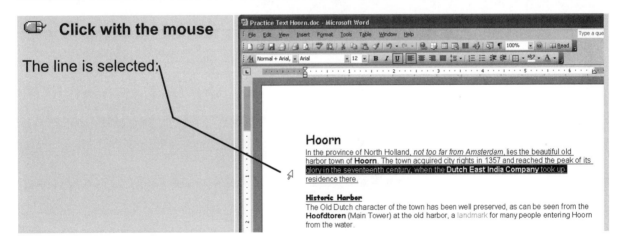

☞ **Click with the mouse**

The line is selected:

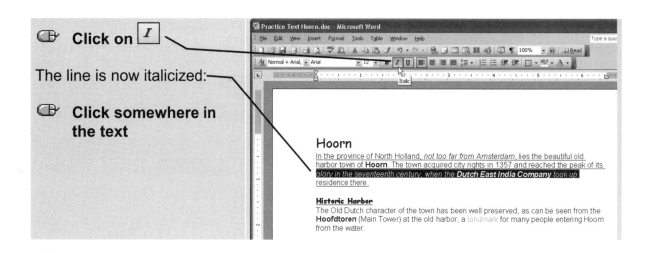

☞ **Click on** I

The line is now italicized:

☞ **Click somewhere in the text**

Selecting a Sentence

A sentence is a block of text that starts with a capital letter and ends with a period, a question mark, or an exclamation point. You can also select one entire sentence. To do that, you use the Ctrl key.

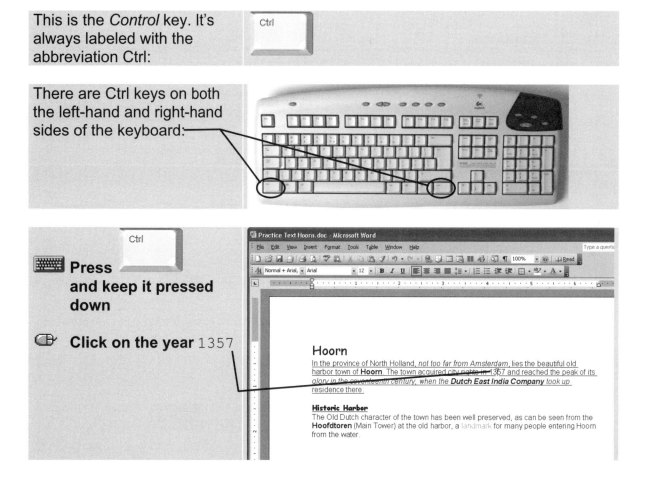

This is the *Control* key. It's always labeled with the abbreviation Ctrl:

There are Ctrl keys on both the left-hand and right-hand sides of the keyboard:

⌨ **Press** and keep it pressed down

☞ **Click on the year** 1357

The whole sentence is now selected:

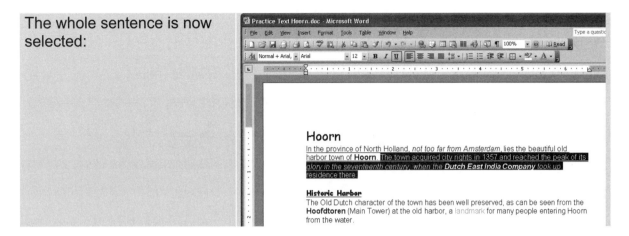

Now you can change the color of the characters in this sentence.

Click on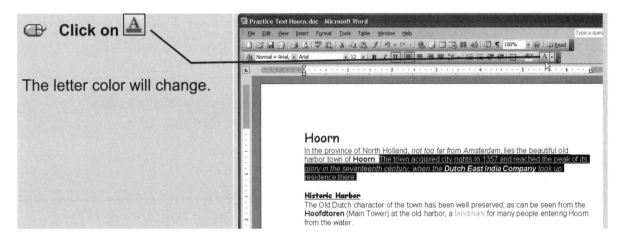

The letter color will change.

Undo

One of the nice features of *Word 2003* is that it keeps track of everything you've done. You can therefore easily *undo* your actions. For example, you can remove the formatting changes you just made. Give it a try:

Click on [↺] **as many times as you need to remove the underlining on the first paragraph**

Click in the text

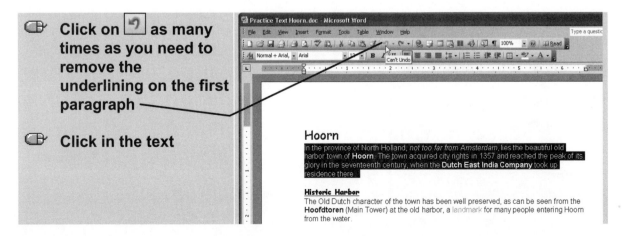

Making Paragraphs Visible

You can also have *Word 2003* clearly display the end of a paragraph.

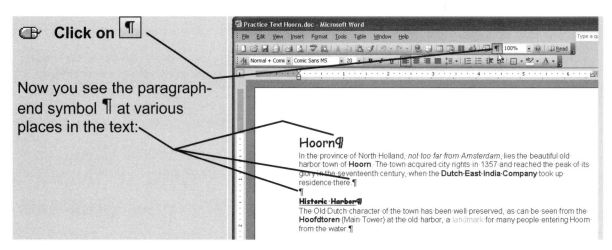

Now you can easily see what makes up a paragraph. Paragraphs can be long and can contain multiple sentences. A paragraph can also be very short. Examples of short paragraphs are the headings **Hoorn** and **Historic Harbor**.

 Tip

When you apply paragraph formatting to the text of your document, *Word* stores it in the paragraph mark (¶) that falls at the end of each paragraph. If you would move text to another part of the document and have forgotten to take the paragraph mark with you, the formatting of that text may change.

Another Way to Select Paragraphs

You can also select a paragraph by clicking twice in the margin. Give it a try:

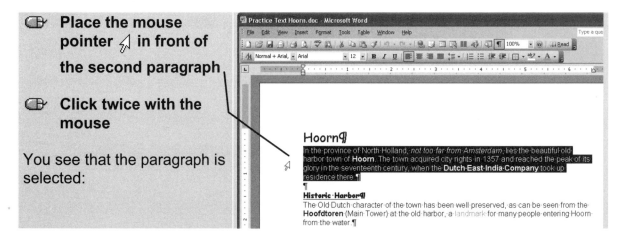

Text Alignment

Word 2003 has four buttons for text alignment. You see them on the formatting toolbar:

Alignment is the way the lines of a paragraph are spaced between the margins. You can use these buttons to align paragraphs in the following ways:

Align Left
The lines are flush against the left margin. The right margin depends on the place where the last word in a line ends. This is the default alignment.

Center
The lines are placed precisely in the middle between the left and right margins.

Align Right
The lines are placed flush against the right margin. This sort of alignment is often used in advertisements.

Justify
The lines begin at the left margin and end precisely at the right margin. This produces straight margins on both sides. To end precisely at the right margin, the space between the words on a line is increased as necessary. Justified text is often used in professional printed matter such as newspapers, books, and magazines.

⇨ Please note:

Alignment is a paragraph function. That means that the selected alignment automatically applies to the whole paragraph, not to a single sentence or line.

You don't have to select a paragraph before changing its alignment. You just have to click in it.

Click in the second paragraph

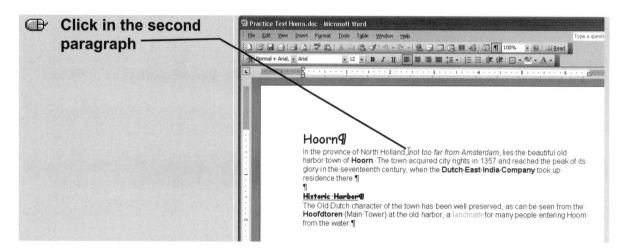

Now you can justify this paragraph.

Click on ≡

Compare the text with the previous image. Pay particular attention to the right margin.
You see that the lines of the paragraph are now flush with both the left and the right margins:

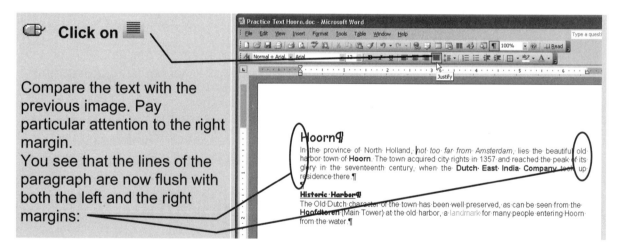

You can also align the lines just on the right margin.

Click on ≡

The lines are neatly lined up along the right margin, but the left margin is now uneven:

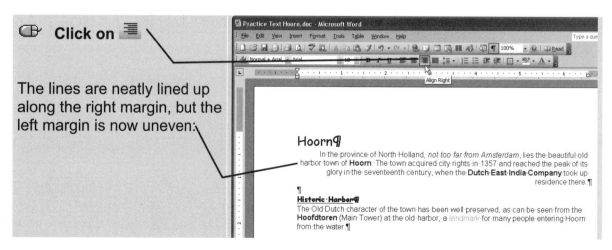

Right alignment is used in special situations such as advertisements. Change the alignment back to left now.

Click on ☰

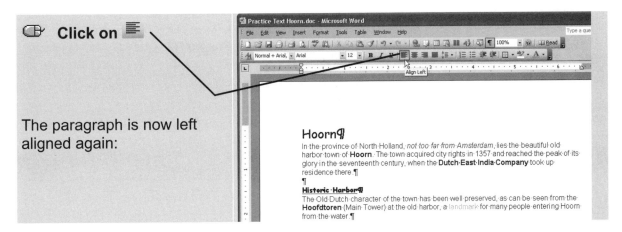

The paragraph is now left aligned again:

The last alignment function is *center*. Just like right alignment, centering is used in special texts. Examples are invitations, menus, poems, or the title of an article.

Click in Hoorn

Now click on ☰

You see that Hoorn is placed in the middle of the page:

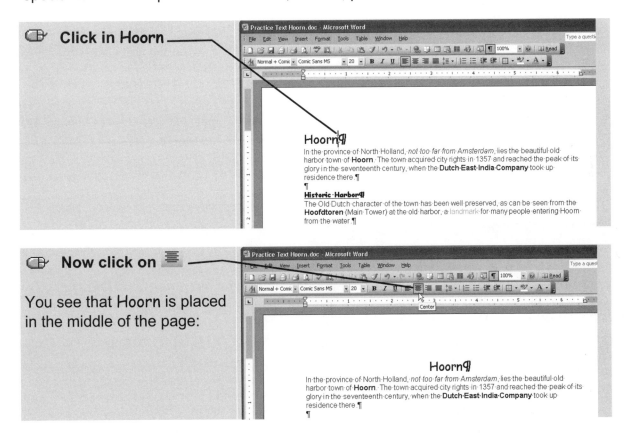

 Tip

You can also specify the alignment beforehand, just as other formatting attributes. Then as you enter new, the alignment is immediately applied.

Selecting Multiple Lines

You can also select multiple lines. You do that by dragging with the mouse.

 **Place the mouse
pointer ⟋ in front of**
Historic Harbor

 **Press the mouse
button and keep it
pressed down**

You see that the line
Historic·Harbor
is selected:

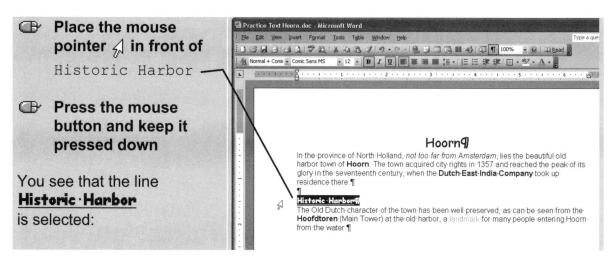

 **Drag the mouse
pointer ⟍ down a
little, keeping the
mouse button pressed
down**

You see that the following line
is also selected:———————

 **Now release the
mouse button**

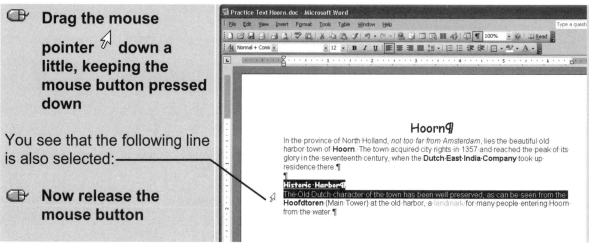

Now you've selected two lines. The first line is in fact a whole paragraph (**Historic
Harbor**). The second line is actually the first line of the next paragraph.

⇨ **Please note:**

Hierarchical structure
Word organizes most document formatting into three levels (font, paragraph, and
section). Paragraph formatting, the second of these and the basic building block of
most documents, includes tasks such as alignment, paragraph spacing and line
spacing.

Remember, *Word* applies alignment on the paragraph level. Take a look at what happens if you now center these lines.

Click on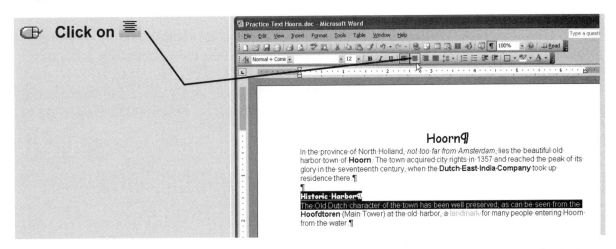

Both paragraphs are now centered:

Please note:
The entire bottom paragraph is centered, not just the first line:

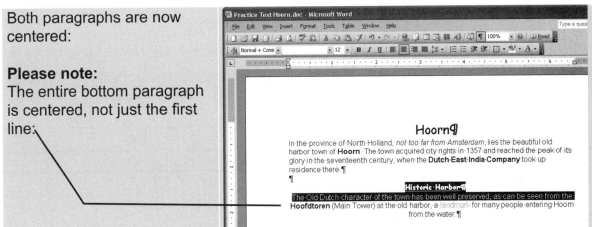

You can undo these last changes.

Click on

Click somewhere in the text

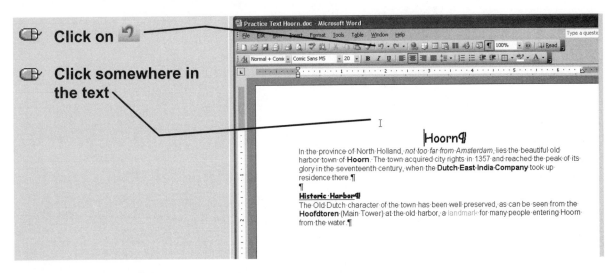

Using Styles

In several situations it can be convenient to use a single formatting style for certain documents. Consider for example companies or organizations that want to keep the font and layout the same for all their reports or letters. You can also use a particular formatting style for your own letters or texts.

Word 2003 has a handy built-in function for this: the *style*. A *style* is a bundle of formatting specifications for a text. For example, a style can define all the following in one stroke:

- font
- font size
- line spacing
- indentation
- color

By selecting a style, you are choosing a particular set of formatting options. Styles can be used for an entire text, but they can also be selected beforehand or afterward on a paragraph-by-paragraph basis.

➡ **Please note:**

Just as for alignment, a style always applies to the whole paragraph.

Because styles apply to whole paragraphs, you don't have to select the paragraph.

👆 **Click in the last line**

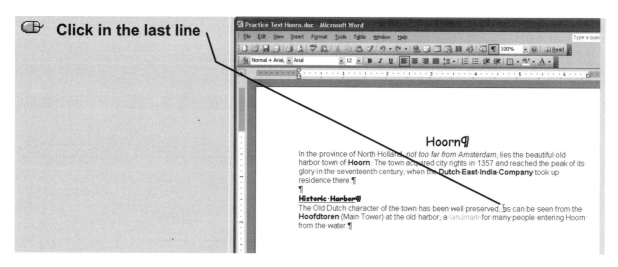

You can select styles in the *Style* box on the far leftside of the formatting toolbar.

Click on ☑ beside

𝐴𝐴 Normal ▼

Now you see a whole list of styles:

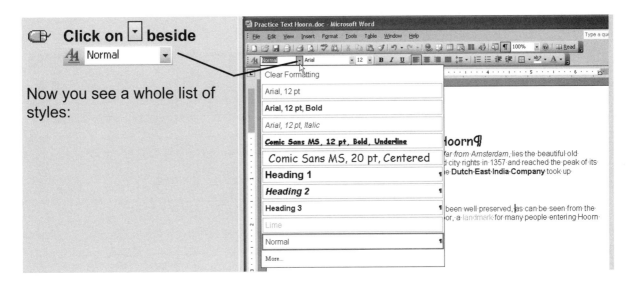

══════════════════

⇨ Please note:

You may see other styles on your computer.

Click on

Heading 2

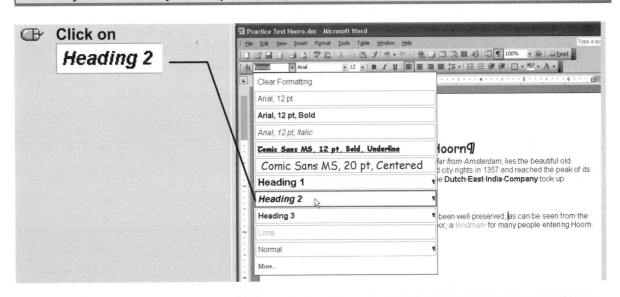

The text in the whole paragraph is now in the style of *Heading 2*:

You can tell by this:

Heading 2

Heading 2 uses large, italic letters.

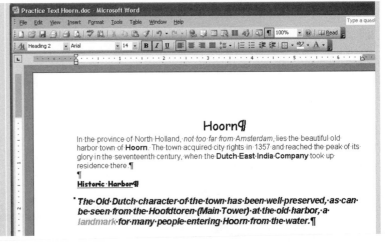

For regular text, use the *Normal* style.

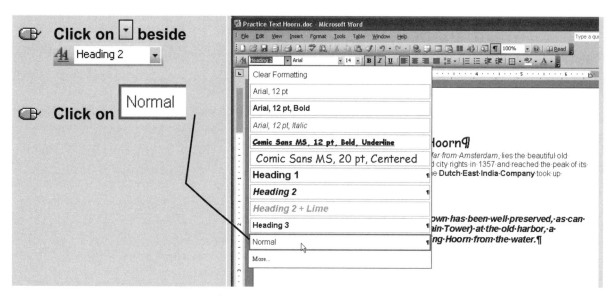

The text has changed back to the default font for this document:

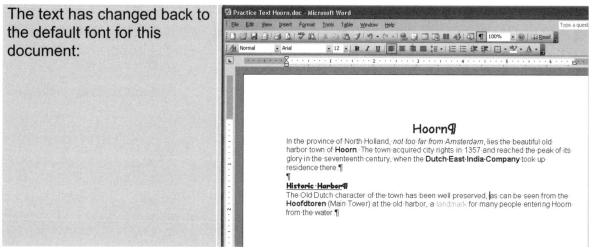

Styles are often used to standardize headings and titles. A company may decide to use **Heading 1** for all the main headings of their documents, **Heading 2** for the second-level headings, and so on.

Format Painter

Word 2003 has a handy function you can use to copy and paste formatting. Say you've formatted a chapter title like this:

Chapter 1

For every subsequent chapter, you'll have to adjust the font size, font, and alignment again. That's a lot of work, and moreover, you'll have to remember or keep looking up what you used the first time. In a situation like this, it's a better idea to use the *Format Painter* function.

That's this button 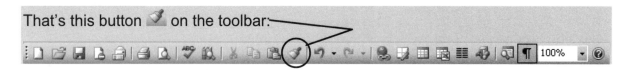 on the toolbar:

Using this button 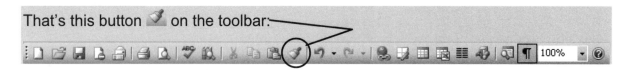 you don't copy the text, but rather the formatting. It happens in three steps:

- Click in the text whose formatting you want to copy (the example)
- Click on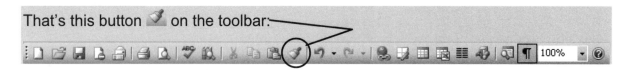
- Drag the mouse pointer along the text that should use the same formatting.

Give it a try:

Click in the heading

Hoorn

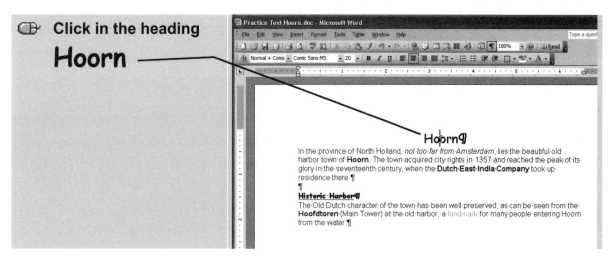

Click on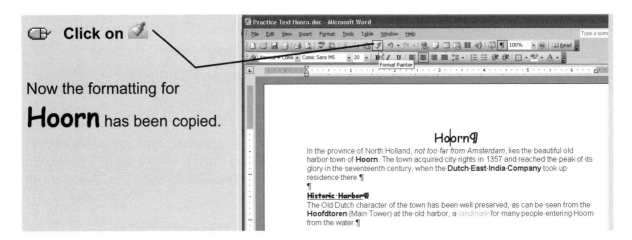

Now the formatting for

Hoorn has been copied.

Now you can apply this style to a different block of text.

Drag the mouse
pointer along
Historic Harbor

Release the button

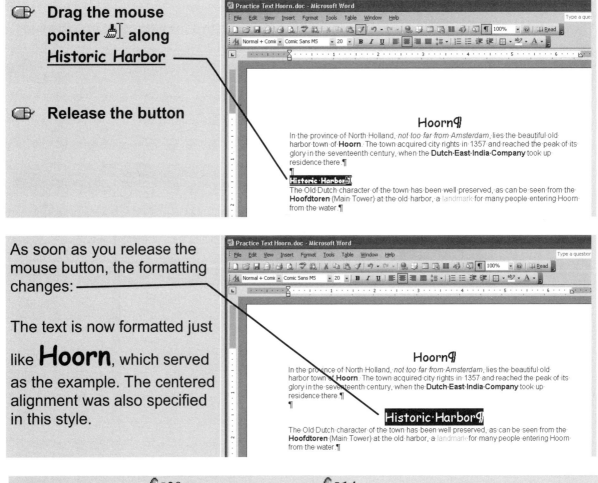

As soon as you release the mouse button, the formatting changes:

The text is now formatted just like **Hoorn**, which served as the example. The centered alignment was also specified in this style.

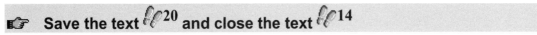 **Save the text 20 and close the text 14**

In this chapter you've seen how you can select larger text sections and change their formatting. You can practice what you've learned in the following exercises.

Exercises

Have you forgotten how to perform a particular action? Use the number beside the footsteps to look it up in the appendix *How Do I Do That Again?*

Exercise: Line Alignment

✓ Open the practice text 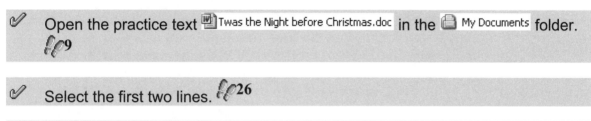 in the My Documents folder. 9

✓ Select the first two lines. 26

✓ Center these lines. 27

✓ Select the first eight lines of the poem. 26

✓ Right align these lines. 28

✓ The text should look like this now:

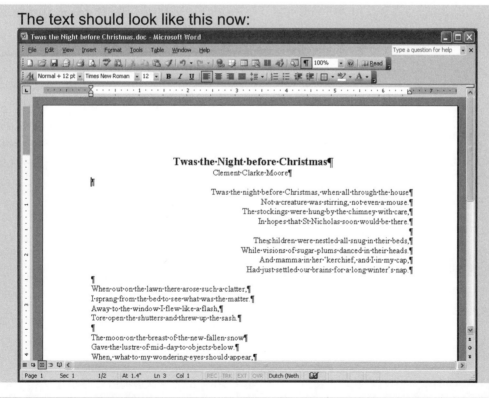

✓ Close the text and don't save the changes. 14

Background Information

Word Alone and Bundled

The very first version of *Word*, version 1.0, came onto the market at the end of 1983, a year after its competitor *WordPerfect* hit the stores. *Word* wouldn't overcome this disadvantage in the race between the word processors for a long time. *WordPerfect* remained the market leader for at least another 10 years.

Many versions later, after *Windows* had replaced *DOS* as the most popular operating system, *Word* passed *WordPerfect* and became the most popular word processing program. That was in no small measure due to the fact that *Word* was part of the popular *Office* package: a collection of programs that were used particularly often in the business world.

Word is still available as a separate program, but it is sold most often in combination with other Microsoft programs. As we mentioned, it is part of *Office*, and it's also part of the latest versions of *Microsoft Works*.

Microsoft Works is a collection of different programs: not only *Word*, but also *Encarta* (an encyclopedia), *Money* (a money management program) and *Picture it!* (a photo editing program).

Microsoft Office is somewhat more serious. In addition to *Word*, it contains the following programs:

- *Excel*: a spreadsheet program. This program makes it easier to work with numbers and their interactions with each other. A spreadsheet is actually a big sheet with lots of little boxes arranged in rows and columns. You can enter mathematical formulas in the boxes, in which the numbers to be used come from boxes elsewhere in the spreadsheet.

- *Access*: a database program. You can store, edit, and view all kinds of data in an organized way with it.

- *PowerPoint*: a presentation program. You can use it to create multimedia presentations, such as a slideshow with sound.

- *Outlook*: an information management program. You can use it to manage your information and communication, such as your e-mail, your appointments, and your schedule.

- *FrontPage*: a website editor. You can use it to make relatively simple websites.

One of the advantages of a package like this is that information can be exchanged easily between the various programs.

Tips

 Tip

Shortcut Keys for Paragraph Formatting

Instead of giving commands with the mouse, you can use the following key combinations to format paragraphs:

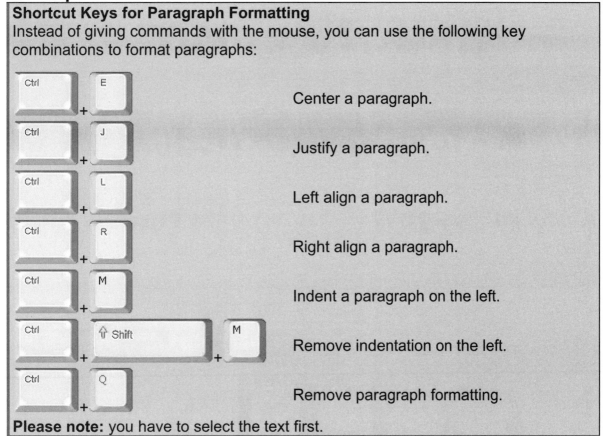

Center a paragraph.

Justify a paragraph.

Left align a paragraph.

Right align a paragraph.

Indent a paragraph on the left.

Remove indentation on the left.

Remove paragraph formatting.

Please note: you have to select the text first.

Tip

Shortcut Keys for Selecting

Instead of giving commands with the mouse, you can use the following key combinations to select text:

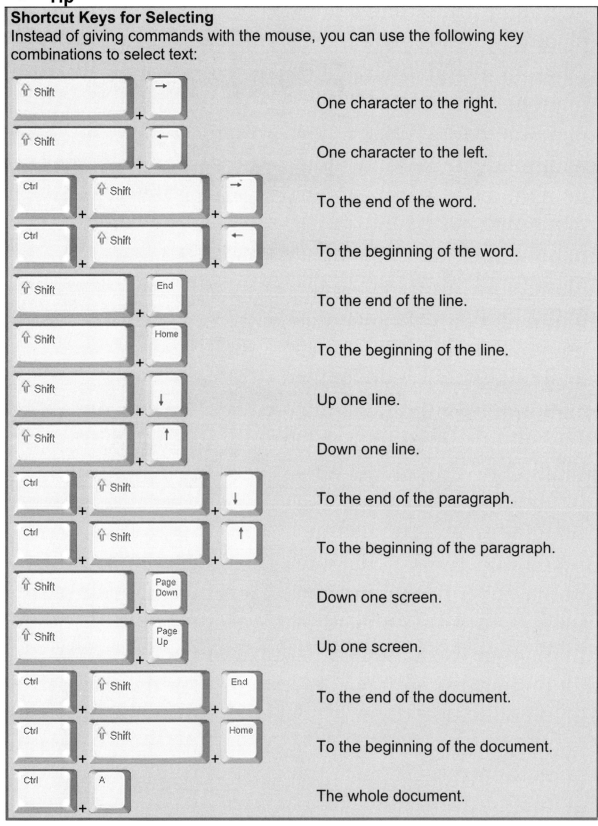

One character to the right.

One character to the left.

To the end of the word.

To the beginning of the word.

To the end of the line.

To the beginning of the line.

Up one line.

Down one line.

To the end of the paragraph.

To the beginning of the paragraph.

Down one screen.

Up one screen.

To the end of the document.

To the beginning of the document.

The whole document.

Tip

Selections at a Glance

What are you selecting?	How:
Text	Drag along the text
A word (but you can only change the formatting)	Click in the word
A word (now you can also delete the word or replace it, etc.)	Double-click in the word
A paragraph	Click in the paragraph three times
A line	Click in front of the line you're pointing to
A paragraph	Double-click in front of the paragraph you're pointing to
A sentence	Click while you hold Ctrl down
Multiple lines	Drag along the lines you're pointing to
The whole text	Click on Edit Click on Select All

5. Formatting Pages

The three *levels* of *Word* formatting available for your documents are Font, Paragraph and Page (*Section*) formatting. To improve the appearance of your documents you can apply *font* and *paragraph* formatting as we have learned in the previous chapters. In this chapter we will take a look at what is commonly called the page layout. Page or *Section* formatting for a typical document includes elements such as margins, paper size, paper orientation, headers and footers, page borders, etc. The margins specify how much white space there is between the edge of the paper and the text. The margins not only ensure that your text looks good on paper but they are also important if you want to have your pages bound.

There may be times when you want to have your text divided into columns such as for a brochure or newsletter. *Word* lets you distribute text over columns any way you like.

Page numbers, headers and footers are also indispensable for improving consistency and legibility in large documents. In *Word 2003* you can add all of these elements to your documents in many different combinations.

In this chapter, you'll learn how to:

- adjust margins
- specify page breaks
- adjust header and footer texts
- insert page numbers

⇨ Please note:

In this chapter you're going to work some more with the practice text from chapter 1: Internet Connections.doc If you don't yet have this file on your computer, then you can download Internet Connections.doc from the website and save it in the My Documents folder.

You can read how to do this in Appendix A at the back of this book.

Page Setup

To see how you can adjust the settings for a page, first open a practice text.

☞ **Start** *Word 2003* ℓℓ⁶

☞ **Open the practice text** 🔲 Internet Connections.doc **in the** 🗁 My Documents **folder** ℓℓ⁹

☞ **For your document display, select** *Print Layout* **view** ℓℓ¹⁰

☞ **Turn off the display of hidden formatting marks** ℓℓ¹¹

Now you see this text:

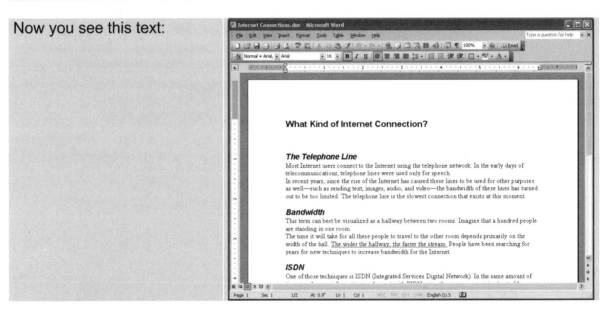

Margins

Every page has blank edges, called margins. Here's how you can make them visible:

👆 **Click on** Tools

👆 **Click on** Options...

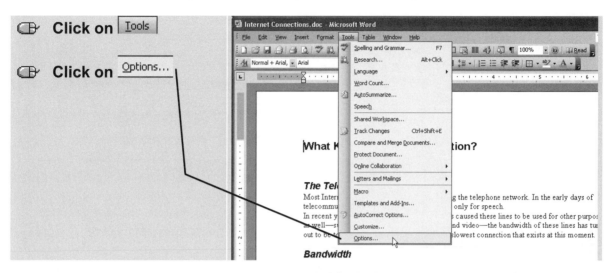

Now you see the *Options* dialog box:

👆 **Click on the tab**
   View

👆 **Click to add a checkmark beside**
   ☐ Text boundaries

👆 **Click on** OK

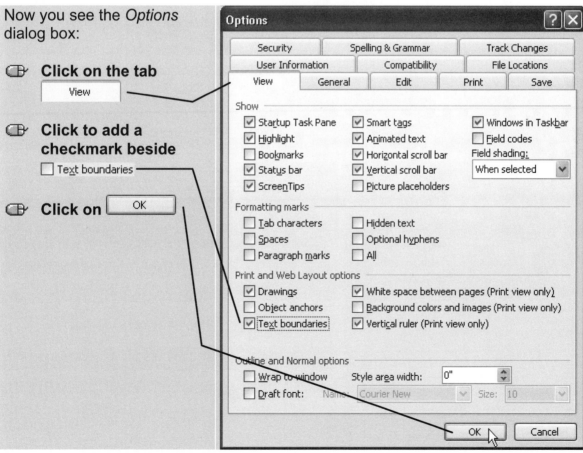

Now you see a dotted line around the text block. The white edges around it are called the margins.

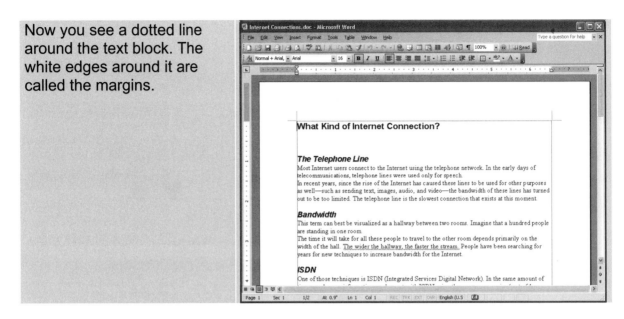

You can adjust the margins like this:

Click on **File**

Click on **Page Setup...**

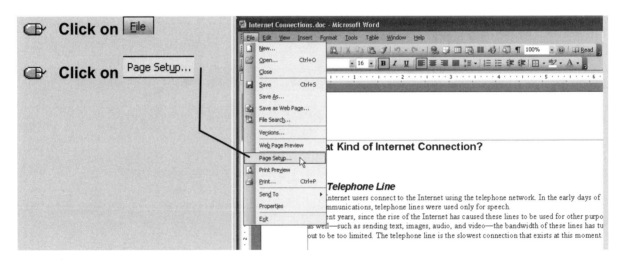

Now you see the *Page Setup* dialog box where you can set margins, page size and page layout.

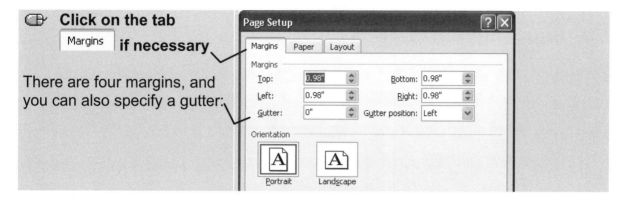

> 👆 **Click on the tab** Margins **if necessary**
>
> There are four margins, and you can also specify a gutter:

You can increase the top margin, for example.

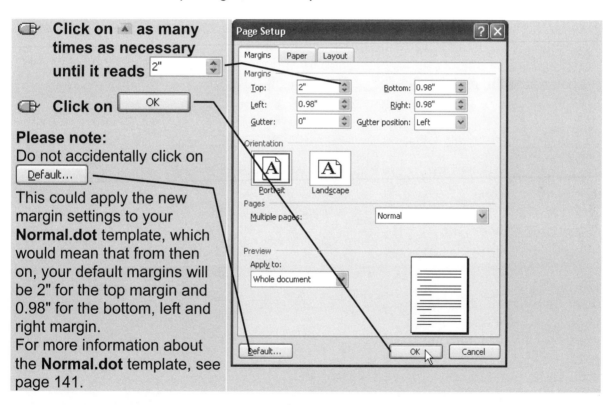

> 👆 **Click on ▲ as many times as necessary until it reads** 2"
>
> 👆 **Click on** OK

Please note:
Do not accidentally click on Default...
This could apply the new margin settings to your **Normal.dot** template, which would mean that from then on, your default margins will be 2" for the top margin and 0.98" for the bottom, left and right margin.
For more information about the **Normal.dot** template, see page 141.

 Tip

Default margins
The top, bottom, left and right margins for this document are set to 0.98". This differs from the default margins for documents in *Word 2003* as shown in the following example:

Top:	1"	Bottom:	1"
Left:	1.25"	Right:	1.25"

You see that there is now more white space at the top of the page:

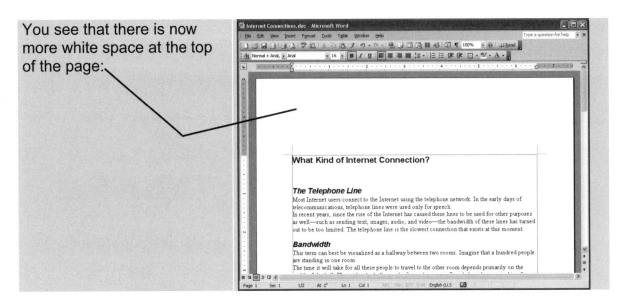

You can adjust the left, right, and bottom margins in the same way. The text will be automatically adjusted to fit inside these margins.

You usually only adjust the margins once for a document. The right amount of white space around the text is a question of taste or efficiency.

💡 Tip

Gutter

In addition to the top, bottom, left, and right margins, *Word 2003* also has a fifth margin: the *gutter*.

The gutter is an extra margin for binding a document. You adjust it here:

`Mirror margins`

If you use even and odd pages, you can have the margins alternate here:

Gutter position: | Left

You can also use the gutter at the top of the page.

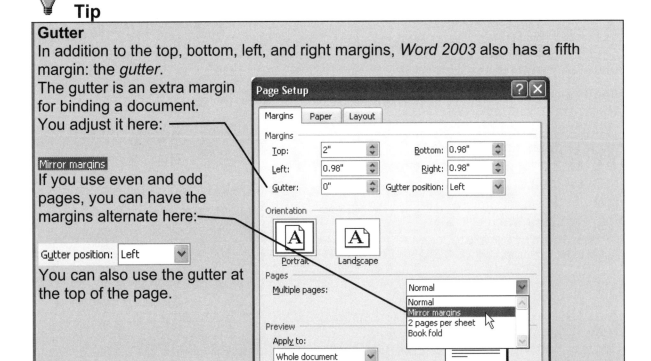

Tip

Minimum Margins

Nearly every printer has a nonprintable area. That's a strip on the paper that can't be printed. Some inkjet printers have a fairly wide nonprintable edge. Laser printers have a very narrow one.

If you make the margins too small, you'll get a warning like this one:

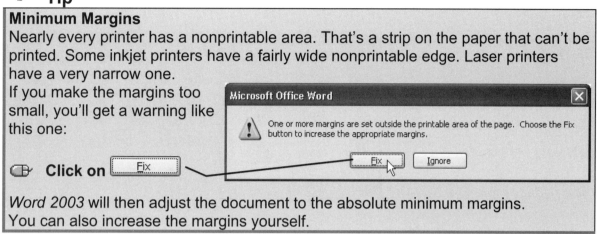

☞ **Click on** Fix

Word 2003 will then adjust the document to the absolute minimum margins. You can also increase the margins yourself.

Page Breaks

You don't need to use the margins to determine how the text is distributed over the pages. There are various other methods for separating blocks or sections of text.

You can:
- insert a page break
- format a paragraph so that it moves to the next page

You can have the page end at a specific place and push a paragraph onto the following page. Here's how you do that:

☞ **Go to the bottom of the first page** ℓℓ**29**

There you see a paragraph with the heading *Cable*:

☞ **Place the cursor before the heading Cable**

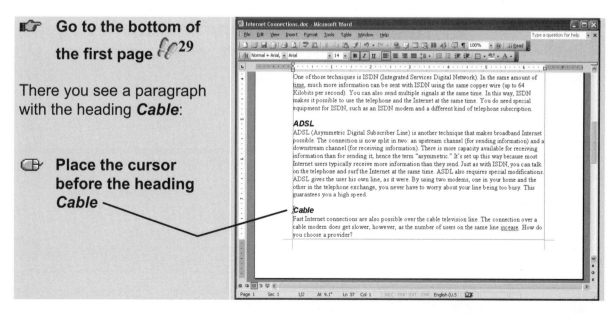

You can insert a **page break** here. This (invisible) symbol specifies that the page ends here and that the rest of the text has to continue on the next page.

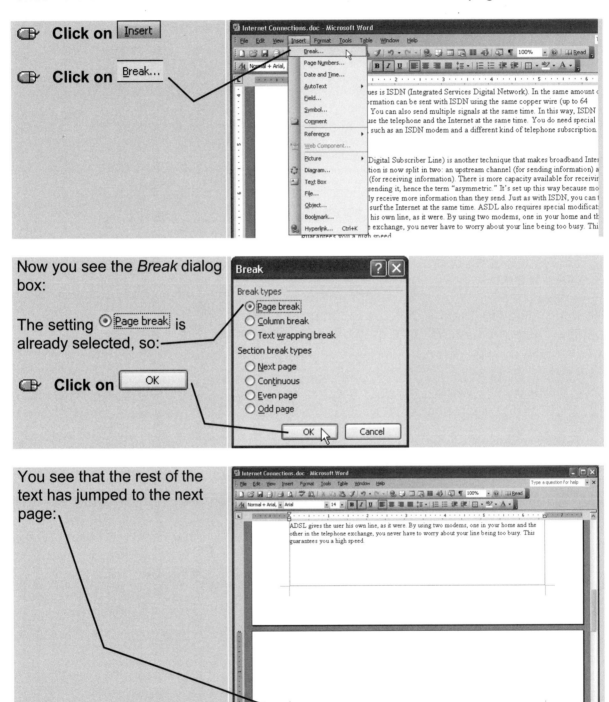

Click on `Insert`

Click on `Break...`

Now you see the *Break* dialog box:

The setting ⊙ `Page break` is already selected, so:

Click on `OK`

You see that the rest of the text has jumped to the next page:

Removing a Page Break

If you want to remove a page break, it's easier to do that in the normal layout than in the print layout.

👆 **Click on** View

👆 **Click on** Normal

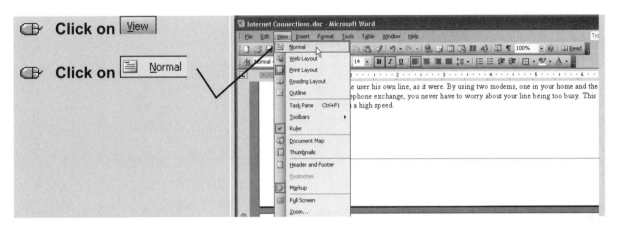

Now you see a line above *Cable* marked *Page Break*:

👆 **Place the cursor on that line**

⌨ **Press** Delete

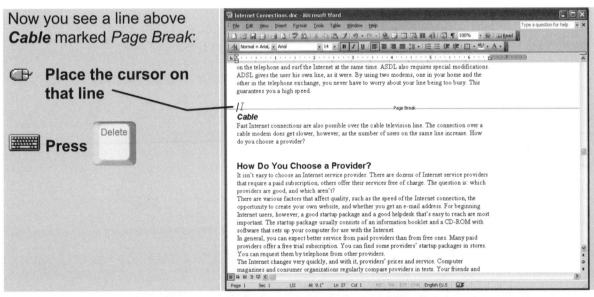

The page break is deleted. You see that a new dotted line indicating the end of the page automatically appears in a different place:

You can't delete or move this dotted line.

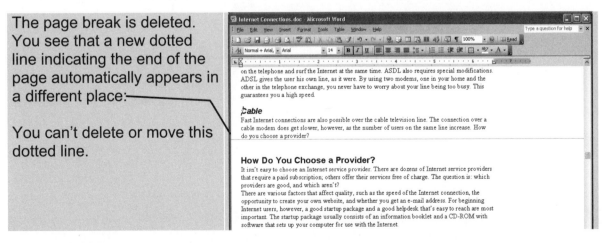

Tip

Page Breaks Using the Keyboard
You can also insert a page break using the keyboard. You do that with the Enter key:

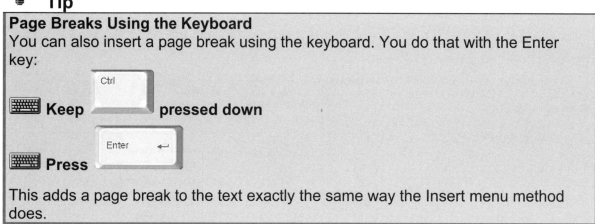

Keep Ctrl **pressed down**

Press Enter

This adds a page break to the text exactly the same way the Insert menu method does.

A Page Break Before a Paragraph

If you want a particular paragraph to start on a new page, you can attach the page break marker to the paragraph itself. Here's how you do that:

Click on *Cable*

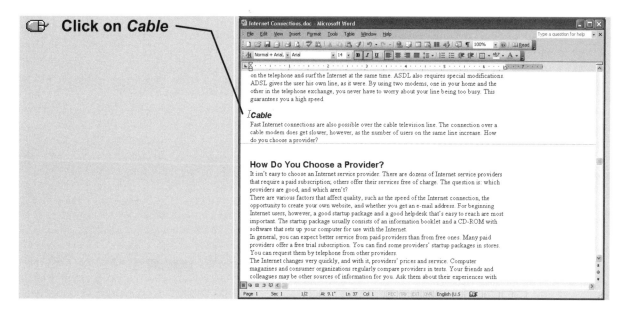

👆 **Click on** Format

👆 **Click on** ≣ Paragraph...

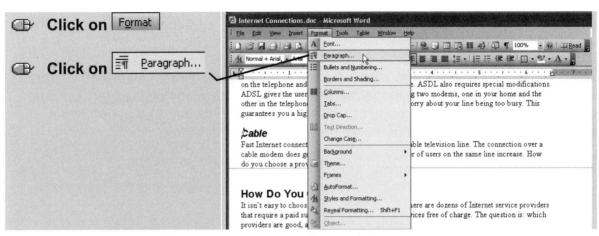

Now you see the *Paragraph* dialog box:

👆 **Click on the tab**
Line and Page Breaks

Now you see several settings for pagination. You can specify a page break before the paragraph here:

👆 **Click to add a checkmark beside**
☐ Page break before

👆 **Click on** OK

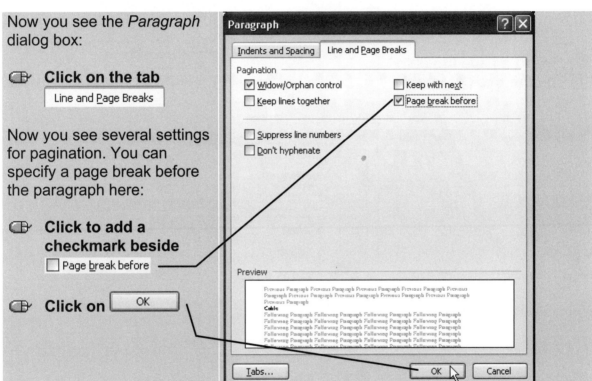

👉 **For your document display, select** *Print Layout* **view**
👣 10

Now you see that the paragraph *Cable* is at the top of the page:

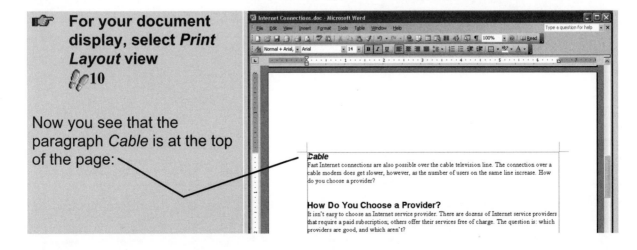

Now you've seen both options for specifying the end of a page at a particular place and continuing on a new page.

Both methods have the same effect. Adding a page break yourself is called a "hard" break. It always stays in the same place in the text, regardless of changes before or after it. You always break a page at a specific paragraph when that page should begin with a particular paragraph, such as a chapter title.

For the next topic, it's convenient if the document has three pages. You can arrange this by creating a new page at the start of the document containing the document title.

👆 **Click in front of *The Telephone Line***

👉 **Insert a page break before this paragraph**
✍30

Now you see that *The Telephone Line* starts on a new page:

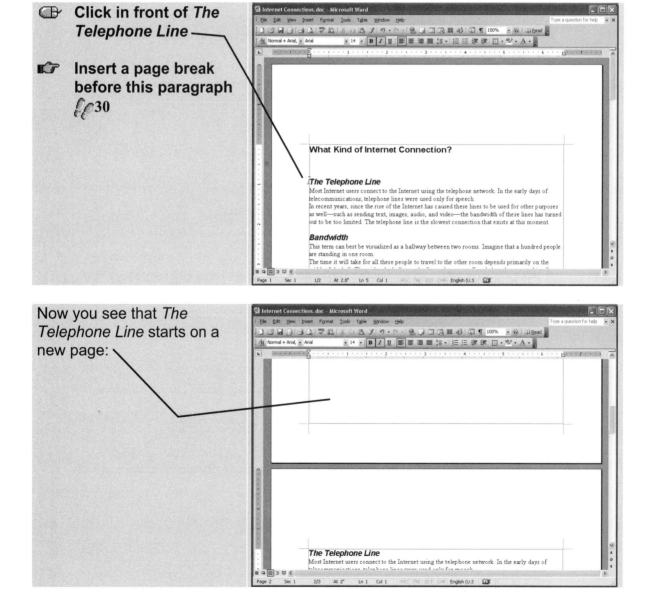

Headers and Footers

Nearly every book has a header. That's a line at the top of the page that usually contains the title of the book or of the chapter, and often the page number.
Some books also have a footer. That's a similar kind of line, but then at the bottom of the page. In many books, that's where the page number is. Of course, you don't have to type in the header or footer on every page; you only have to specify it once. Regardless of the number of pages in the document, *Word 2003* prints this header or footer on every page.

The header and footer are printed in the top and bottom margins of the page, respectively. Here's how you add a header or a footer:

☞ Click on View

☞ Click on
Header and Footer

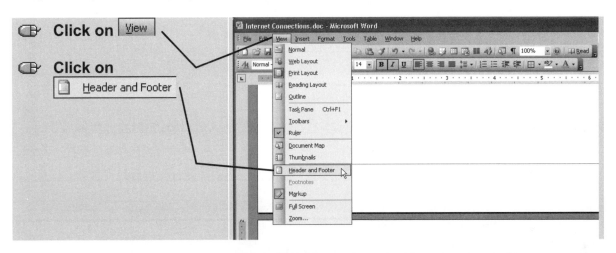

Now the top margin is visible:

You also see a long toolbar:

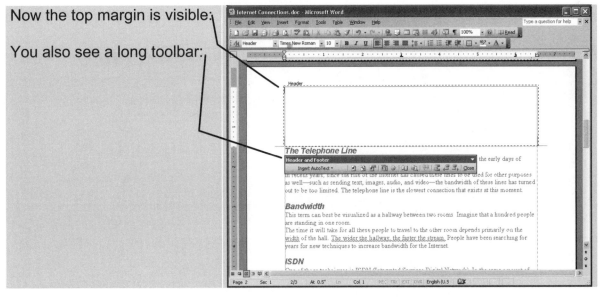

You can use this toolbar to specify several preferences for the header and footer:

You can also use it to move to the footer.

Click on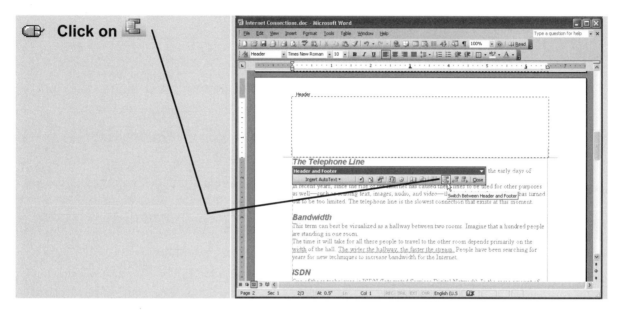

Now you see the bottom margin, where the footer will go:

Click on again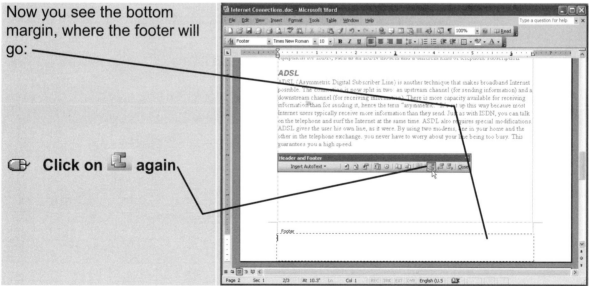

Now you see the header location. You can start typing in a header line.

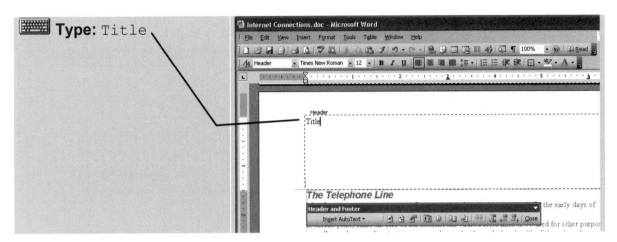

Type: Title

A header or footer can be formatted like any other text.

Page Numbers

Headers often contain the page number. You can add that in like this:

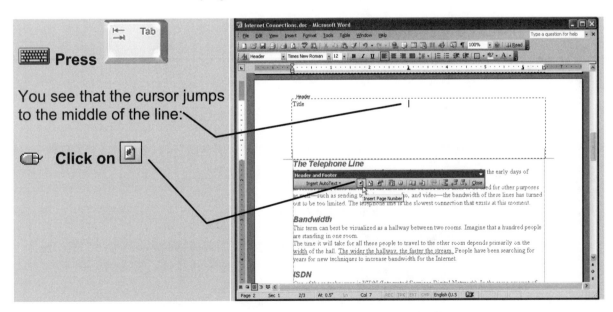

Press Tab

You see that the cursor jumps to the middle of the line:

Click on

You see that the page
number 2 is filled in:

That's correct; you're on the
second page now.

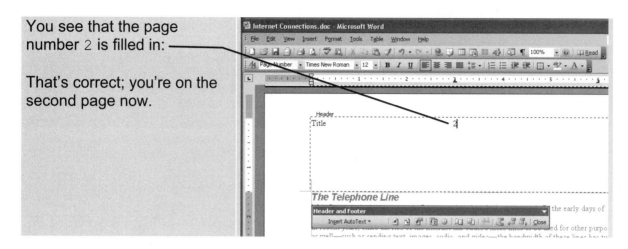

Word 2003 can also display the total number of pages. You can use that in an
important document where no pages should be missing, for example. You can have it
say *page 1 of 4*. You can add this kind of page numbering to the footer, for example.

Click on

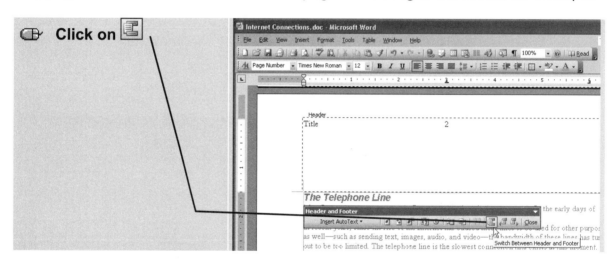

Now you see the footer area.

First, type in the text:

Type: Page

Type a space

Now you can add in the page
number:

Click on

Type a space

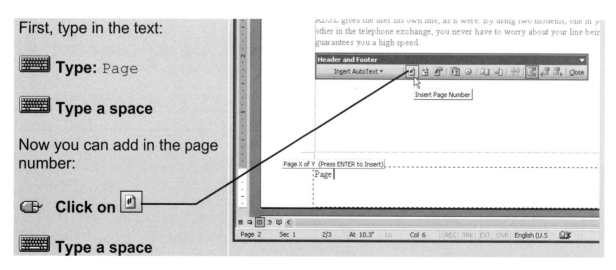

Type: of

Type a space

Now you can add in the total number of pages:

☞ **Click on**

The total number of pages (3) is filled in:
This number automatically changes as the number of pages in the document changes.

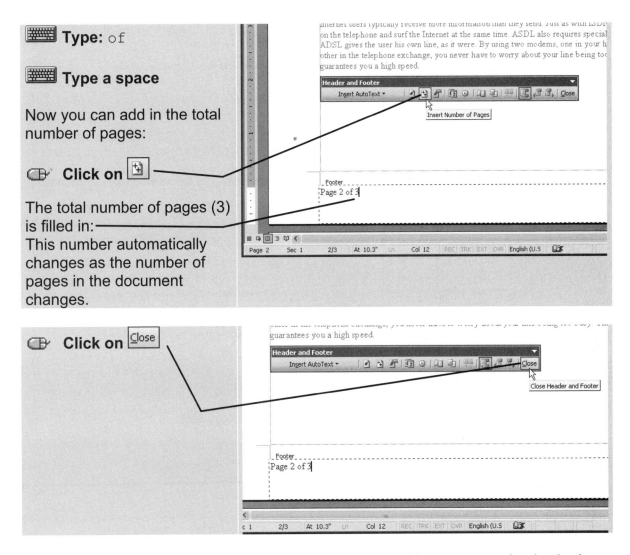

☞ **Click on** Close

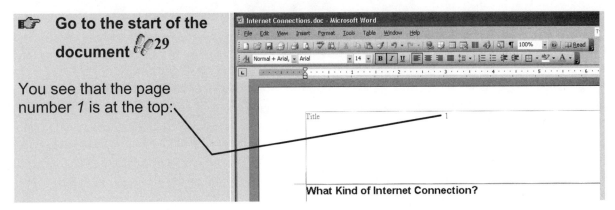

The toolbar disappears and you see the regular layout. Now you can check whether the page numbers are filled in correctly.

☞ **Go to the start of the document** 𝓁𝓁²⁹

You see that the page number *1* is at the top:

☞   Go to the bottom of the page 🐾29

You see that *Page 1 of 3* is at the bottom:

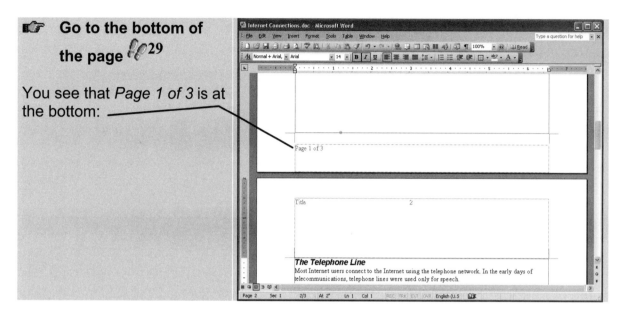

You see that you can use page numbers in very flexible ways.

☞   Close this document and don't save the changes 🐾14

You can practice what you've learned in the following exercises.

Exercises

Have you forgotten how to perform a particular action? Use the number beside the footsteps to look it up in the appendix *How Do I Do That Again?*

Exercise: Page Formatting

In this exercise, you'll practice formatting a page.

✅ Start *Word 2003.* 6

✅ Open the document Internet Connections.doc in the My Documents folder. 9

✅ Make sure that *Text boundaries* are on. 31

✅ For your document display, select *Print Layout* view. 10

✅ Adjust the top margin of the page to 1.8". 32

✅ Add a page break before the heading **Bandwidth**. 30

✅ For your document display, select *Normal* view. 12

✅ Remove the page break. 33

✅ Add a header with the text *Exercise.* 34

✅ Add a footer containing the page number. 35

Tips

 Tip

Formatting Page Numbers
You can select different kinds of numbering, such as *I, II* or a, b, and so forth.
You do that by clicking on the toolbar on:

Then you see the *Page Number Format* dialog box where you can select the numbering style:

You can also start with a page number other than 1:

You can use this if two documents belong together, for example, such as separate chapters in a book.

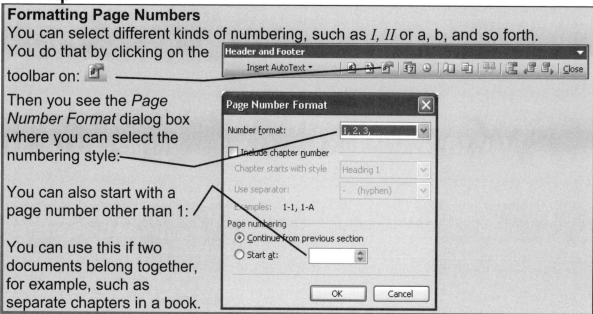

 Tip

Header Types
Books often have three different headers. The even pages often contain the title of the book, while the uneven pages contain the title of the chapter. The first page of a chapter usually doesn't have any header text, just the page number. You can specify all these kinds of headers in *Word 2003*.

You do that by clicking on the toolbar on:

Then you see the *Page Setup* dialog box where you can specify the headers:

By default, *Word 2003* creates only one header which is used for even, odd, and first pages.

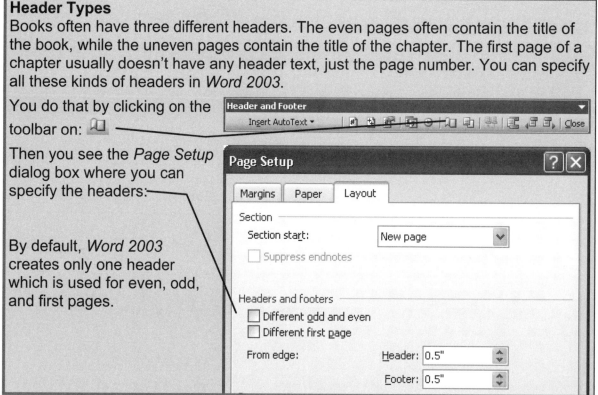

Tip

The header is usually in the top margin. The position of the header is specified by giving the distance to the edge of the paper. Of course, this distance has to be within the top margin. You specify that here:

Click on File

Click on Page Setup...

Click on the tab Layout

You specify the distance here:

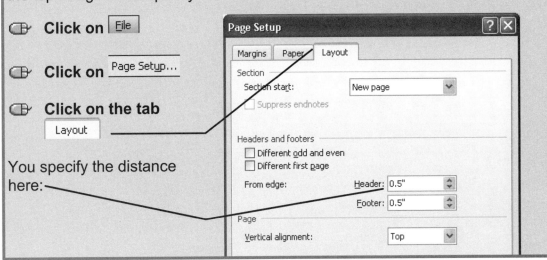

 Tip

Normal.dot

When you create a new document, *Microsoft Word* bases your new document on a template. If you choose *Blank document*, *Word* will base your document on the *Normal* template, normal.dot. When a document is created, it inherits three things from its parent template:

- styles
- content (e.g. text, pictures, any content in headers and footers)
- page settings (e.g. margins, paper size, paper orientation, settings for headers and footers)

If a document is created from a template other than normal.dot, the document has no connection to normal.dot. That is, no styles in normal.dot affect the document, no content in normal.dot is brought into the document, and no page settings in normal.dot affect the document. A new document only inherits these things from its parent template. So at the moment a document is created, the styles of its parent template are copied to the document. From that moment, a document only has access to the styles stored in the document.

6. Pictures and Clip Art

"A picture is worth a thousand words," so goes the saying. A photo or illustration can enhance your document, making the text easier to read and more attractive.
In *Word 2003*, it is very easy to add all kinds of graphics such as pictures, illustrations or drawings to your documents. You can modify each graphic by adjusting the size, color or by changing its brightness or contrast. You can position each graphic so that it appears exactly where you want it to in your text.

In this chapter, you'll learn how to:

- insert a picture
- open the *Picture* toolbar
- move a picture
- change the size of a picture
- crop a picture
- edit a photo
- create a watermark
- delete a picture
- insert clip art
- format clip art

⇨ Please note:

To work through this chapter, you'll first need to download the files
The North Carolina Landscape.doc , Ben Franklin.doc , smokies.jpg , and jockeys ridge.jpg from the website and save them in the My Documents folder (if you haven't already).

You can read how to do this in Appendix A at the back of this book.

Inserting a Picture

In *Word 2003*, the word "picture" is an umbrella term for different kinds of images. The image might be an illustration (line drawing), a drawing (bitmap), or a photo.

☞ **Start *Word 2003*** ᶜ⁶

☞ **Close the *Getting Started* Task Pane** ᶜ⁶⁹

☞ **Open the document** 📄 The North Carolina Landscape.doc **in the** 📁 My Documents **folder** ᶜ⁹

☞ **For your document display, select *Normal* view** ᶜ¹²

Now you see this text. You're going to add a photo to it.

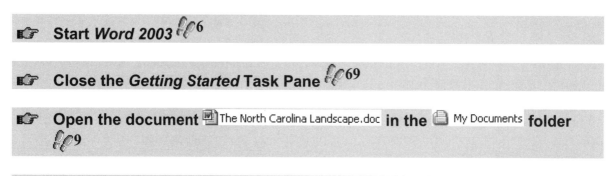

First place the cursor at the location where the photo should be inserted. Later you'll see that you can move the photo to any desired spot in the text.

🖱 **Click below the first paragraph of text**

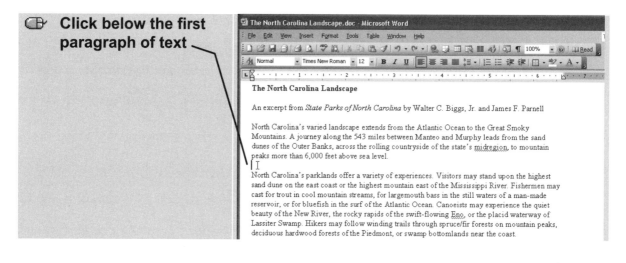

Now you can insert the photo. Here's how you do that:

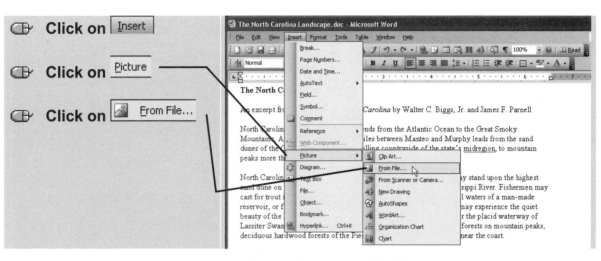

Click on [Insert]

Click on [Picture]

Click on [From File...]

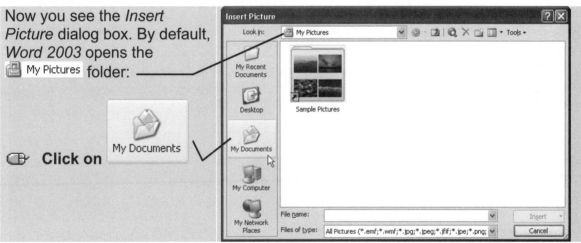

Now you see the *Insert Picture* dialog box. By default, *Word 2003* opens the [My Pictures] folder:

Click on [My Documents]

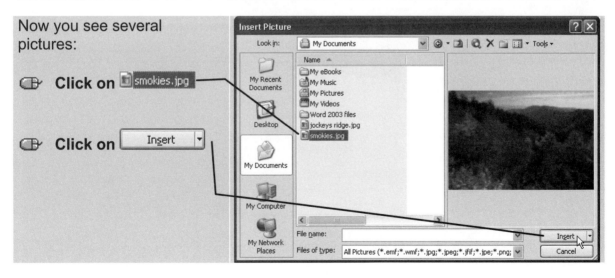

Now you see several pictures:

Click on [smokies.jpg]

Click on [Insert]

HELP! My window looks different.

You can easily change the way the window is displayed:

☞ **Click on** ▾ **beside** 🔲 ▾

Now you can select a display style:

☞ **Click on** 📄 **Preview**

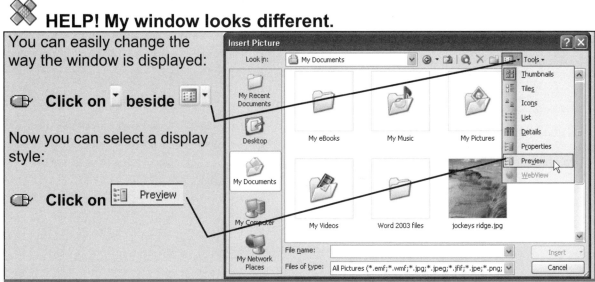

You see a photo of fall foliage in the Smoky Mountains:

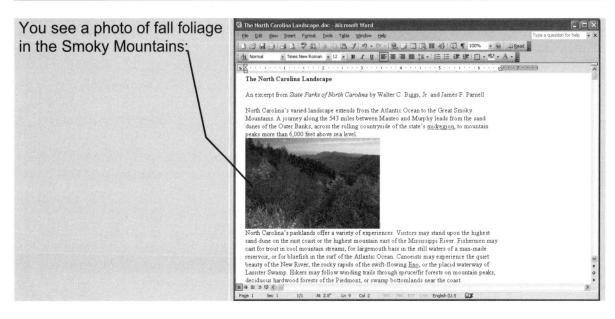

The Picture Toolbar

Before you get started with this photo, it's a good idea to bring up the *Picture* toolbar. You can display it in the window like this:

☞ **Click on the photo**

☞ **Click on** View

☞ **Click on** Toolbars

☞ **Click on** Picture

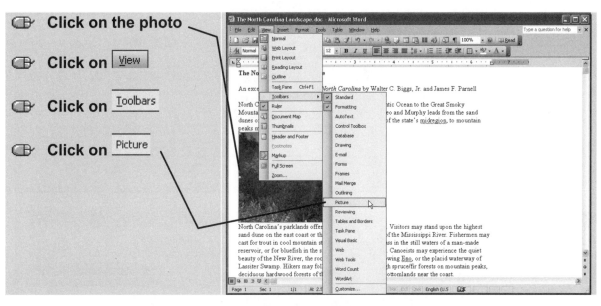

The toolbar automatically appears:

☞ **Click somewhere beside the photo**

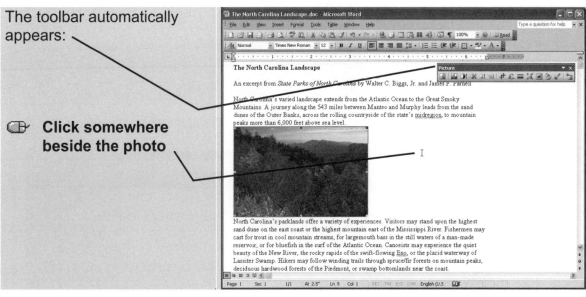

Now the toolbar is gone
again:

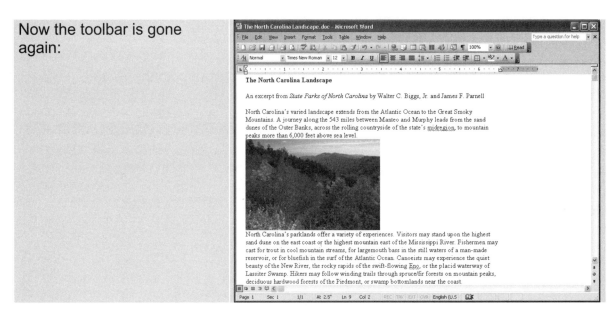

👆 **Click on the photo**

The toolbar reappears:

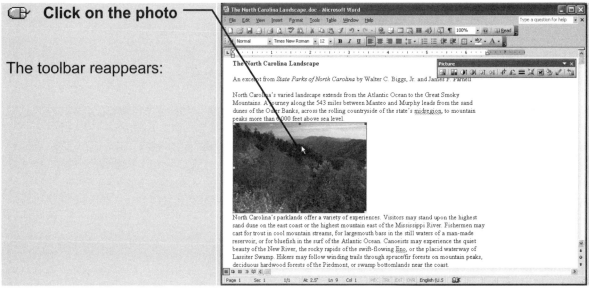

You see that the toolbar automatically appears when you click on the photo.

Moving a Picture

You can place the photo in the text in different ways. For example, there are different ways to have the text flow around the picture. You can best select the way like this:

Double-click on the photo

Click on Layout

Now you see the various ways you can place the picture within the text:

The default setting is for the picture to be placed in line with the text:

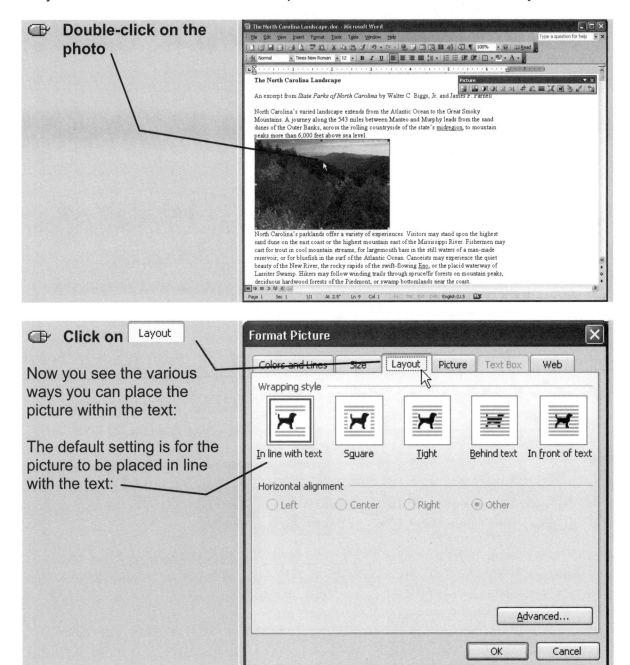

Now you can see what happens if you want to have the text flow around the picture.

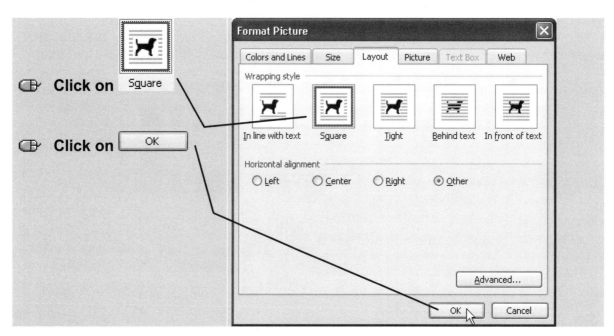

Click on Square

Click on OK

You see that the text now runs along the right side of the photo:
The program automatically jumps to the print layout view now.

Now you can drag the photo more toward the center of the page:

Place the mouse pointer on the photo

Press the mouse button

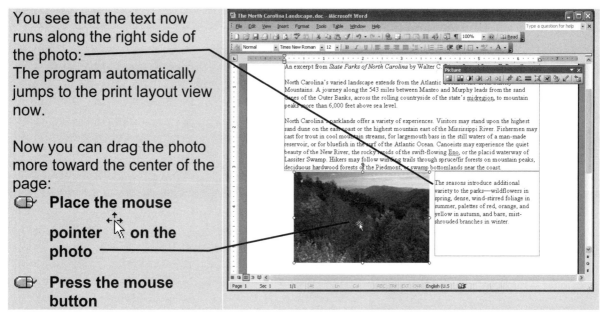

Drag the photo to the center

Release the mouse button

You see that the text now runs along both sides of the photo:

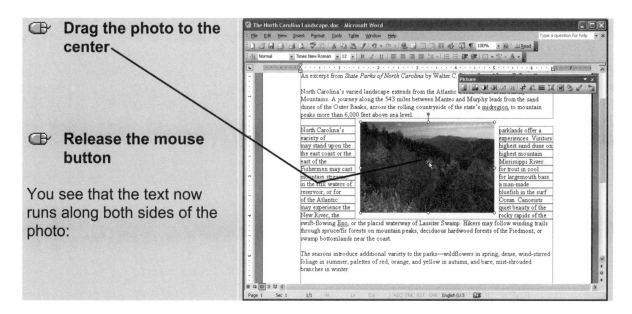

Word 2003 has many more settings for positioning a photo. Take a look at all the options:

Double-click on the photo

Click on Layout

Click on Advanced...

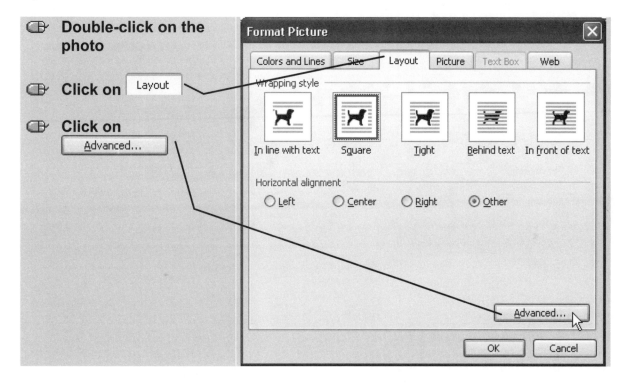

Click on [Text Wrapping]

Now you see these extra settings for placing the text:

You see that the text is being placed on both sides of the photo. You can also restrict it to the right side.

Click on ⊙ Right only

Click on [OK]

Click on [OK] **again**

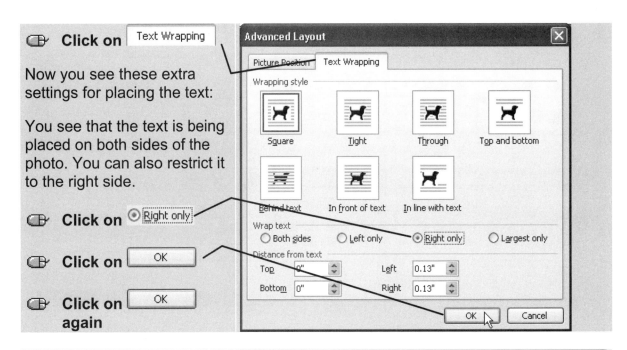

You see that the text only runs down the right side of the photo now:

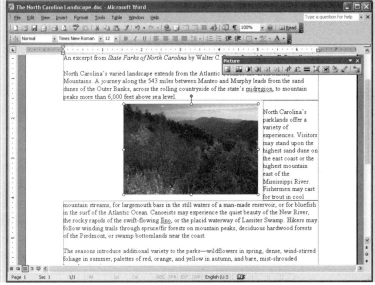

 Tip

Other Kinds of Text Wrapping Styles
There are several more kinds of text wrapping styles. You'll learn about these later in this book.

 Please note:

You can't drag a picture with the mouse if you've chosen the *In line with text* wrapping style. The photo will just stay in place on the line.

Scaling Pictures

You can "scale" a picture, in other words, make it larger or smaller. It's very easy to do this with the mouse.

Click on the photo

Now you see dots around the edges of the photo.
These are called **handles**:

You can drag the handles in the **corners** with the mouse to make the photo larger or smaller.

Place the mouse
pointer on the bottom
right corner

The mouse pointer changes
into ↘.

Press the left mouse
button and keep it
pressed down

Drag the corner to the
top and the left

You can see from the dotted
line what size the photo will
become:

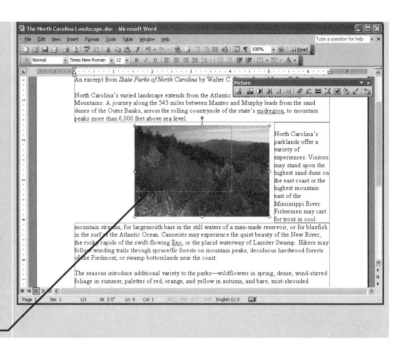

Release the mouse
button

You see that the photo is
quite a bit smaller:

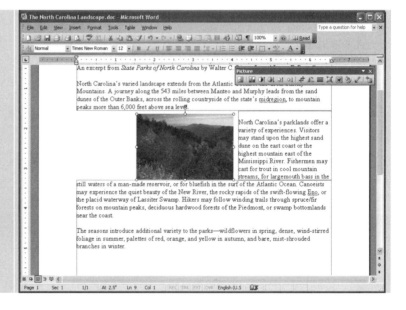

You can increase the size of the photo in the same way, by dragging the corner outward.

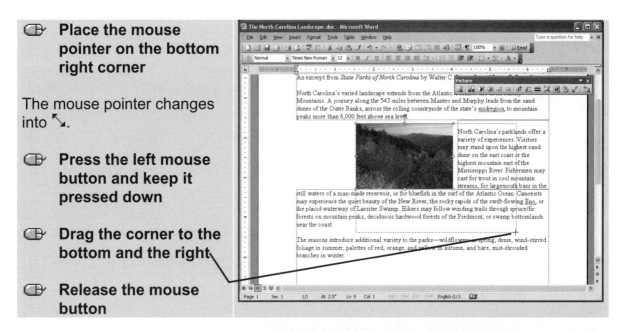

☞ **Place the mouse pointer on the bottom right corner**

The mouse pointer changes into ↘.

☞ **Press the left mouse button and keep it pressed down**

☞ **Drag the corner to the bottom and the right**

☞ **Release the mouse button**

You see that the photo has gotten larger:

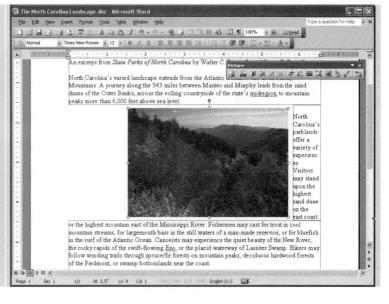

Going Back

If you've changed something about a picture's size, you can return to its original state this way:

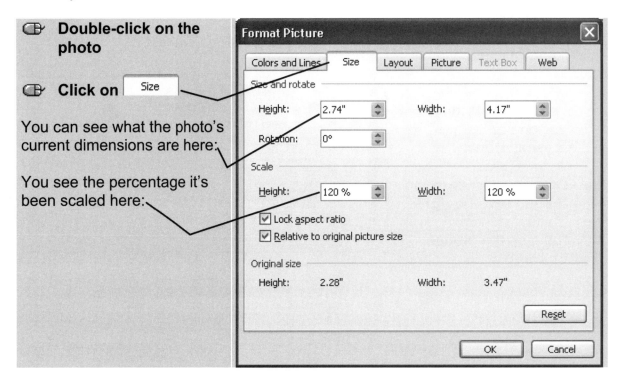

- **Double-click on the photo**

- **Click on** Size

You can see what the photo's current dimensions are here:

You see the percentage it's been scaled here:

Here's how to return the picture to its original values in one go:

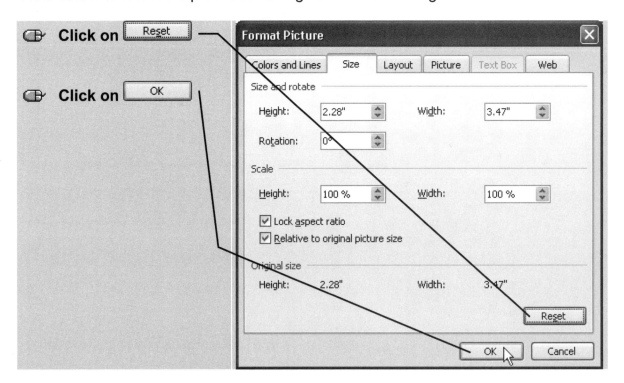

- **Click on** Reset

- **Click on** OK

You see that the photo has regained its original size:

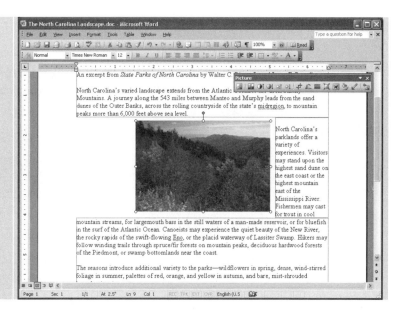

 Tip

The Toolbar
You can also use the toolbar to go to the *Format Picture* dialog box:

🖱️ **Click on the photo**

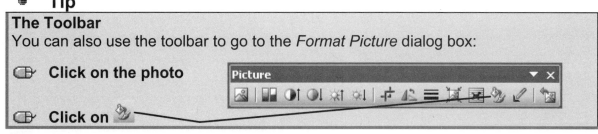

🖱️ **Click on** 🖼️

 Tip

Not on the Corners
If you drag a handle in the middle of one of the sides instead of on the corner, the photo will be "deformed." The photo will be stretched or shrunk accordingly.

For example, you can "flatten" the photo:

Cropping a Picture

You can also cut off part of a picture. Perhaps you don't want to use a part of the picture or you want to focus attention on a particular area. You could cut off part of the trees in the practice photo so that the sky stands out better. You do that with the mouse, but first you need to select the cropping tool.

☞ **Click on the photo**

You see the handles around the edges of the photo:

☞ **Click on the toolbar on**

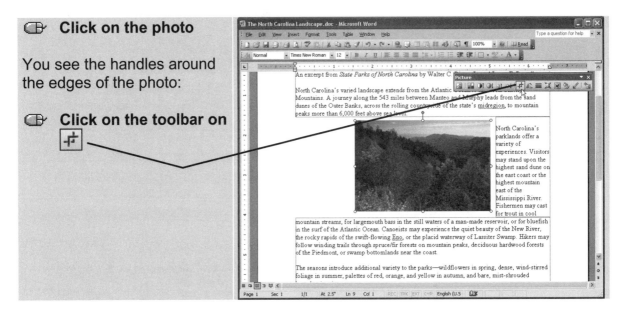

Now you can cut off the bottom of the photo, for example.

☞ **Place the mouse pointer on the bottom handle**

☞ **Press the left mouse button and drag the handle upward**

☞ **Release the mouse button**

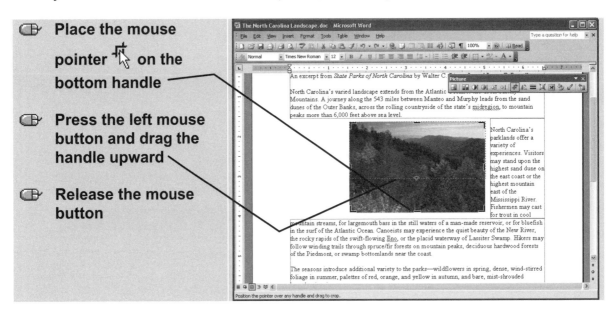

You see that the bottom of the photo has been cut off:

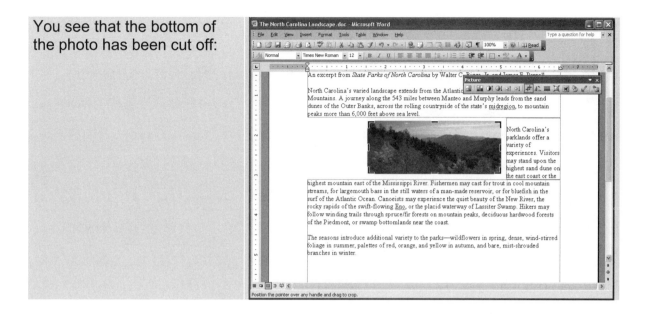

The Original State

The *Reset Picture* command will allow you to restore your graphic to its original state. This will undo any changes you have made to a picture's contrast color, brightness or size. You do that with the toolbar.

Click on the toolbar on

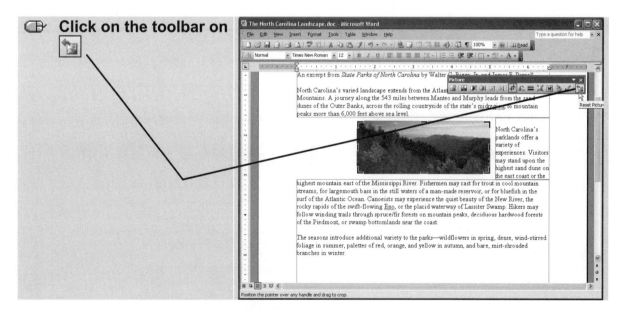

The photo returns to its original state.

Editing Photos

Word 2003 has a few features for editing photos. You can change the following things:
- the brightness
- the contrast

You can also turn the photo into:
- a grayscale photo
- a black-and-white photo
- a watermark

You can apply these effects using the toolbar. For example, you can change the photo's brightness.

☞ **First click on the photo**

☞ **Click on** ⊡ **a few times**

You see that the photo becomes lighter:

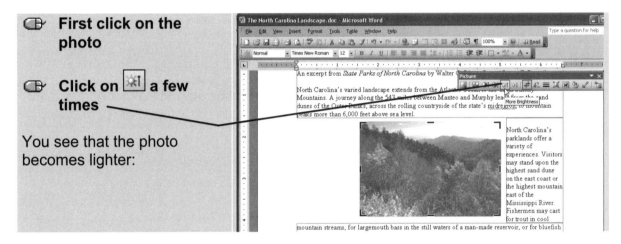

You can also increase the contrast.

☞ **Click on** ⊡ **a few times**

You see that the contrast between the colors increases:

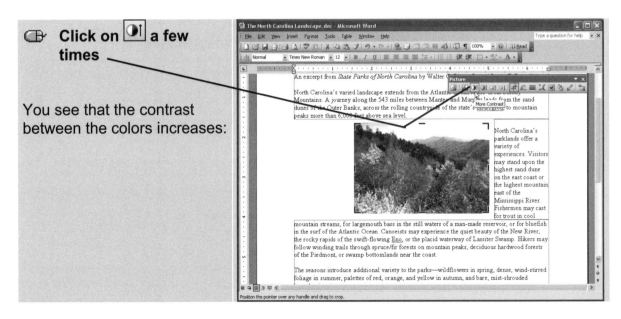

You can always remove these effects with the *Reset Picture* command.

Click on 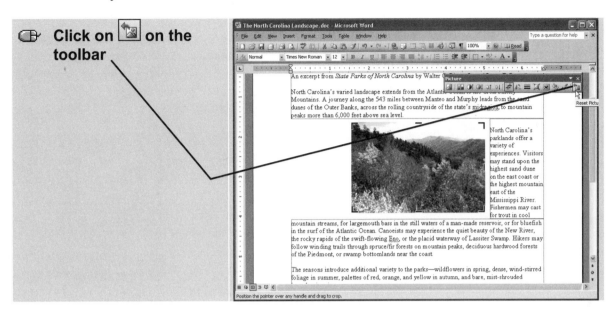 on the toolbar

One unusual effect is turning a color photo into a photo containing only shades of gray. The result looks a lot like a color photo that's been printed with a black-and-white printer. You can also convert the photo completely to black and white. Take a look:

Click on

Click on Grayscale

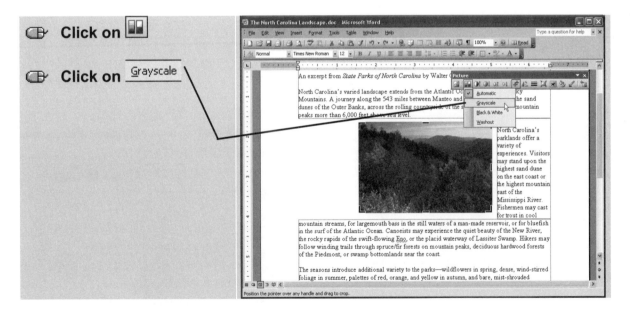

You see that the photo has become gray:

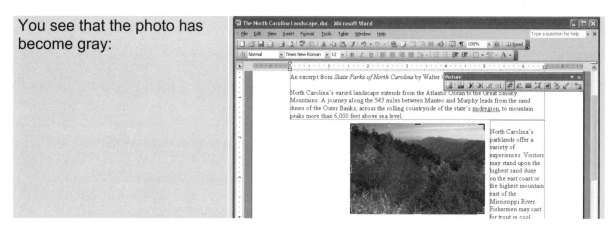

Click on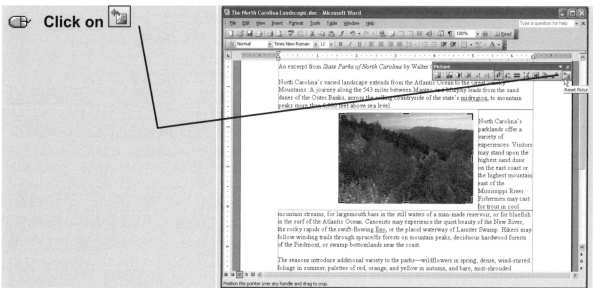

You see the original photo again:

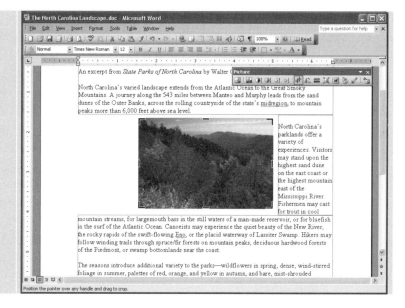

Washing Out a Photo

Word 2003 has a nice effect you can use to turn a photo into a light watermark on the paper. We call this effect "washing out" a photo. You can print the text out over the watermark if desired.

First, turn the photo into a watermark:

☞ **Click on** [icon]

☞ **Click on** Washout

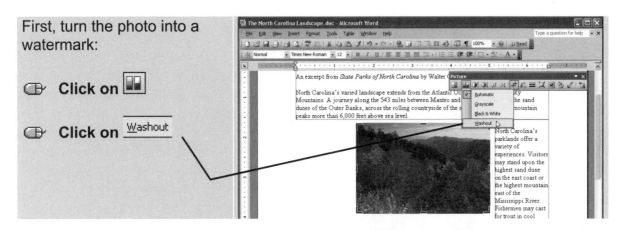

Now the photo looks like a very light watermark:

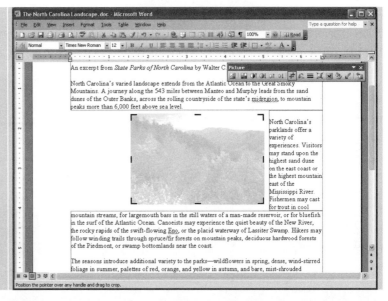

If the crop tool is still selected, you can deselect it like this:

☞ **Click on** [icon]

The tool is no longer selected.

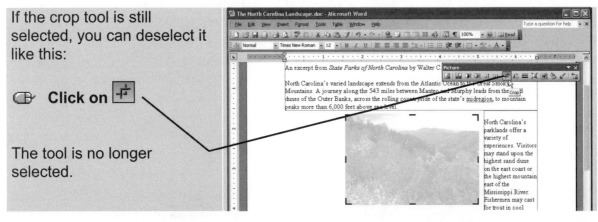

Now you're going to increase the size of the photo, for example, to the same width as the lines of text.

☞ **Increase the size of the photo** *✎36*

🖰 **Drag the photo flush against the left margin**

The watermark has now pushed part of the text down:

You can change the wrapping style of the picture now so that the text flows over the watermark. You can do that with the help of the toolbar.

🖰 **Click on**

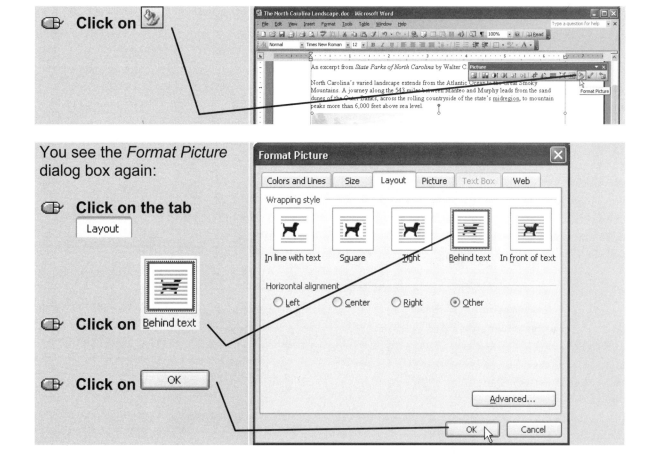

You see the *Format Picture* dialog box again:

🖰 **Click on the tab** Layout

🖰 **Click on** Behind text

🖰 **Click on** OK

You see that the text now flows over the watermark:

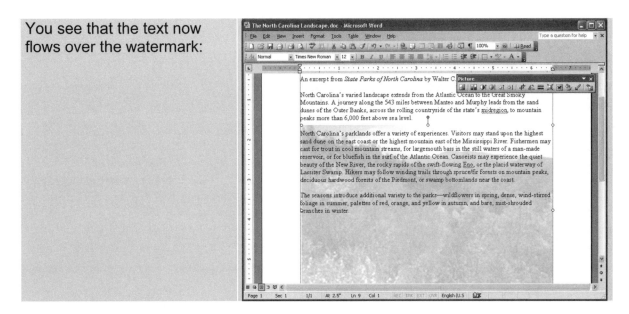

You can create nice stationery or certificates with a watermark.

Deleting a Picture

You can delete a picture very easily.

Click on the photo

The photo should be selected.

Press

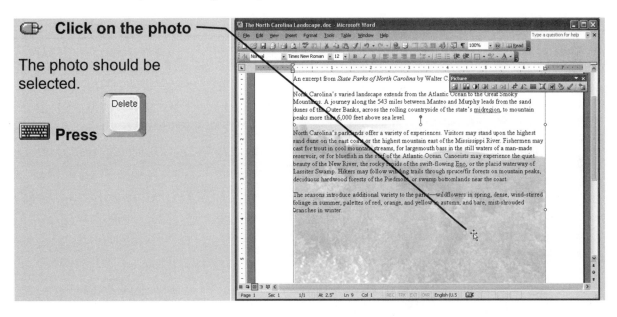

The photo is removed.

Tip

Cutting

Instead of deleting a picture, you can cut it. Then you can paste the same picture somewhere else if you'd like. Here's how you do that:

☞ **Click with the <u>right</u> mouse button on the photo**

☞ **Click on** ✂ Cut

☞ **Click with the <u>right</u> mouse button on the place you want to insert the photo**

☞ **Click on** 📋 Paste

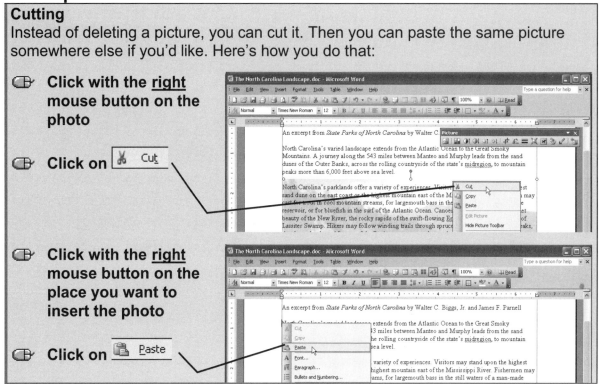

Inserting Clip Art

Word 2003 has a large number of illustrations you can use. These illustrations are called "clip art." Depending on your installation of *Word 2003*, there may be a lot or only a little clip art available. You can view the available clip art this way:

First, place the cursor on the spot where the clip art should be inserted.

☞ **Place the cursor below the second paragraph**

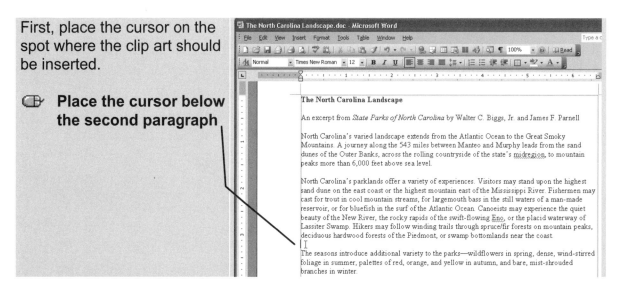

Then you can insert the clip art.

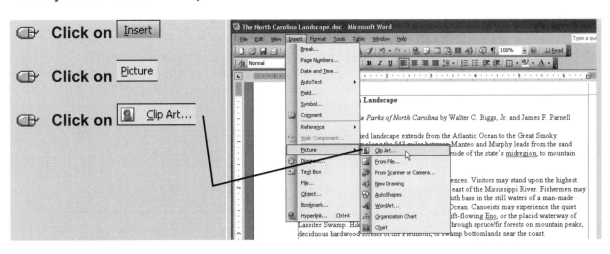

Click on Insert

Click on Picture

Click on 🔲 Clip Art...

Now you see the *Clip Art* Task Pane:

You can use this Task Pane to search for clip art, add new clip art, and organize clip art into categories in the Media Gallery.

⌨ **Type the word** mountain **in the search box**

Click on Go

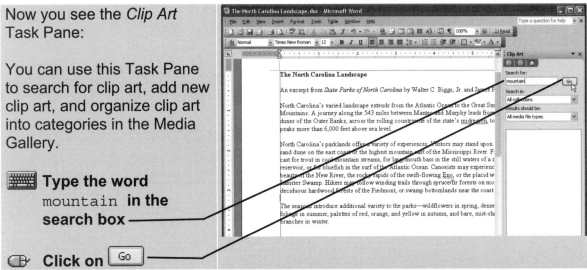

Now you see the clip art available in this category:

Click on a clip art illustration

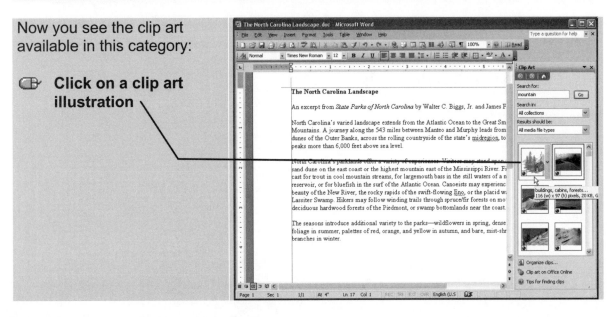

The clip art is immediately inserted:

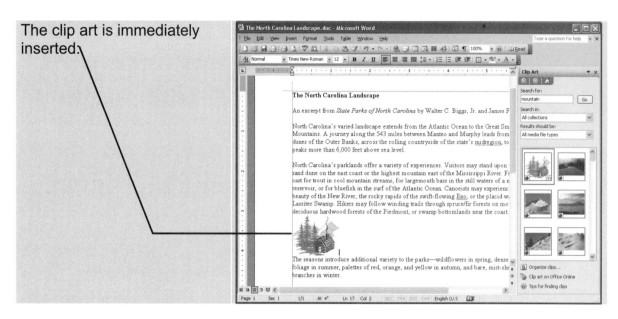

 HELP! I don't see that one.

If you don't see the same clip art on your computer, then:
☞ **Click on a different clip art illustration**

You can close the Task Pane now:

☞ **Click on** ☒

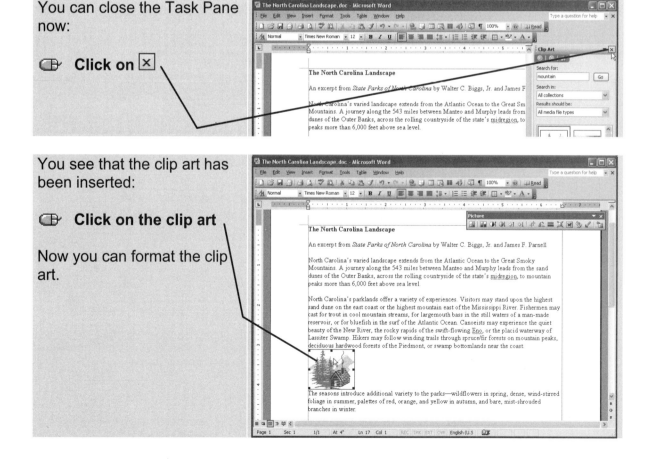

You see that the clip art has been inserted:

☞ **Click on the clip art**

Now you can format the clip art.

Formatting Clip Art

You can format clip art the same way you format a photo. For example, you can have the text flow around the clip art. Give it a try:

First, change the clip art to the desired size:

☞ **Increase the size of the clip art** 👣³⁶

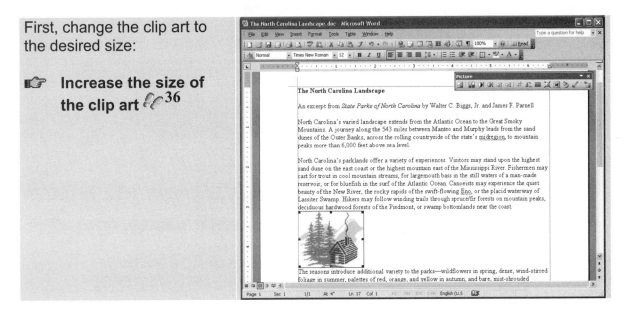

Now that the clip art is the desired size, you can have the text flow around it. Because the clip art contains white space, the text will flow nicely around the drawn areas. Give it a try:

👆 **Click on the clip art**

👆 **Click on the tab**
     Layout

👆 **Click on** Tight

👆 **Click on** OK

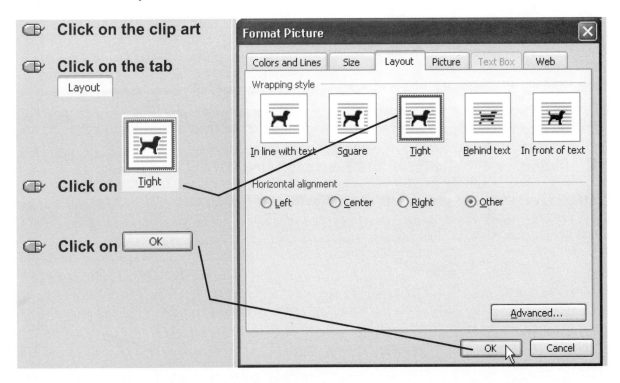

You see that the text to the right of the clip art comes right up to the drawing:

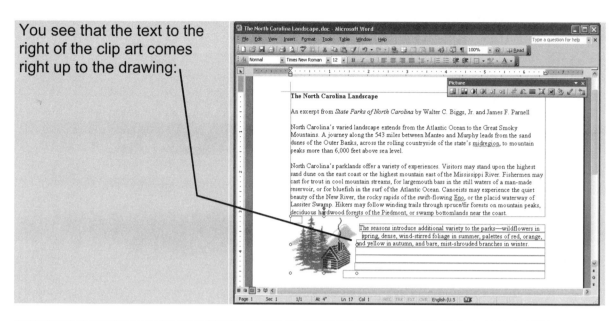

You can see the text wrapping better if you place the clip art in the center of the text.

👈 **Drag the clip art to the center of the page**

You see that the text now runs down the left and right sides of the clip art:

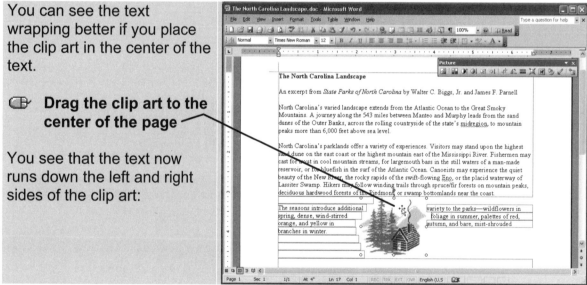

☞ **Close this document and don't save the changes** 👣14

You can practice what you've learned in the following exercises.

Exercises

Have you forgotten how to perform a particular action? Use the number beside the footsteps to look it up in the appendix *How Do I Do That Again?*

Exercise: Photo

In this exercise, you'll practice inserting a photo into a text and editing it.

✓ Start *Word 2003*. ^{6}

✓ Open the document Ben Franklin.doc in the My Documents folder. ^{9}

✓ Insert the photo jockeys ridge.jpg from the My Documents folder. ^{37}

✓ Call up the *Picture* toolbar. ^{38}

✓ Have the text wrap square around the photo. ^{39}

✓ Place the photo in the center of the text. ^{40}

✓ Have the text run down only the right side of the photo. ^{41}

✓ Increase and decrease the size of the photo. ^{36}

✓ Return the photo to its original settings. ^{42}

✓ Crop the photo. ^{43}

✓ Lighten the photo. ^{44}

✓ Increase the color contrast in the photo. ^{45}

✓ Make the photo black and white. ^{46}

✓ Turn the photo into a watermark in the text. ^{47}

✓ Delete the photo. ^{48}

Background Information

Magnifying and Shrinking without Loss of Sharpness
At first glance, it seems like a simple thing to increase and decrease the size of a photo. It's actually a lot of work for the program you use to do it, however. All kinds of calculations have to be made before the larger or smaller version of the picture is displayed on your screen. This might not seem very important to you. Nonetheless, the degree of image quality may be profoundly affected if you make huge adjustments to your graphics.
A program can display images in two ways: using dots, called *pixels*, or using vector drawings. Images built out of pixels include the well-known *bitmaps*. The photo you inserted in this chapter is a bitmap. Examples of vector drawings include the clip art you can search for and insert in *Word 2003*.
The difference between a picture made up of pixels and a vector drawing is easiest to see if you increase or decrease the size of the picture. Pictures containing pixels become jagged as the size changes: they become less sharp. Vector drawings, on the other hand, stay just as sharp as the original image, however large or small you make them.

A magnified bitmap   A magnified vector drawing

Tips

 Tip

Magnifying and Shrinking in Percentages
To very precisely magnify or shrink a picture, you'll need to use the *Format Picture* dialog box:

👉 **Double-click on the photo**

👉 **Click on the tab**
   Size

Height: and Width: in inches:

Height: and Width: in percentages:

Keep the relationship between the height and the width constant, so that the picture isn't deformed:

Percentage is relative to the original size of the figure:

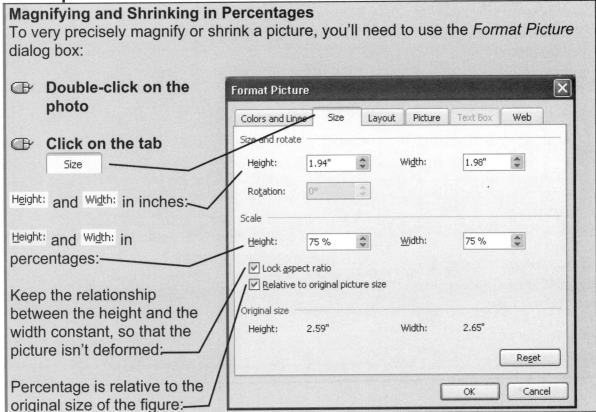

 Tip

Cropping: Cut to Size
You can't crop very precisely with the mouse. But you can with the *Format Picture* dialog box:

👉 **Double-click on the photo**

👉 **Click on the tab**
   Picture

Choose how much you want to crop off the picture on each side:

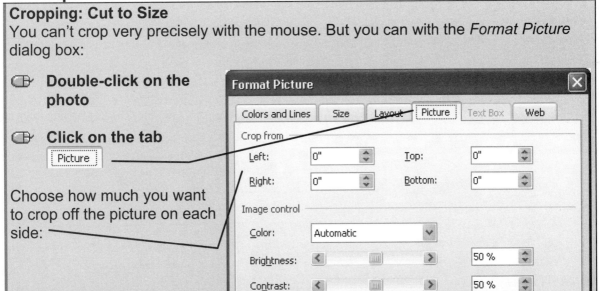

Tip

Moving the Picture with the Text
You can specify that a picture should move along with the text. This only works if the wrapping style is not *In line with text*.

☞ **Double-click on the photo**

☞ **Click on the tab**
Layout

☞ **Click on**
Advanced...

☞ **Click on the tab**
Picture Position

The picture slides along with the text:

Another picture may cover this picture:

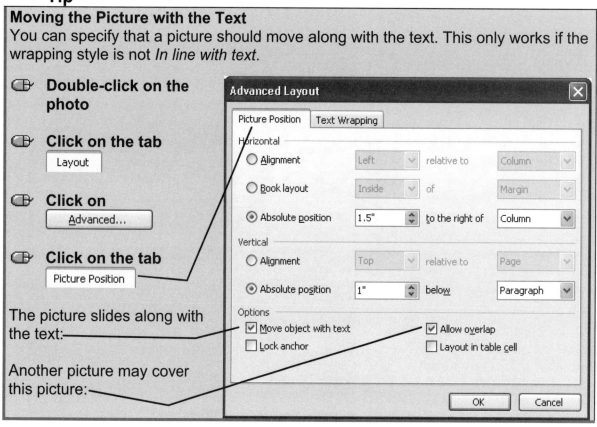

7. Drawings, Shapes, and Other Effects

A document that contains only text can seem boring. *Word 2003* offers several features for fixing that. You can add all kinds of *objects* to a text. These objects may be photos or illustrations, but they can also be drawings, such as a line or an ellipse. You can also add special objects in *Word 2003*. For example, the *AutoShape* feature contains a whole collection of images, varying from arrows to text balloons. You can decorate text in all kinds of ways using *WordArt*. You can also add borders and shading to the page.

In this chapter, you'll learn how to:

- insert drawings
- insert *AutoShapes*
- insert *WordArt*
- add borders and shading
- add a text box
- anchor objects

Please note:

To work through this chapter, you'll first need to download the files
The North Carolina Landscape.doc and Ben Franklin.doc from the website and save them in the My Documents folder (if you haven't already).

You can read how to do this in Appendix A at the back of this book.

Drawings

Word 2003 contains tools you can use to add line drawings into your text. Give it a try:

☞ **Start *Word 2003*** $\ell\ell^6$

☞ **Open the document** 📄 The North Carolina Landscape.doc **in the** 📁 My Documents **folder** $\ell\ell^9$

☞ **For your document display, select the *Print Layout* view** $\ell\ell^{10}$

☞ **Close the *Getting Started* Task Pane** $\ell\ell^{69}$

Now you see this text:

You're going to draw in it.

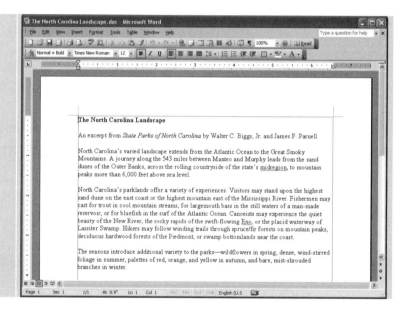

First you need to turn on the *Drawing* toolbar. Here's how you do that:

Click on [icon]

Now you see the toolbar at the bottom of the window:

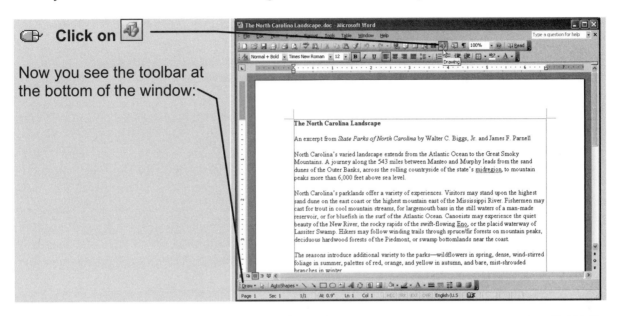

You can achieve all kinds of effects using this toolbar:

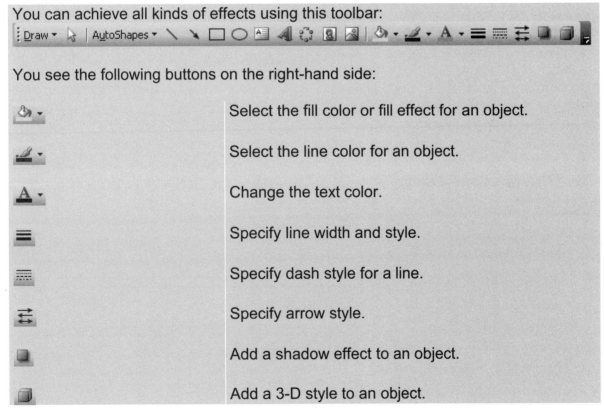

You see the following buttons on the right-hand side:

Select the fill color or fill effect for an object.

Select the line color for an object.

Change the text color.

Specify line width and style.

Specify dash style for a line.

Specify arrow style.

Add a shadow effect to an object.

Add a 3-D style to an object.

On the left-hand side of the toolbar, you see various buttons you can use to draw with or to insert something. It would take us too far afield to describe all these functions in detail. We'll cover only the most important ones here. Then you can experiment with the other options at a later time.

You start a drawing like this:

The simplest shape is a straight line. You draw one like this:

☞ **Click on** ![line tool] **on the** *Drawing* **toolbar**

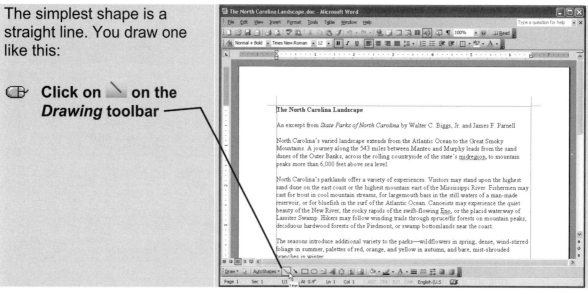

Now you see a large box, the drawing canvas, in which you can create a drawing:

You don't need this box to draw a line in the text. Scroll down a little until you see the text again.

☞ **Click on** ☑ **a few times**

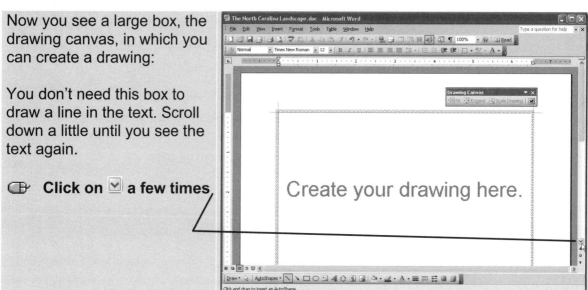

Now you can draw by dragging with the mouse.

🖱 **Place the mouse pointer ┼ on the text**

🖱 **Press the mouse button and drag down diagonally** ──

🖱 **Release the mouse button**

You see that a line has been drawn:

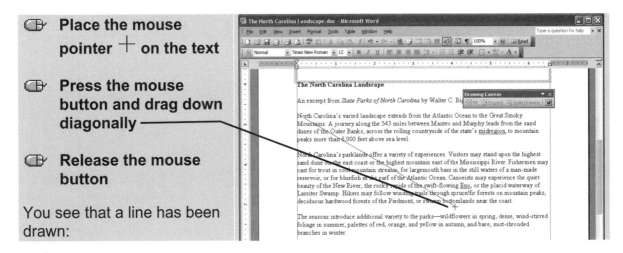

❋ HELP! The line jumps somewhere else.

When you draw a line outside the drawing canvas, the text may "jump back" so that the line is outside the text. You can move the line into the text by hand.

🖱 **Place the mouse pointer on the line**

The mouse pointer changes into ⁺⇕⁺:

🖱 **Drag the line upward** ──

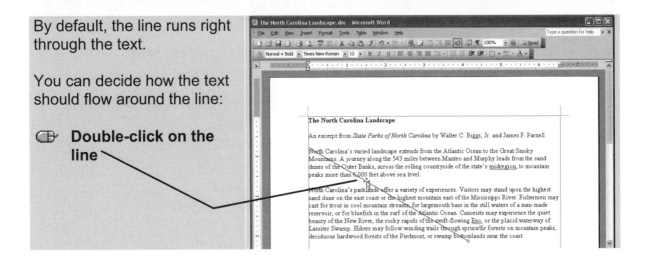

By default, the line runs right through the text.

You can decide how the text should flow around the line:

🖱 **Double-click on the line** ──

The *Format AutoShape*
dialog box appears.

👆 **Click on the tab**

> Layout

On this tab, you can specify
how the text should wrap
around the line.

👆 **Click on** Tight

👆 **Click on** OK

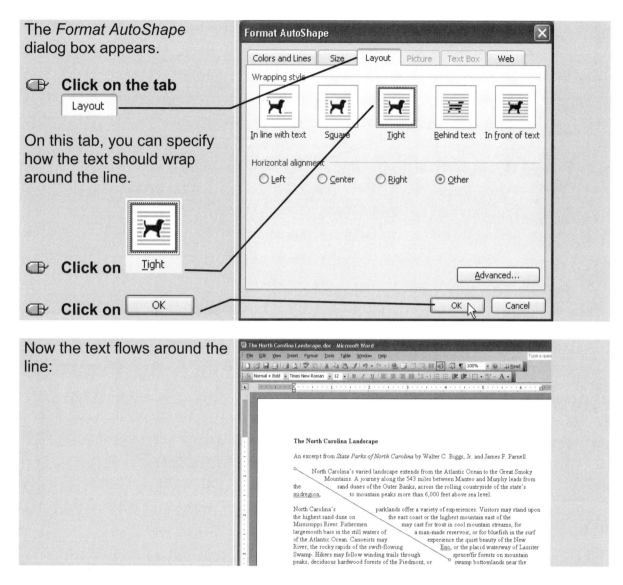

Now the text flows around the
line:

You can ensure that this setting will also apply to your subsequent drawings. Here's
how you do that:

👆 **Click on the line**

The line is selected:

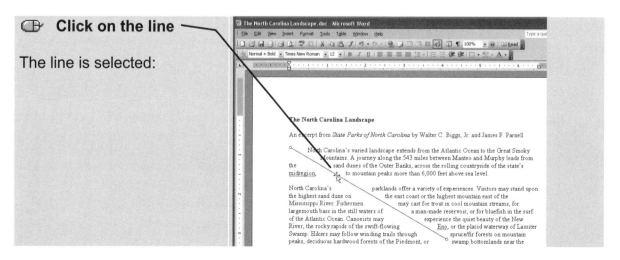

☞ **Click on** Draw ▾ **on the** *Drawing* **toolbar**

☞ **Click on**
Set AutoShape Defaults

Subsequent drawings will now use the same formatting as this line.

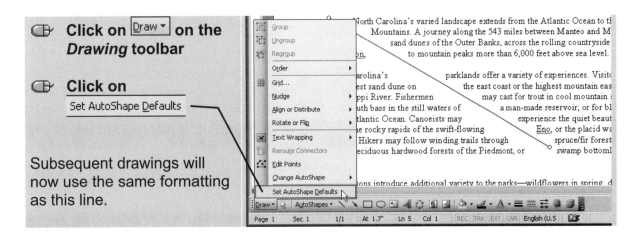

You can move the line if you'd like.

☞ **Place the mouse pointer** ⇖ **on the line**

☞ **Drag the line upward and to the right**

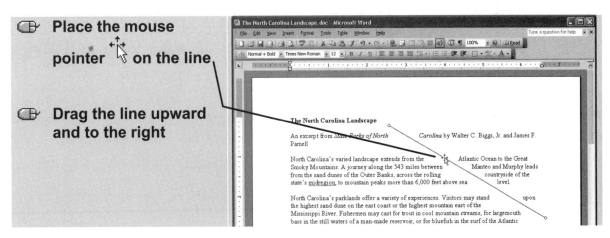

In addition to lines, *Word 2003* can draw arrows, rectangles, and ellipses. You draw these shapes in the same way.

☞ **Click on the** *Drawing* **toolbar on** ▢

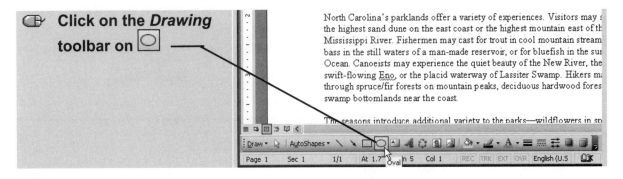

Place the mouse pointer ┼ on the text

 Press the mouse button and drag down diagonally

 Release the mouse button

You see the ellipse you've drawn. There are handles around the ellipse. You can use these to shrink or magnify the ellipse:

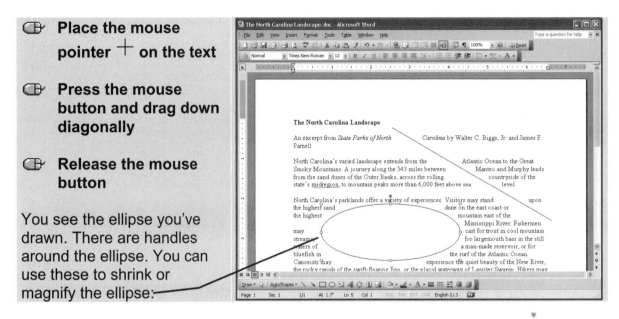

💡 **Tip**

┌───┐
│ **Selected?**   │
│ If a shape has handles, then it is selected and you can go on to format it. If you have │
│ multiple shapes on a page and you want to change one of them, first select the │
│ shape you want to change by clicking on it.   │
└───┘

You can further modify this shape in various ways. For example, you can color in the ellipse and even give it a shadow effect.

 Click on ⌐ beside 🖫 on the *Drawing* toolbar

Now you see various colors from which you can choose:

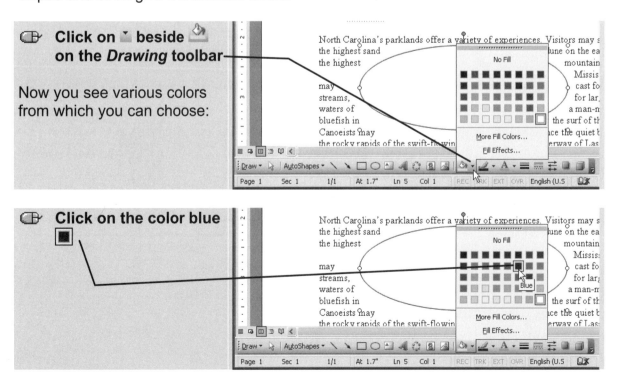

 Click on the color blue ■

The ellipse has now turned blue:

☞ **Click on** ▣ **on the**
   Drawing **toolbar**

You see various shadow effects:

☞ **Click on** ▣ **(Shadow Style 2)**

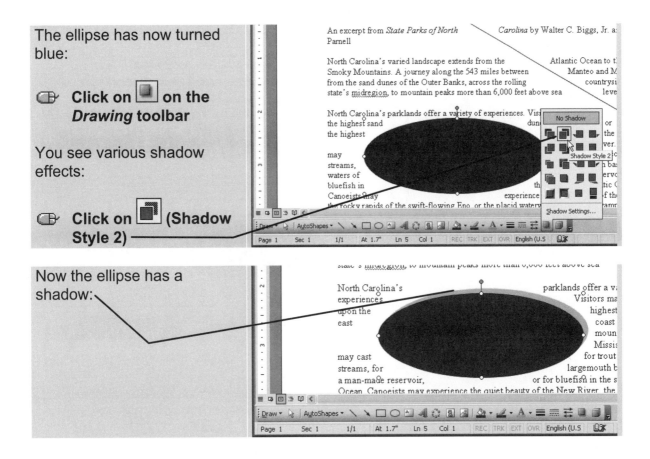

Now the ellipse has a shadow:

AutoShapes

Word 2003 has other ready-made shapes you can use. These are called *AutoShapes*. You can insert them like this:

☞ **Click on** [AutoShapes ▾]

☞ **Click on**
   ☆ Stars and Banners

You see all kinds of shapes:

☞ **Click on** ▯

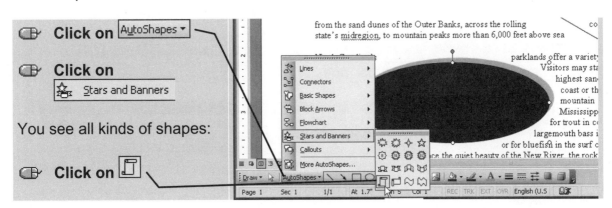

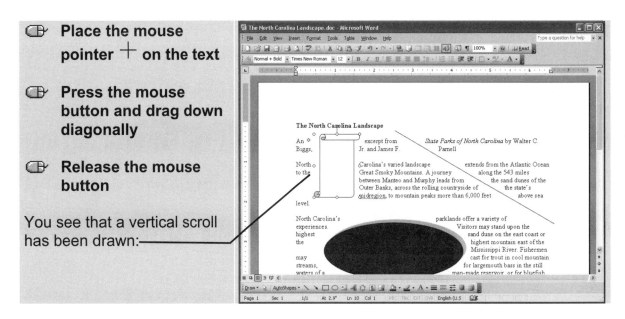

Place the mouse pointer ┼ on the text

Press the mouse button and drag down diagonally

Release the mouse button

You see that a vertical scroll has been drawn:

You can draw all kinds of shapes this way.

💡 **Tip**

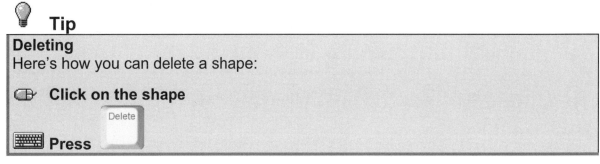

Deleting
Here's how you can delete a shape:

Click on the shape

⌨ **Press** Delete

☞ **Delete all drawings** 🦶⁴⁸

💡 **Tip**

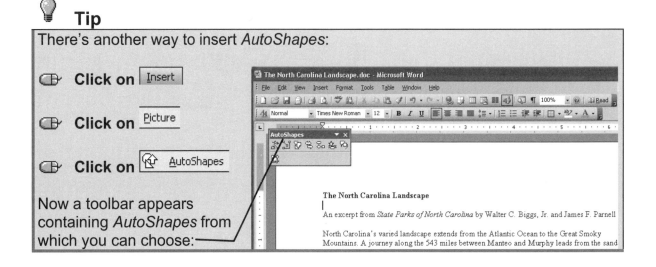

There's another way to insert *AutoShapes*:

Click on Insert

Click on Picture

Click on 🔲 AutoShapes

Now a toolbar appears containing *AutoShapes* from which you can choose:

Tip

Does the mouse pointer look funny?
After working with an object, the mouse pointer may look different than what you're

used to. For example, it might look like this: 👆 You can return it to its normal shape
this way:

☞ **Click somewhere in the text outside the object**

WordArt

Word 2003 also contains a fun function for creating special effects with letters. This
function is called *WordArt*. You create a *WordArt* object by first selecting the text you
want to use.

☞ **Select the title *The North Carolina Landscape*** 👣26

☞ **Click on** 🄰

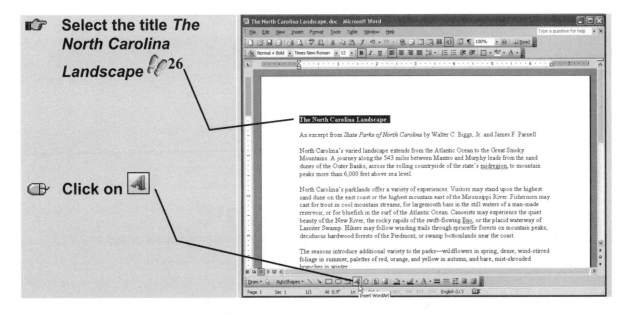

You see the *WordArt Gallery* dialog box with various effects:

☞ **Click on**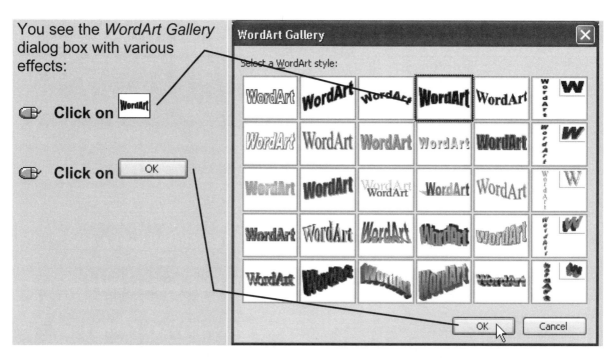

☞ **Click on** OK

Now you see the *Edit WordArt Text* dialog box:

You can change the text here if you'd like.

☞ **Type the title in the box**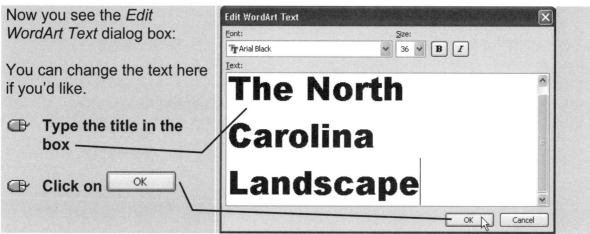

☞ **Click on** OK

You see the *WordArt* effect inserted into the page:

☞ **Click on the *WordArt* object**

A small toolbar appears with which you can further edit this effect: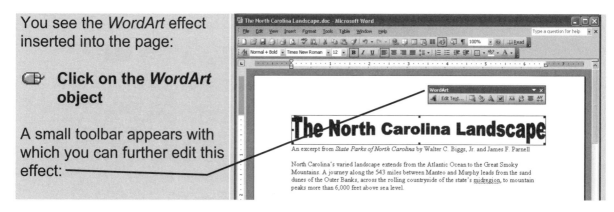

Using this toolbar, you can format the *WordArt* object in various ways:

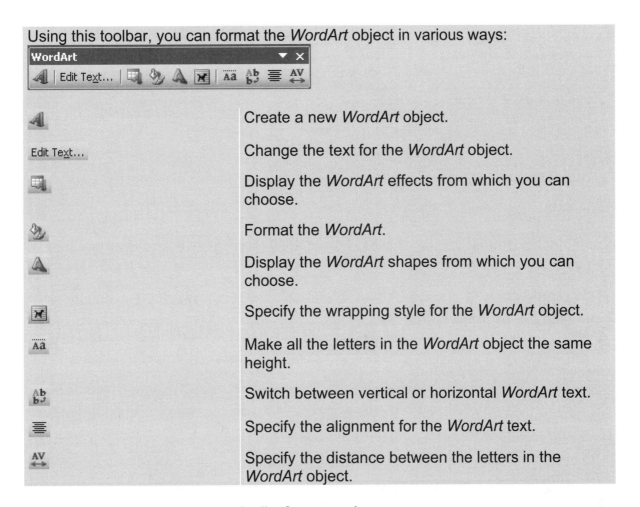

	Create a new *WordArt* object.
Edit Text...	Change the text for the *WordArt* object.
	Display the *WordArt* effects from which you can choose.
	Format the *WordArt*.
	Display the *WordArt* shapes from which you can choose.
	Specify the wrapping style for the *WordArt* object.
Aa	Make all the letters in the *WordArt* object the same height.
	Switch between vertical or horizontal *WordArt* text.
	Specify the alignment for the *WordArt* text.
AV	Specify the distance between the letters in the *WordArt* object.

You can make the text run vertically, for example.

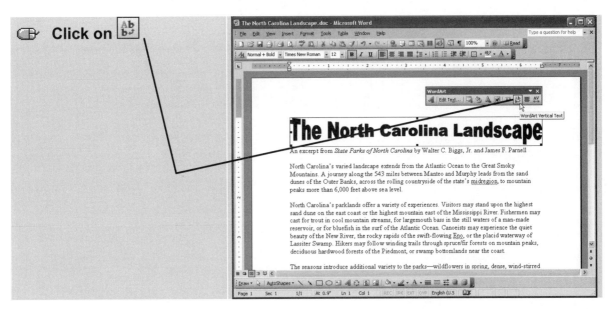

You see that the object now runs vertically in the text:

☞ **Click on** [Ab/b₃] **again**

The text runs horizontally again.

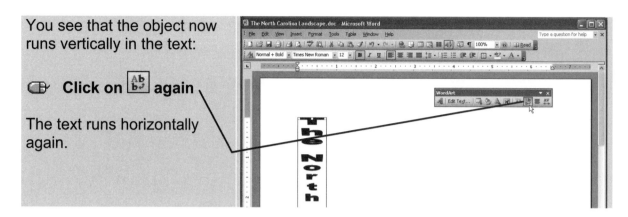

Earlier in this chapter you saw how to format the wrapping style for a drawing. You can do that for a *WordArt* object in the same way.

You see that the default formatting places the *WordArt* object as a block in the text:

North Carolina's varied landscape extends from the Atlantic Ocean to the Great Smoky

The North Carolina Landscape

Mountains. A journey along the 543 miles between Manteo and Murphy leads from the sand dunes of the Outer Banks, across the rolling countryside of the state's midregion, to mountain peaks more than 6,000 feet above sea level.

You can change the style for the *WordArt* on the toolbar:

☞ **Click on** [icon]

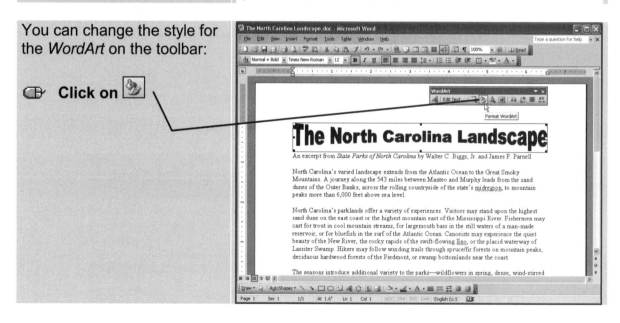

You see the *Format WordArt* dialog box:

⊞ **Click on the tab** Layout

⊞ **Click on** Square

⊞ **Click on** OK

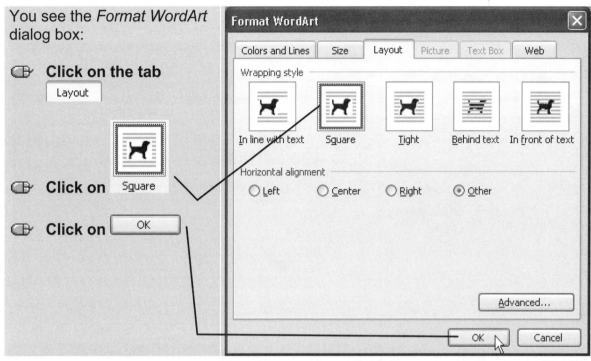

You see that the text flows around the *WordArt* object:

The object has also acquired a handle you can use to rotate it.

⊞ **Place the mouse pointer on the green dot on the handle**

Now the mouse pointer changes into a circular arrow ↻ :

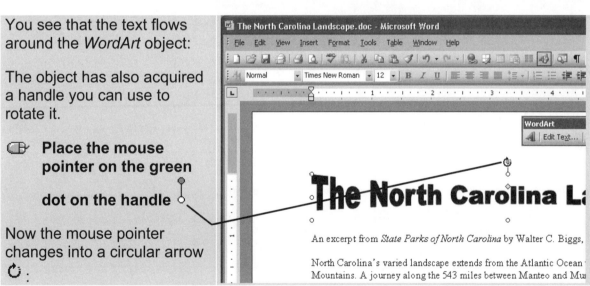

You can rotate the object now. Give it a try:

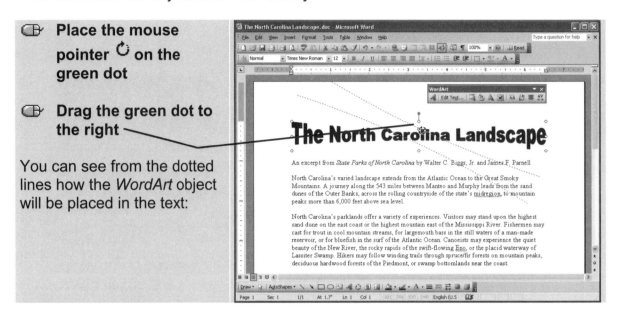

- ☞ **Place the mouse pointer ↻ on the green dot**

- ☞ **Drag the green dot to the right**

You can see from the dotted lines how the *WordArt* object will be placed in the text:

After you release the mouse button, you see the *WordArt* object's new position:

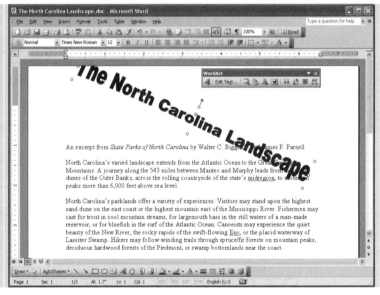

☞ **Close this document and don't save the changes** ✍14

Borders and Shading

Word 2003 offers other ways to format paragraphs. You can give a paragraph a background color. This is called *shading*. You can also place lines (a *border*) around a paragraph. Take a look:

☞ **Open the document** Ben Franklin.doc **in the** My Documents **folder** 🐾⁹

First, place the cursor in the paragraph:

🖰 **Click several times on**
☑ **until you see the second paragraph** ⟍

🖰 **Click in the second paragraph** ⟍

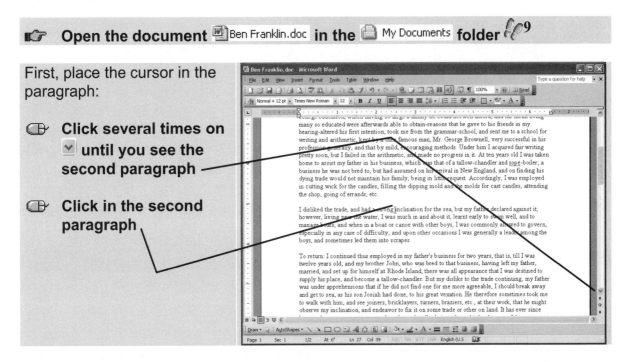

You can give this paragraph a background color first.

🖰 **Click on** Format

🖰 **Click on**
Borders and Shading...

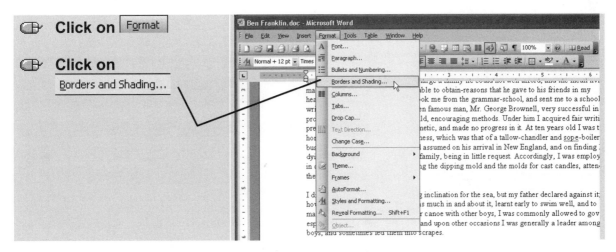

Now you see the *Borders and Shading* dialog box:

☞ **Click on the tab**
   Shading

☞ **Click on ▇ turquoise, for example**

You can see the effect in the preview pane at the right:

☞ **Click on** OK

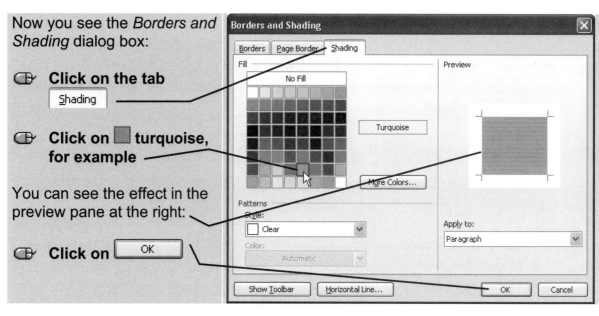

Now you see that the paragraph has a light blue-green color:

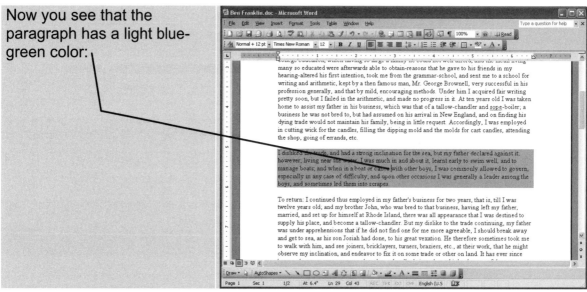

☞ **Click on** Format

☞ **Click on**
   Borders and Shading...

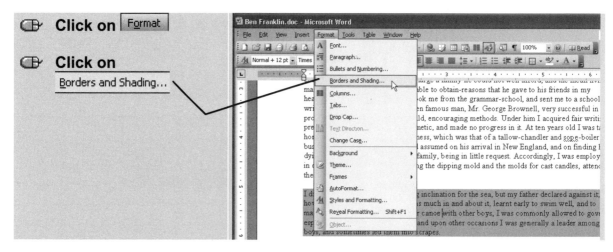

☞ Click on the tab

Borders

☞ Click on Box

You can see the effect in the preview pane at the right:

☞ Click on OK

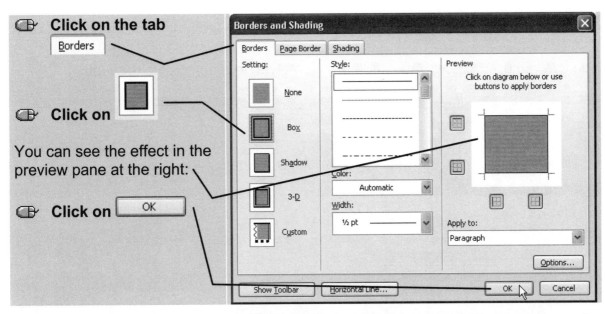

You see that the paragraph now has a border:

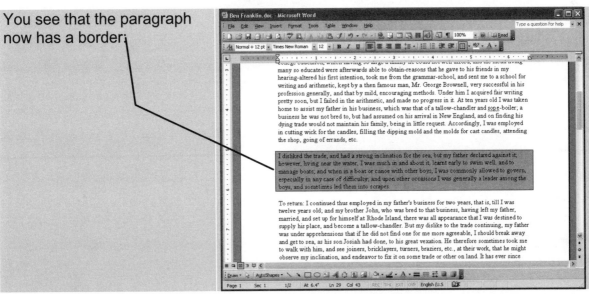

Take It Away, Sam

You can remove borders and shading you've given to a paragraph this way:

☞ **Make sure the cursor is in the paragraph** ✌51

☞ **Click on** Format

☞ **Click on**
Borders and Shading...

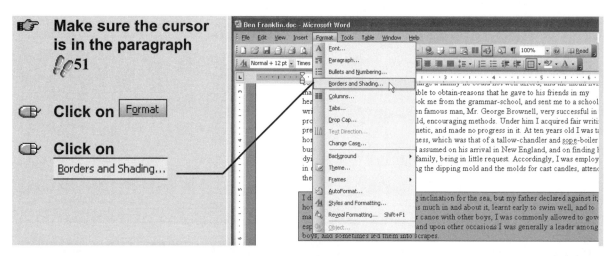

☞ **Click on the tab**
Borders

☞ **Click on**

You see in the preview pane that the edge has been removed:

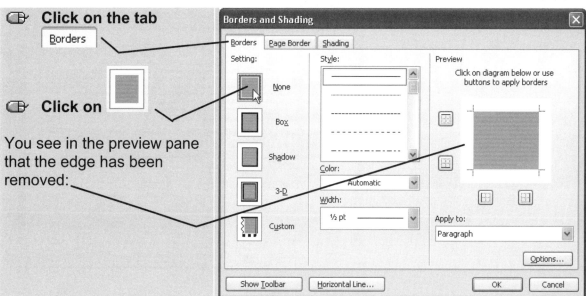

Click on the tab
Shading

Click on
No Fill

You can see the effect in the preview pane at the right:

Click on OK

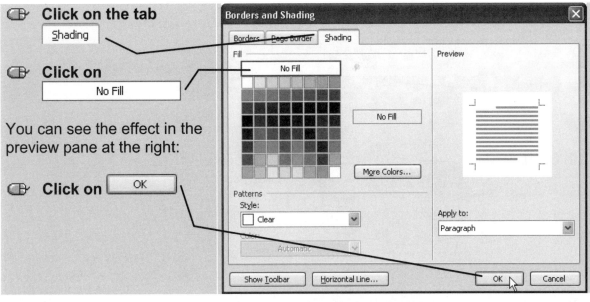

The border and the background color have disappeared:

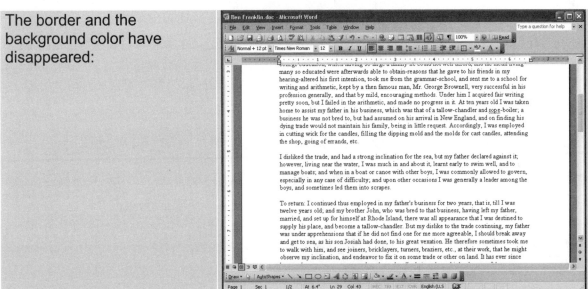

You've seen that with the help of borders and shading, you can format a paragraph so that it clearly stands out from the rest of the text.

Tip

You can specify exactly how you want the border of the paragraph to look:

The border's style:

The border's color:

The border's width:

Click on one of these four
buttons to add or remove the
associated edge:

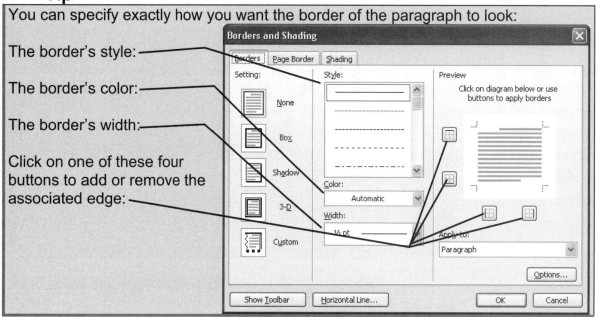

Page Borders

You can also add a border around the whole page. Here's how you do that:

👉 **Click on** `Format`

👉 **Click on**
   `Borders and Shading...`

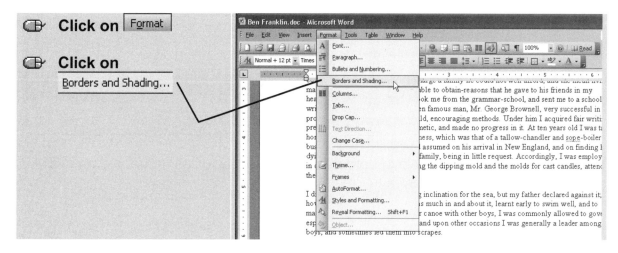

Click on the tab
Page Border

Click on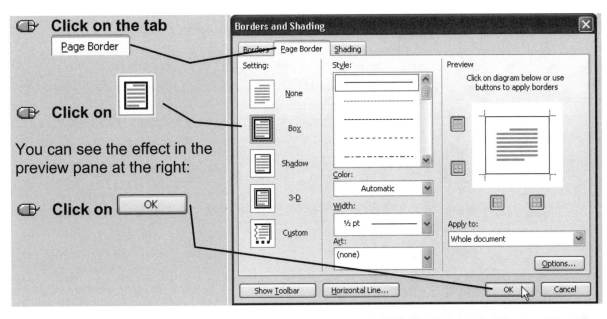

Click on

You can see the effect in the preview pane at the right:

Click on OK

Click several times on

Now you see a border around the text:

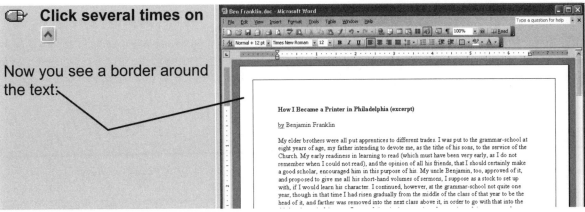

💡 **Tip**

You can specify exactly how you want the page border to look:

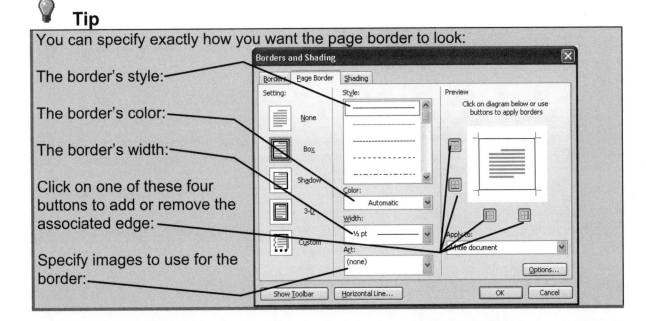

The border's style:

The border's color:

The border's width:

Click on one of these four buttons to add or remove the associated edge:

Specify images to use for the border:

You can also remove a page border. Here's how you do that:

👆 **Click on** Format

👆 **Click on**
Borders and Shading...

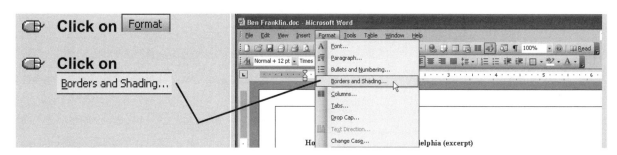

👆 **Click on the tab**
Page Border

👆 **Click on**

You can see the effect in the
preview pane at the right:

👆 **Click on** OK

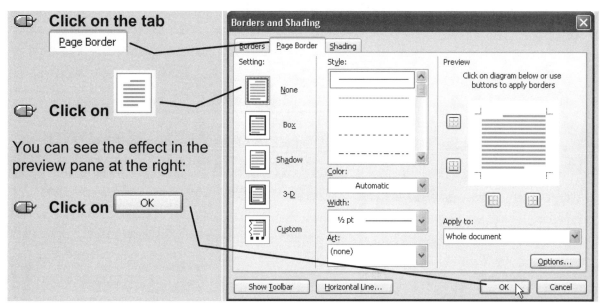

You see that the border
around the text is now gone:

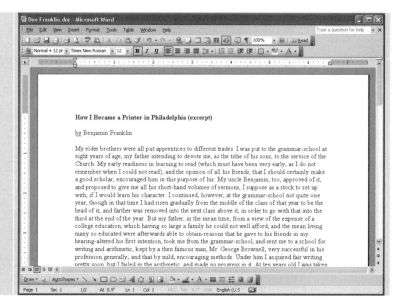

Inserting a Text Box

A text box is a separate box where you can enter and format text. You can place the text box anywhere in the text, just like a drawing or a *WordArt* object. Here's how you insert a text box:

➡ Please note:

☞ **Make sure no text is selected** 🐾⁵²

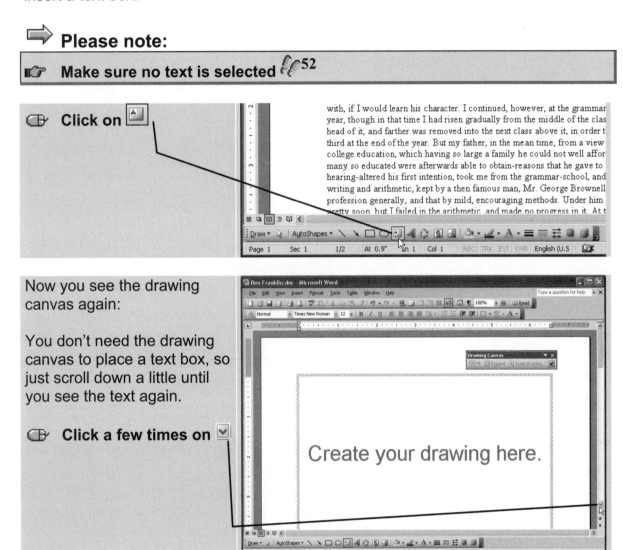

Now you see the drawing canvas again:

You don't need the drawing canvas to place a text box, so just scroll down a little until you see the text again.

☞ **Click a few times on** ▾

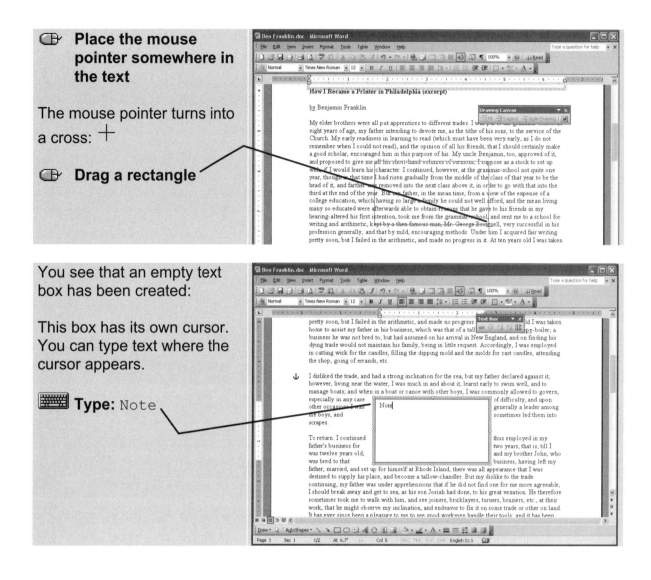

☞ **Place the mouse pointer somewhere in the text**

The mouse pointer turns into a cross: +

☞ **Drag a rectangle**

You see that an empty text box has been created:

This box has its own cursor. You can type text where the cursor appears.

⌨ **Type:** Note

Anchoring Objects

You may already have noticed that there's a little anchor in the margin when clip art, a shape, or a *WordArt* object is selected. That's also the case for a text box.

The anchor shows you where the text box is located in the text:

HELP! I don't see an anchor.

If you don't see an anchor:

☞ **Click on** Tools

☞ **Click on** Options...

☞ **Click on the tab** View

☞ **Click to add a checkmark beside** ☐ Object anchors

☞ **Click on** OK

You see the anchor when you're using the *Print Layout* view.

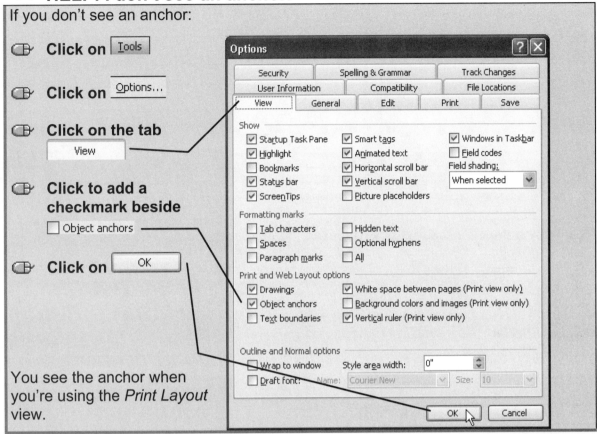

By default, a shape or text box is bound to that position in the text. If the text moves, the text box will move with it. Take a look:

☞ **Click in front of the paragraph**

You can add a few empty lines here now:

⌨ **Press** Enter ↵ **a few times**

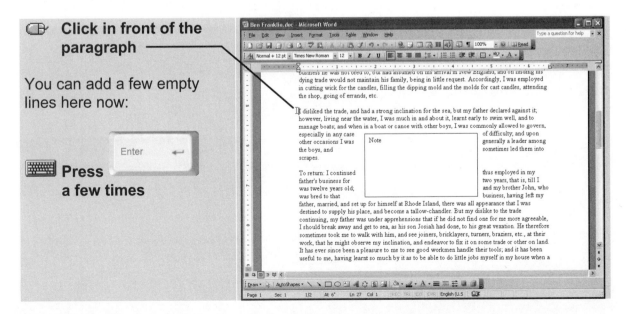

You see that the text box slides down along with text (after a short delay):

You can undo these changes.

☞ **Click a few times on** ⤺

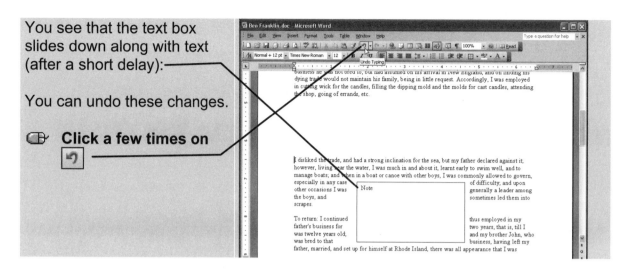

Now you can anchor the text box to a fixed location in the text. Here's how you do that:

☞ **Click on the text box**

☞ **Click on** Format

☞ **Click on** Text Box...

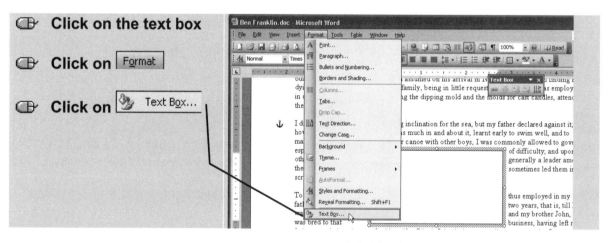

Now you see the *Format Text Box* dialog box:

☞ **Click on the tab** Layout

☞ **Click on** Advanced...

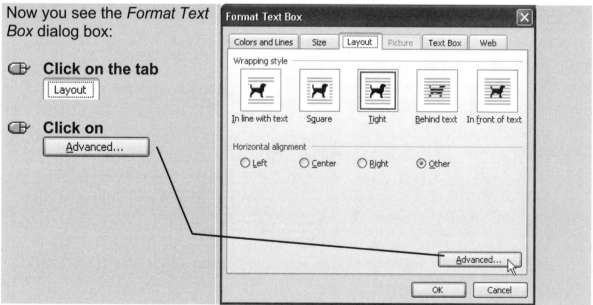

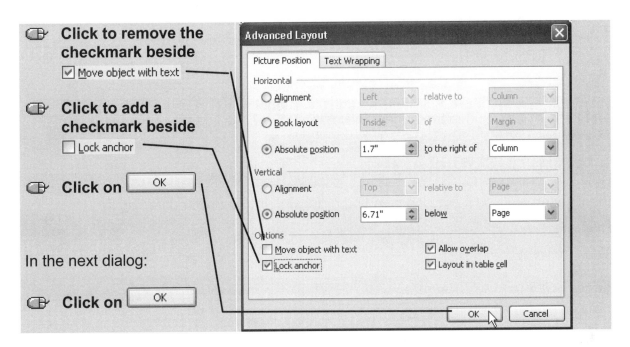

Now the anchor has a lock ⚓. You can add some more empty lines to the top of the paragraph and see what happens.

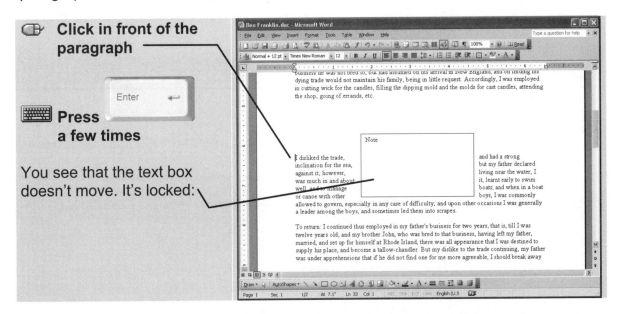

You can lock any kind of object to a fixed position on the page this way. You can do this for objects such as pictures, clip art, *AutoShapes*, a *WordArt* object or a text box. You can also choose to anchor an object to a paragraph. That's convenient if a photo belongs with a particular paragraph, for example, and you want to make sure the two stay together.

☞ **Close the document and don't save the changes** 🖋14

Exercises

Have you forgotten how to perform a particular action? Use the number beside the footsteps to look it up in the appendix *How Do I Do That Again?*

Exercise: Drawing

In this exercise, you'll practice inserting a drawing into a text and editing it.

✔ Start *Word 2003*. $\ell\ell^6$

✔ Open the document 📄Ben Franklin.doc in the 📁 My Documents folder. $\ell\ell^9$

✔ Turn on the *Drawing* toolbar. $\ell\ell^{53}$

✔ Draw an ellipse. $\ell\ell^{54}$

✔ Have the text wrap square around the drawing. $\ell\ell^{39}$

✔ Move the drawing to another spot in the text. $\ell\ell^{40}$

✔ Magnify the drawing. $\ell\ell^{36}$

✔ Make the ellipse red. $\ell\ell^{55}$

✔ Apply *Shadow Style* 7 to the drawing. $\ell\ell^{56}$

✔ Delete the drawing. $\ell\ell^{48}$

Exercise: WordArt

In this exercise, you'll practice inserting a *WordArt* object into a text and editing it.

✓ Add a *WordArt* object to the text. ☞**57**

✓ Rotate the *WordArt* object. ☞**58**

✓ Set the wrapping style for the *WordArt* object to square. ☞**39**

✓ Delete the *WordArt* object. ☞**48**

Exercise: Borders and Shading

In this exercise, you'll practice inserting and deleting borders and shading.

✓ Add a red background to the first paragraph in the text. ☞**59**

✓ Add a border to the first paragraph in the text. ☞**60**

✓ Remove the shading from the text. ☞**61**

✓ Remove the border from the text. ☞**62**

✓ Close *Word 2003* without saving your changes. ☞**13**

Tips

 Tip

More Colors
In addition to the default fill and line colors, *Word 2003* will let you choose from more colors:

☞ **Click on the object you want to color**

☞ **Click on ▾ beside 🎨 or beside 🖊 on the** *Drawing* **toolbar**

☞ **Click on** More Fill Colors... **or** More Line Colors...

Now you see the *Colors* dialog box:
Now you can select exactly the color you want on both tabs.

☞ **Click on** OK

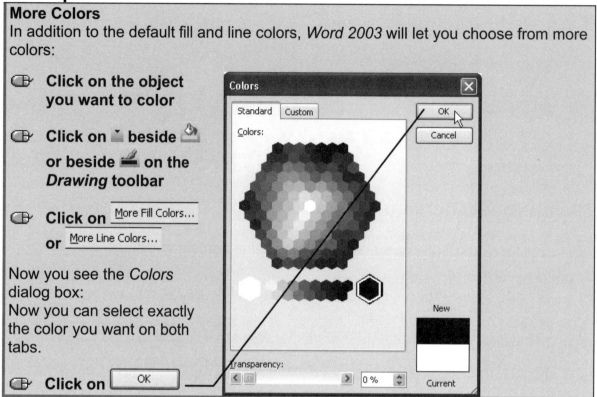

 Tip

Background Color for a Document
You can add a background color to the whole document:

☞ **Click on** Format

☞ **Click on** Background

☞ **Click on a color**

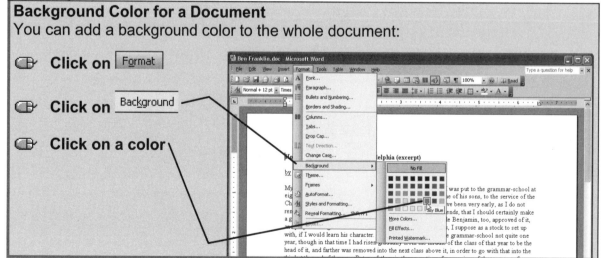

Tip

Add Color to Your Text
You can also add a background color to just part of the text on a page:

☞ **Select the text**

👆 **Click on** Format

👆 **Click on**
Borders and Shading...

Now you see *the Borders and Shading* dialog box:

👆 **Click on the tab** Shading

👆 **Click on the color**

👆 **Click on** Text

👆 **Click on** OK

The selected text now has the desired background color.

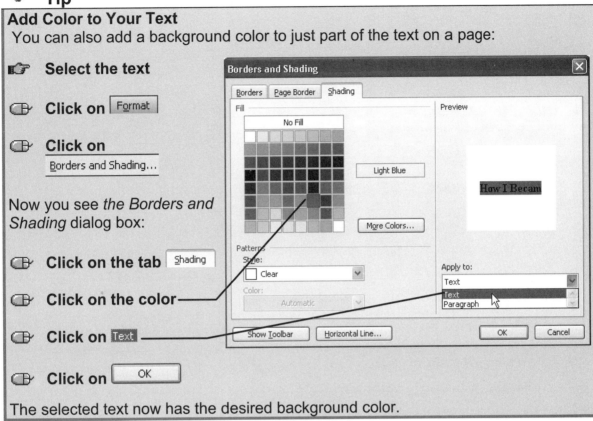

 Tip

Grid and Line Patterns
When you add a color, you can also specify a particular pattern:

👆 **Click on the tab**
Shading

👆 **Click on** ∨ **beside the list** Style:

👆 **Click on a pattern**

👆 **Click on** OK

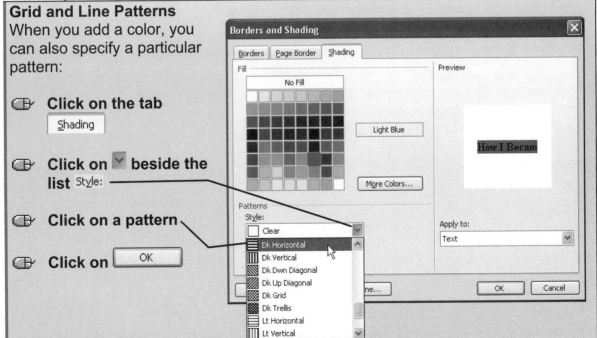

8. Bullets, Numbering, and Tabs

Word processing programs such as *Microsoft Word 2003* contain an enormous number of functions to help you create any kind of printed matter you can think of, from simple letters to entire books including an automatically generated table of contents and index. You can also create other printed matter, such as labels and envelopes.

Lists, charts, and tables are frequently used forms of text formatting. In this chapter, you're going to create bulleted and numbered lists first. Then you'll see how to use the Tab key to set up tab stops. You can create orderly rows and columns for a chart that way.

In this chapter, you'll learn how to:

- use bullets in lists
- determine the formatting for new paragraphs
- number paragraphs
- use tabs
- place tab stops
- delete tab stops
- specify portrait or landscape page orientation

Bulleted Lists

List are useful tools for emphasizing important points and enabling rapid scanning of text. *Word 2003* has special formatting options for lists, such as:

- first
- second
- et cetera

There's a button for this: ⫶☰
You see this button on the right side of the formatting toolbar:

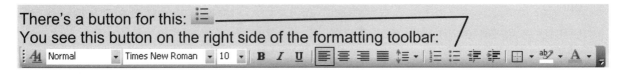

 HELP! I don't see the formatting toolbar.

If you don't see a toolbar with the ⫶☰ button, then click on View , Toolbars , Formatting .

 HELP! I don't see the button.

If you don't see the ⫶☰ button on the toolbar, then click on ⯆ on the right side of the toolbar. The button will then become visible.

☞ **Start *Word 2003* 𝕝𝕝⁶**

☞ **For your document display, select the *Print Layout* view 𝕝𝕝¹⁰**

☞ **Close the *Getting Started* Task Pane 𝕝𝕝⁶⁹**

☞ **Select the *Times New Roman* font 𝕝𝕝²¹ and select font size 12 𝕝𝕝²²**

You'll see that you can format bulleted lists before or after you type. First, we will start by adding a bulleted list to a text already typed. Type in the text for the list now:

⌨ **Type:**
List
first
second
third

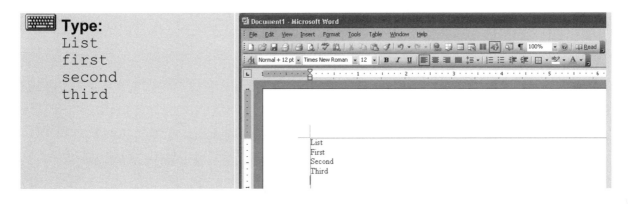

Tip

You see that *Word 2003* automatically begins the typed words with a capital letter. This is called *autocorrection*.

You can turn off autocorrection by clicking on ⬚ Tools , ⬚ AutoCorrect Options...

To format the lines as a list, you're going to select them first.

☞ **Select the bottom**
three lines ✐26

☞ **Click on** ⬚

You see that the lines are indented and preceded by a *bullet:*

Note that the ⬚ button now has a border:

☞ **Make sure the list is**
still selected

☞ **Click on** ⬚

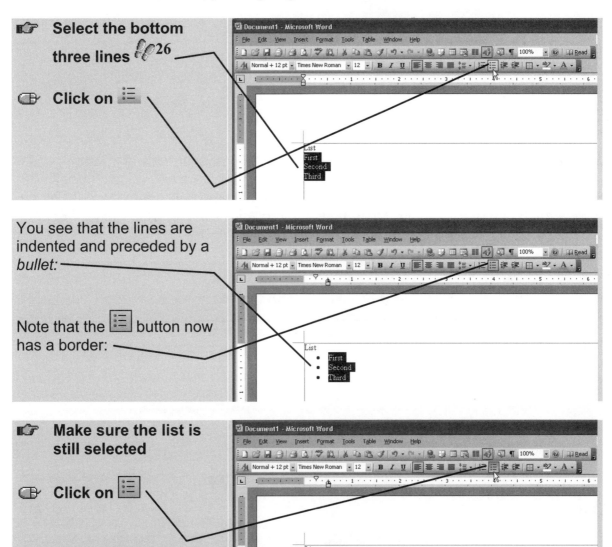

You see that the list
formatting has disappeared:

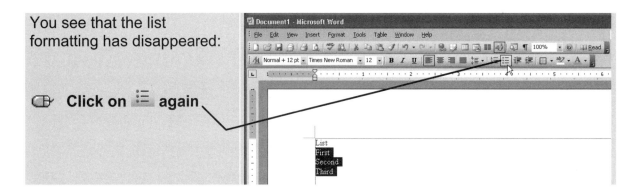

☞ **Click on** ≣ **again**

The list formatting is active again.

Hierarchy and Inheritance in Word

Word's formatting functionality is based on a hierarchy of character, paragraph, and page settings, each of which gives you an easy way to create and adjust formatting. Information regarding paragraph formatting is stored in the paragraph mark (¶) at the end of each paragraph. If you create a new paragraph, it will automatically *inherit* the attributes of the previous paragraph. Let's take a look:

☞ **Click at the end of the last line**

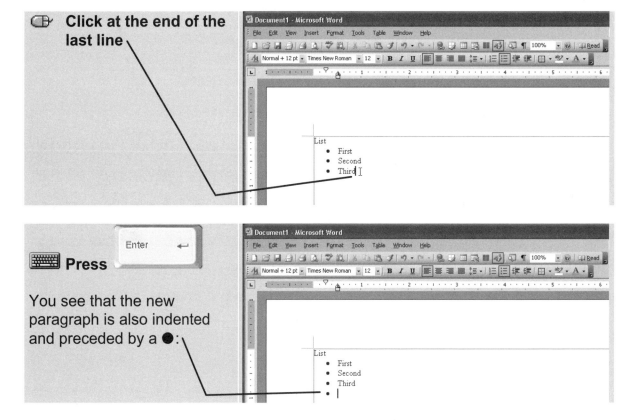

⌨ **Press** `Enter ⏎`

You see that the new paragraph is also indented and preceded by a ●:

The new paragraph receives the same formatting as the previous paragraph.

Tip

If the paragraph mark (¶) at the end of a paragraph is deleted, the next paragraph will merge with the preceding one, and adopt its formatting and style. Some people work with the paragraphs marks visible, so that they can avoid accidentally deleting this symbol. If you accidentally delete the paragraph mark and want to restore the paragraph mark and the original formatting:

☞ **Click on**

An Empty List?

If you do not type anything on these new lines, the formatting will revert back to the regular paragraph formatting that you were using before you started the bulleted list. You can not create empty lists—see for yourself:

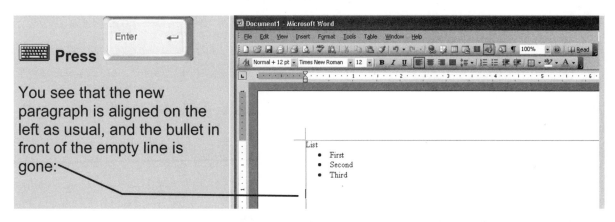

Press Enter ←

You see that the new paragraph is aligned on the left as usual, and the bullet in front of the empty line is gone:

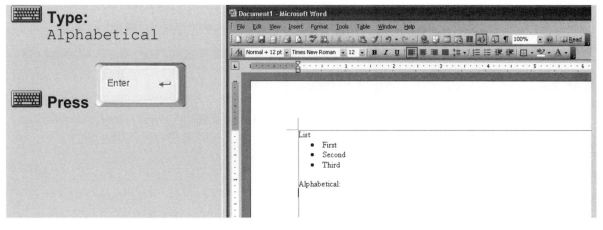

Type: Alphabetical

Press Enter ←

Now you can give the command that the next lines should be a list. This time you're specifying the list beforehand. Give it a try:

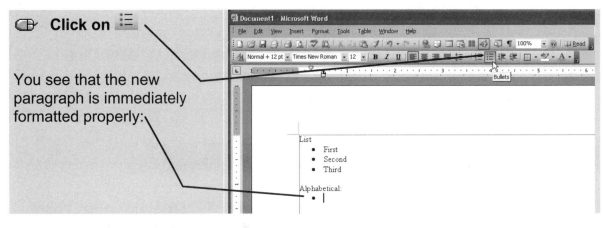

Click on

You see that the new paragraph is immediately formatted properly:

Type:
Ape
Bear
Cobra

You see that all these new paragraphs are also formatted correctly:

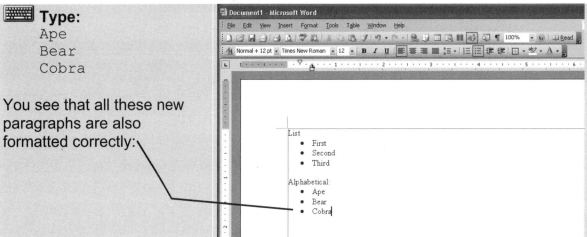

You can turn off the list when you want to begin a new regular paragraph.

Press Enter

Click on

Type:
Animals

You see that this is now a regular paragraph:

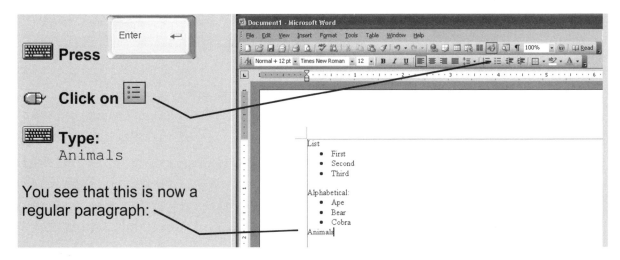

Tip

Other List Symbols
You can select different list symbols:

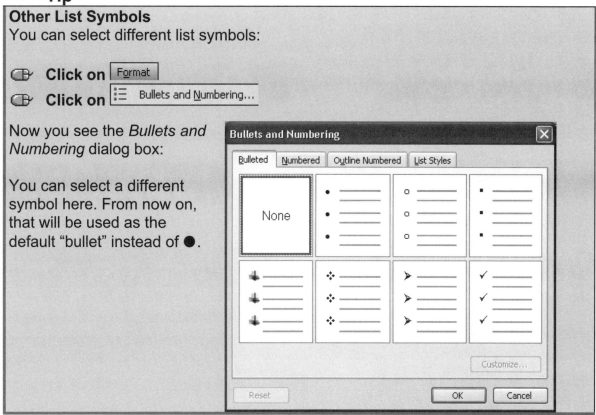

👆 **Click on** Format

👆 **Click on** 📋 Bullets and Numbering...

Now you see the *Bullets and Numbering* dialog box:

You can select a different symbol here. From now on, that will be used as the default "bullet" instead of ●.

Numbering

You've seen how to format text using bullets. *Word 2003* also has special formatting for numbered lists, such as:

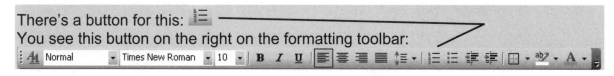

1. beginning
2. next
3. et cetera

There's a button for this: 📋
You see this button on the right on the formatting toolbar:

| 🔠 | Normal | ▼ | Times New Roman | ▼ | 10 | ▼ | **B** | *I* | U | ≡ | ≡ | ≡ | ≡ | ↕≡ ▾ | ≣ | ≣ | ≢ | ≢ | ⊞ ▾ | ᵃᵇ⁄ ▾ | A ▾ |

 HELP! I don't see the button.

If you don't see the 📋 button on the toolbar, then click on ▾ on the right side of the toolbar. The button will then become visible.

☞ **Begin a new document** ✏️53

☞ **Specify font size 12** ✏️22

⌨️ **Type:**
One
Two
Three

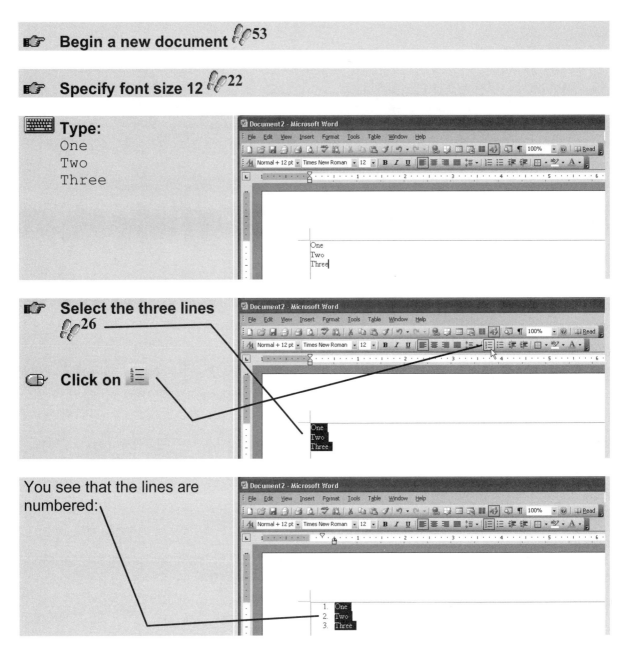

☞ **Select the three lines** ✏️26

🖱️ **Click on** ▤

You see that the lines are numbered:

You can turn the numbering back off. Here's how you do that:

☞ **Make sure the lines are selected** ✏️26

🖱️ **Click on** ▤

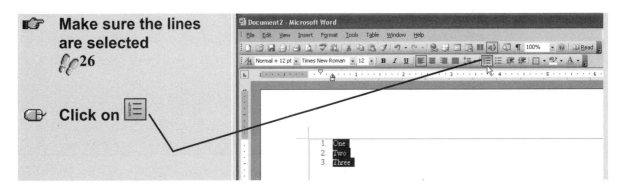

You see that the numbering is gone again:

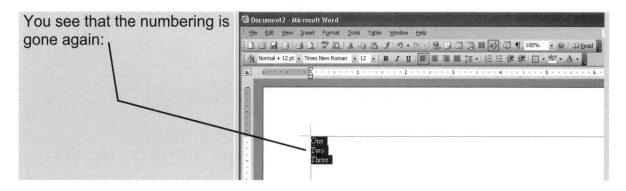

Now you know how to format lists using bullets and numbering.

Tabs

A chart consists of horizontal rows and vertical columns. It isn't hard to create a chart in which the columns are lined up properly, such as a points chart for a game:

Points	Chris	Marian	Bill	John	Allan
Game 1	20	10	30	20	15
Game 2	10	20	10	20	25
	---	---	---	---	---
Total	30	30	40	40	40

You have to use a special key for this. If you try to do it using spaces, the columns will never line up correctly, and the chart will probably look something like this:

Points	Chris	Marian	Bill	John	Allan
Game 1	20	10	30	20	15
Game 2	10	20	10	20	25
	---	---	---	---	---
Total	30	30	40	40	40

You create nicely aligned charts with the help of the Tab key:

The Tab key is at the top left of the letters on the keyboard;

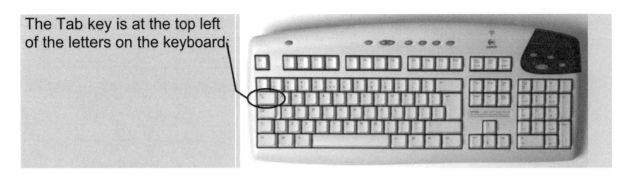

You can create the points chart now.

☞ **Begin a new document** 🦶53

☞ **Close the *Getting Started* Task Pane** 🦶69

☞ **Turn off the *Text boundaries* option** 🦶31

☞ **Set all four margins of the document to 0.98"** 🦶32

☞ **Select font size 12** 🦶22

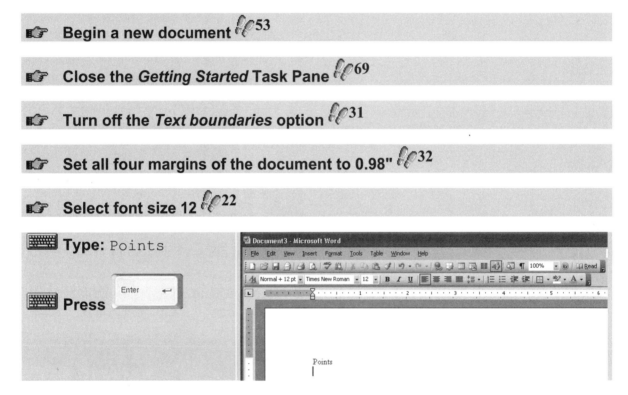

⌨ **Type:** Points

⌨ **Press** [Enter ↵]

Now you can type in the names, pressing the Tab key between them.

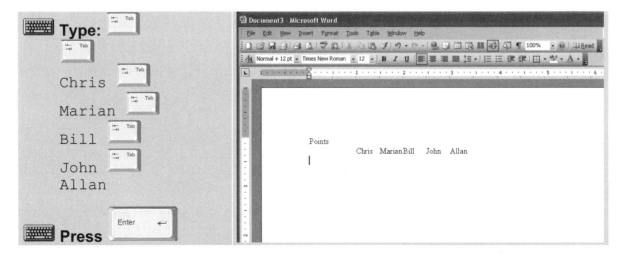

⌨ **Type:** [Tab]
[Tab]
Chris [Tab]
Marian [Tab]
Bill [Tab]
John [Tab]
Allan

⌨ **Press** [Enter ↵]

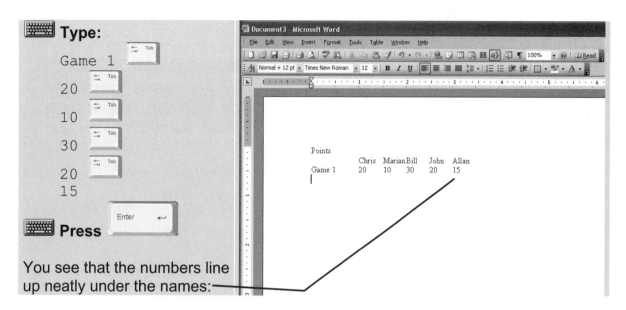

You see that the numbers line up neatly under the names:

That's because you used the Tab key. You can create another row under this one.

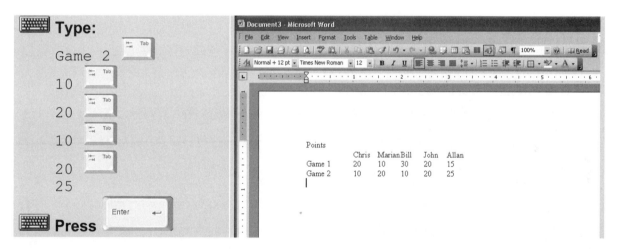

Type a row of lines under this one.

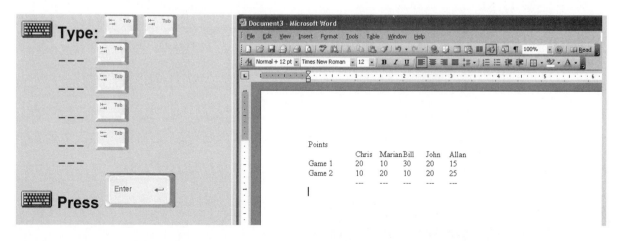

And finally, type in a row of totals.

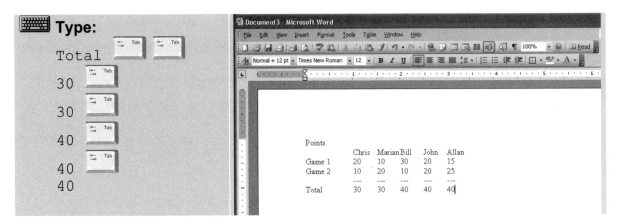

All the columns are neatly lined up. Sometimes, however, you may want to change the amount of space between the columns.

Tab Stops

You see that the columns aren't neatly spaced. That's because of *Word 2003*'s tab stops. A *tab stop* is a location that indicates how far text should be indented when you press the Tab key. *Word 2003* has a default setting for tab stops.

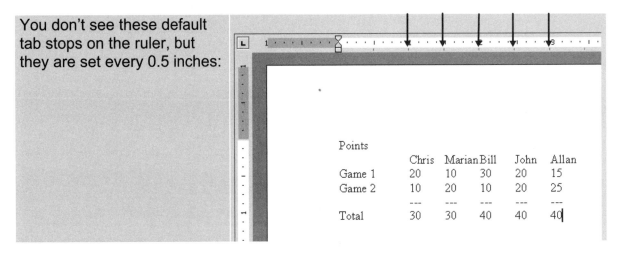

You don't see these default tab stops on the ruler, but they are set every 0.5 inches:

In this case, it works out fine, and all the names and numbers fit into this width. But look what happens if you use a longer name:

Click after `Bill`

Type a space

Type: `Silverstein`

You see that the data in the last columns no longer line up properly:

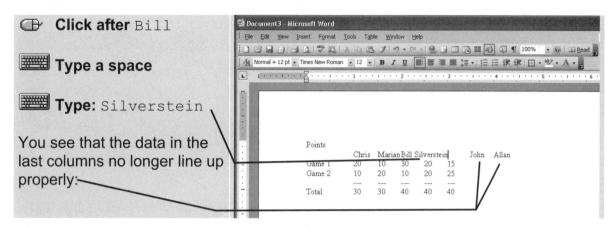

You can fix this by inserting your own tab stops into the ruler. Before you do that, you need to select the chart first.

⇨ **Please note:**

First select ... then act.

☞ **Select the columns and rows in the chart** *26*

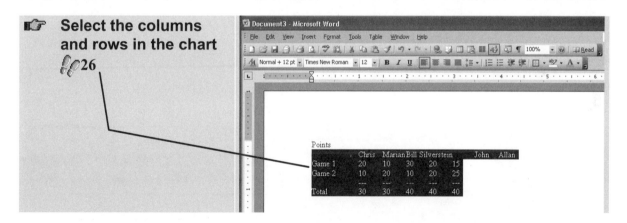

Once all the columns and rows are selected, you can insert the new tab stops.

Click on *1* on the ruler

You see that a small right angle **L** is placed on the ruler. This symbol is a tab stop.

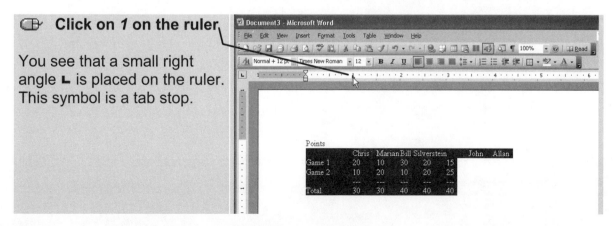

Now you can add in the rest of the tab stops, one every inch, for example.

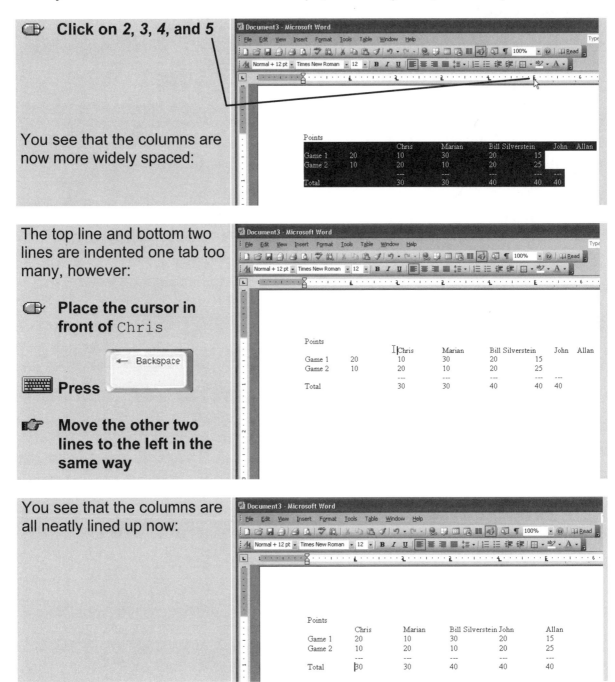

☞ **Click on 2, 3, 4, and 5**

You see that the columns are now more widely spaced:

The top line and bottom two lines are indented one tab too many, however:

☞ **Place the cursor in front of** Chris

⌨ **Press** ← Backspace

☞ **Move the other two lines to the left in the same way**

You see that the columns are all neatly lined up now:

You can adjust this spacing column by column to suit your tastes. You do that by dragging the tab stops in the ruler.

➡ **Please note**

 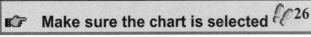 **Make sure the chart is selected** ℓℓ26

👉 **Place the mouse pointer on the tab stop ∟ at *2***

👉 **Press the mouse button and keep it pressed down**

👉 **Drag the tab stop to the left, to *1.6***

👉 **Release the mouse button**

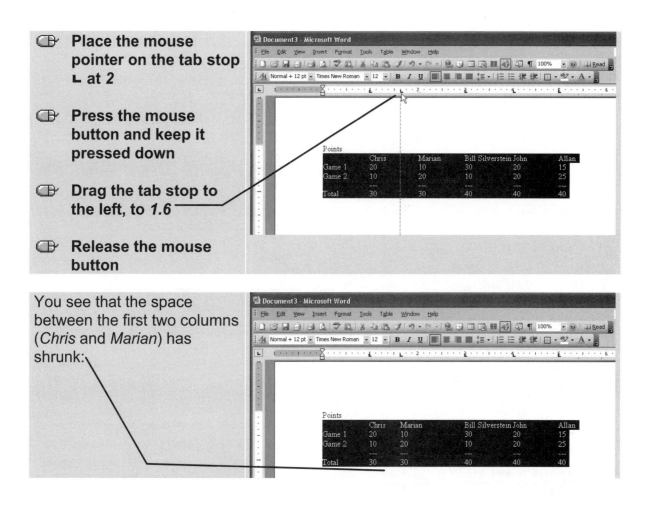

You see that the space between the first two columns (*Chris* and *Marian*) has shrunk:

Removing a Tab Stop

You can delete tab stops too, if for example you've added one too many. Give it a try:

➡️ **Please note:**

👉 **Make sure the chart is selected** 👣**26**

👉 **Click on *2.5* on the ruler**

This adds an extra tab stop, but now parts of the last two columns have jumped back to the left:

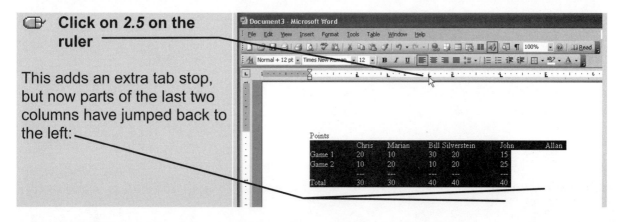

This occurs because the columns adjust themselves to the new tab stop. That works fine for the numbers in the columns, but not for the long name. That's why the numbers have jumped to the new tab stop at 2.5 inches but the names haven't; the name *Bill Silverstein* is too wide.

You can delete the tab stop at 2.5 inches by dragging it off the ruler.

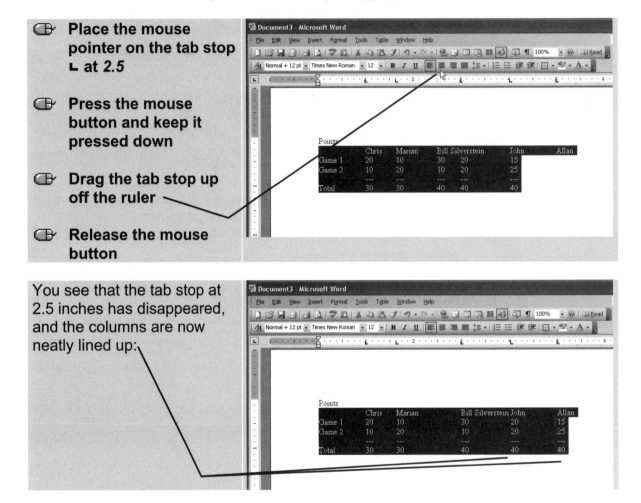

☞ **Place the mouse pointer on the tab stop ∟ at 2.5**

☞ **Press the mouse button and keep it pressed down**

☞ **Drag the tab stop up off the ruler**

☞ **Release the mouse button**

You see that the tab stop at 2.5 inches has disappeared, and the columns are now neatly lined up:

Select All

There is an important rule of thumb you can use to keep from getting confused with charts:

Before you change anything: **always select all the rows and columns**.

Take a look at what happens if you don't do that:

☞ Select the row *Game 1*

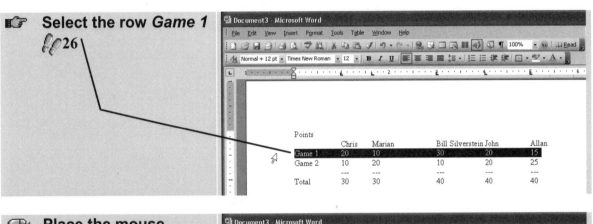

🖰 Place the mouse pointer on the tab stop ⌐ at *4*

🖰 Drag the tab stop to *3*

🖰 Release the mouse button

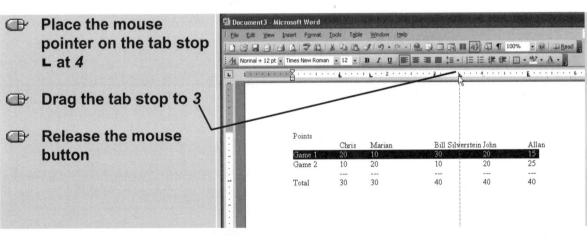

You see that only the number 20 in the row *Game 1* moves to the tab stop at 3:

The row *Game 2* remains unchanged, because it wasn't selected.

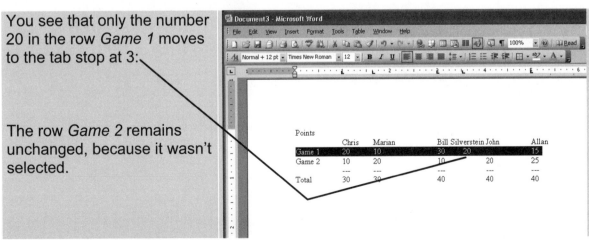

You can undo this indentation by selecting the affected row and dragging the tab stop back.

☞ **Select the row *Game 1* again** 🦶26

☞ **Drag the tab stop ∟ at 3 back to *4***

☞ **Click in the text**

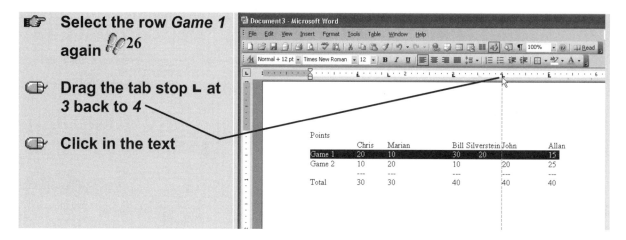

The columns are neatly lined up again.

☞ **Save the chart and name it *Points Chart*** 🦶20

Portrait or Landscape

By default, *Word 2003* uses *portrait* orientation for pages. When you create charts or tables, however, the page probably won't be wide enough that way. In that case, you can select *landscape* orientation. You can see the difference in the *Print Preview*:

☞ **Click on** 🔍

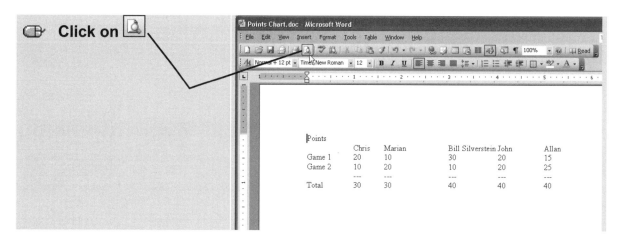

You see this preview of a *portrait* page:

☞ **Click on** Close

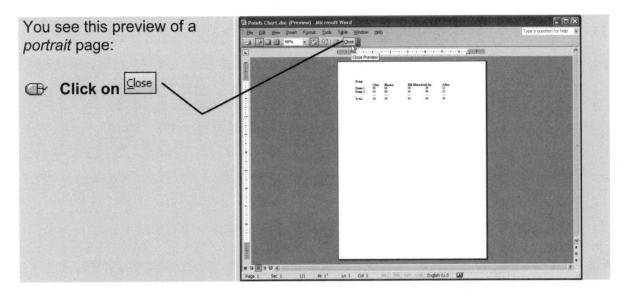

Now you can select landscape instead of portrait orientation.

☞ **Click on** File

☞ **Click on** Page Setup...

☞ **Click on** Landscape

You see that the paper turns 90 degrees.

☞ **Click on** OK

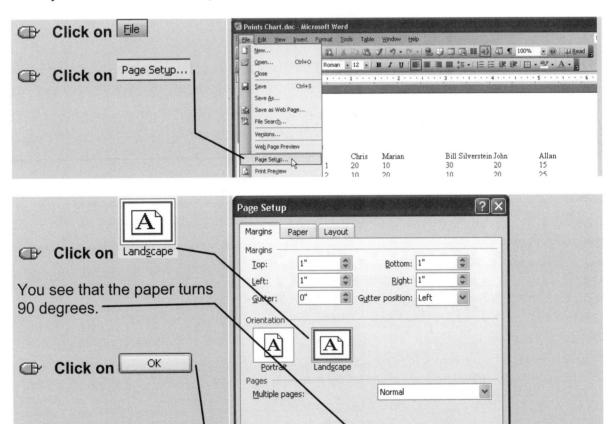

You can see the effect well in the *Print Preview*:

Click on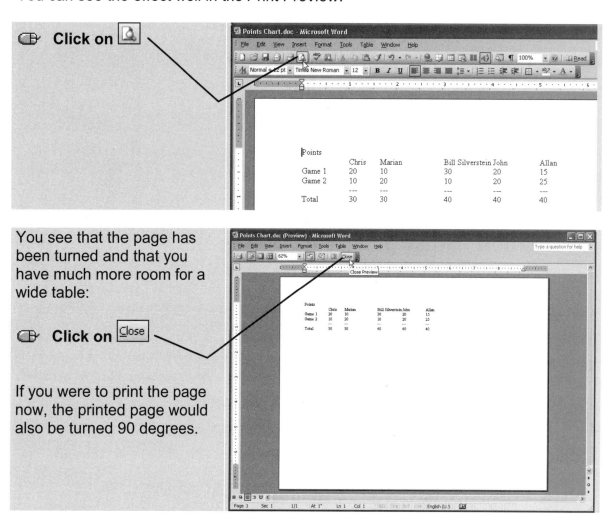

You see that the page has been turned and that you have much more room for a wide table:

Click on Close

If you were to print the page now, the printed page would also be turned 90 degrees.

Save the chart &&⁵⁴

You can practice what you've learned in the following exercise.

Exercises

Have you forgotten how to perform a particular action? Use the number beside the footsteps to look it up in the appendix *How Do I Do That Again?*

Exercise: Tidying Up the Chart

In this exercise, you'll practice working with charts.

✓ Open the text you saved earlier under the name *Points Chart.* 9

✓ Reduce the space between the columns, using tab stops at: 1, 1.6, 2.5, 3.8, and 4.5 inches: 55

Points	Chris	Marian	Bill Silverstein	John	Allan
Game 1	20	10	30	20	15
Game 2	10	20	10	20	25
	---	---	---	---	---
Total	30	30	40	40	40

✓ Save this text. 54

✓ Print this text. 56

Tips

 Tip

Deleting All Tab Stops in *Word 2003*

Here's how you can delete all newly inserted tab stops in one go:

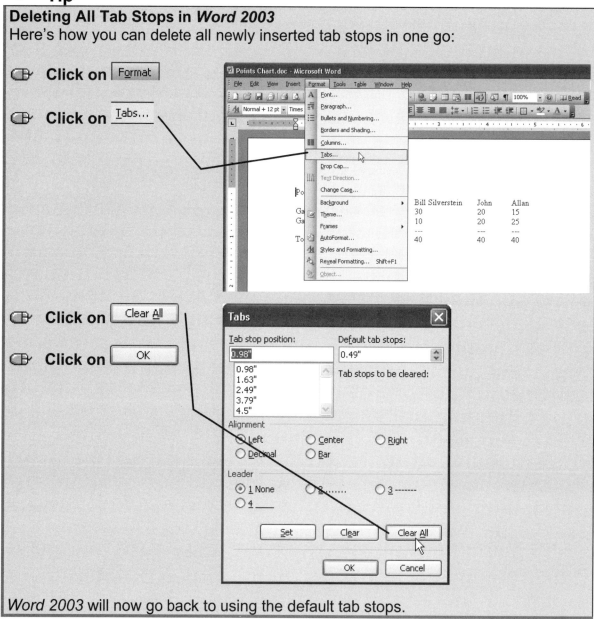

 Click on Format

 Click on Tabs...

 Click on Clear All

 Click on OK

Word 2003 will now go back to using the default tab stops.

 Tip

Tab Types

Word 2003 has different kinds of tab stops. You'll read more about them in the next chapter.

Tip

Selecting the Whole Chart

If the entire text consists of a chart, then you can quickly select the whole chart this way:

Click on Edit

Click on Select All

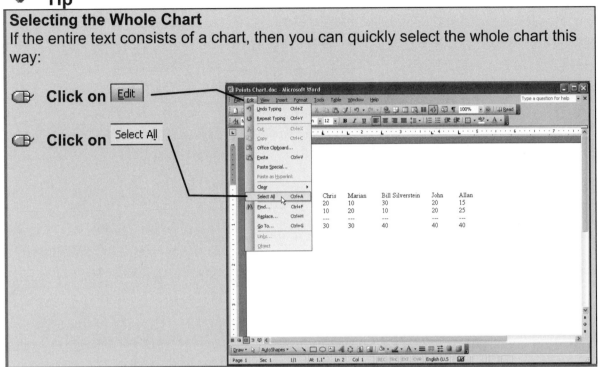

9. Tables

Tables are often used to format text. A table consists of horizontal *rows* and vertical *columns*. The little boxes created this way are called *cells*. In this chapter, you'll see that *Word 2003* has extensive options for creating tables. For example, you can add borders or shading. You can also format the text in the cells in a host of ways—you can even turn the text 90 degrees. If a table contains numbers, *Word 2003* can even perform simple calculations on them.
Once you've learned how to create tables, you'll have a powerful tool for enhancing your text.

In this chapter, you'll learn how to:

- create a new table
- adjust the column widths
- adjust the row heights
- automatically adjust the rows and columns
- add borders and shading to a table
- autoformat a table
- add text to a cell
- change the text direction
- perform simple calculations
- line amounts up neatly under one another
- merge and split cells
- draw a table

Creating a New Table

Word 2003 has a special formatting function you can use to make simple tables like this:

	January	February
	5	6

You use these buttons to do that:
You see these on the standard toolbar:

☞ **Start *Word 2003*** 🐾6

☞ **Close the *Getting Started* Task Pane** 🐾69

☞ **For your document display, select the *Print Layout* view** 🐾10

☞ **Set all four margins of the document to 0.98"** 🐾32

☞ **Select the font *Times New Roman*** 🐾21

☞ **Select font size *12*** 🐾22

✖ HELP! I don't see any buttons.

If you don't see the toolbar:

👆 **Click on** View

👆 **Click on** Toolbars

👆 **Click on** Standard **and**
Formatting

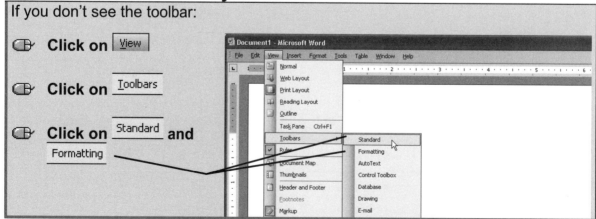

You're going to create a table three cells wide and two cells high, for example.

Click on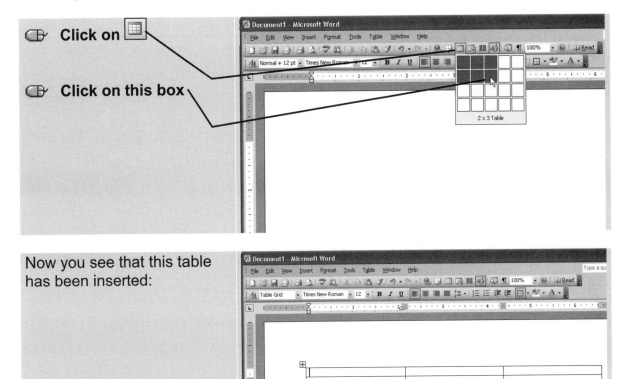

Click on this box

Now you see that this table has been inserted:

You can insert text into the boxes in this table. These boxes are called *cells* in *Word 2003*. You can move the cursor into a cell by clicking in it.

Click in the second cell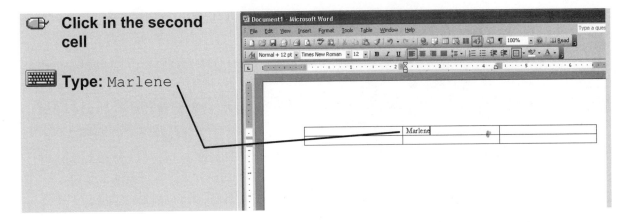

Type: Marlene

You can quickly jump to the next cell by pressing the Tab key.

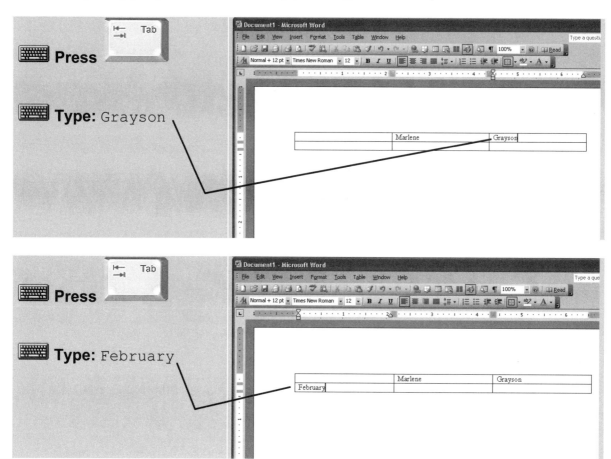

Adding a Row

You can easily add a new row at the bottom of a table. It happens automatically when you press the Tab key. Give it a try:

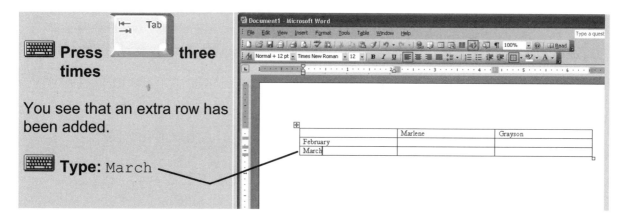

There's another way to add rows or columns to a table.

Adding Columns

To do that, you first have to move the cursor into the desired column.

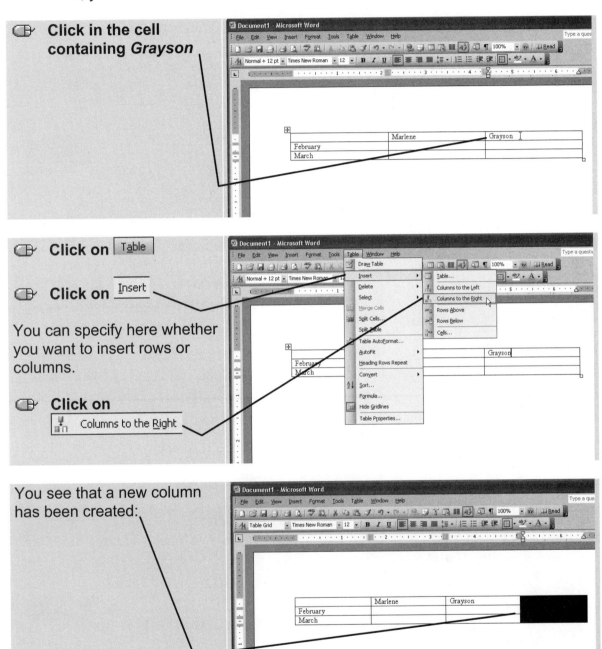

Click in the cell containing *Grayson*

Click on Table

Click on Insert

You can specify here whether you want to insert rows or columns.

Click on
Columns to the Right

You see that a new column has been created:

Adjusting the Column Widths

You can adjust column widths using the mouse. Here's how you do that:

Place the mouse pointer on the line between columns 1 and 2

The mouse pointer turns into ⊦‖⊦:

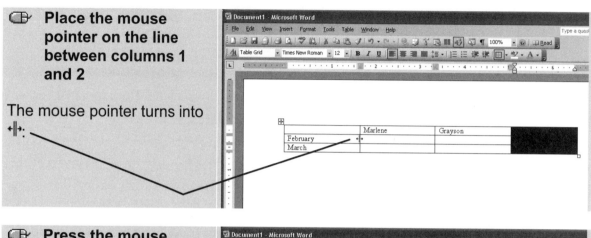

Press the mouse button and keep it pressed down

Drag the mouse to the left

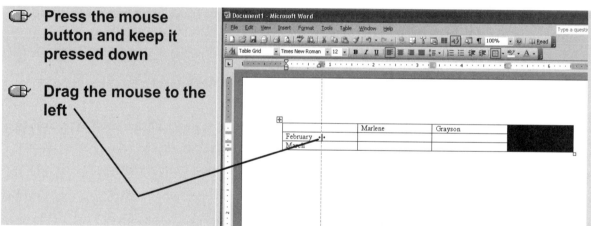

Release the mouse button

You see that the second column containing *Marlene* has become wider:

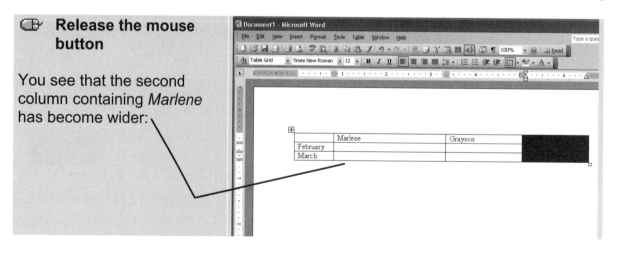

Changing Row Heights

You can also change the height of a row.

Place the mouse pointer on the line between rows 1 and 2

The mouse pointer ⊥ changes into ‡:

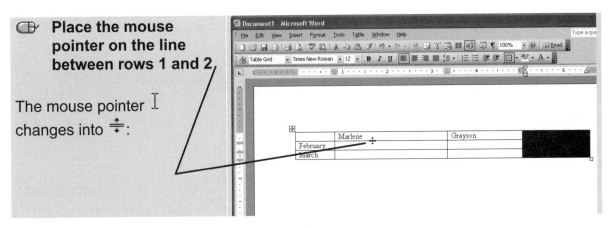

Press the mouse button and keep it pressed down

Drag the mouse downward

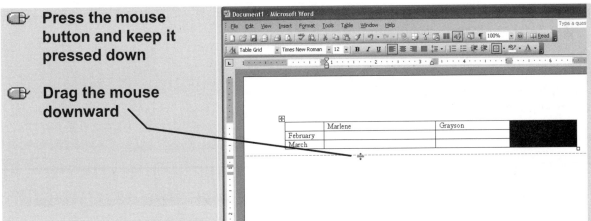

Release the mouse button

The row is taller now:

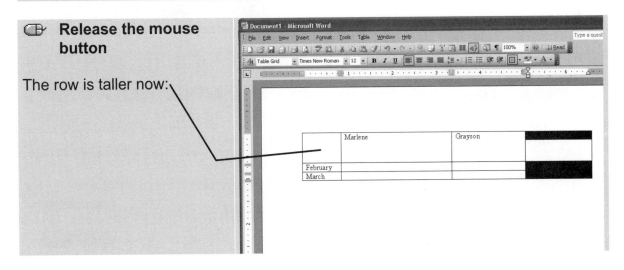

AutoFit

You now have a table with unequal row heights. Some columns are also wider than others. You can try to correct this by dragging the cell boundaries with the mouse some more but the results are usually not as accurate as you would like. Fortunately, *Word 2003* has a command to help you out.

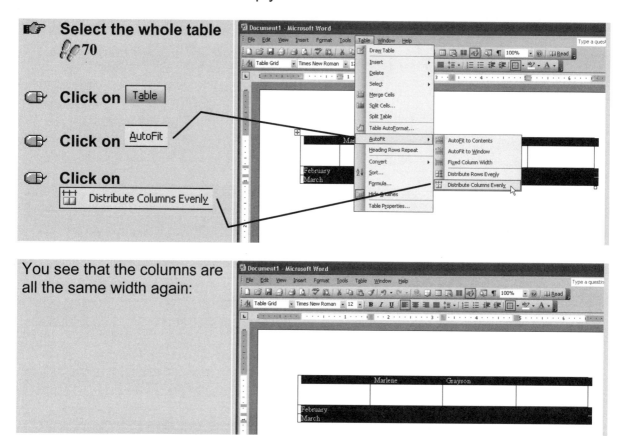

☞ **Select the whole table**
✐70

🖱 **Click on** Table

🖱 **Click on** AutoFit

🖱 **Click on**
Distribute Columns Evenly

You see that the columns are all the same width again:

You can make all the rows the same height in the same way.

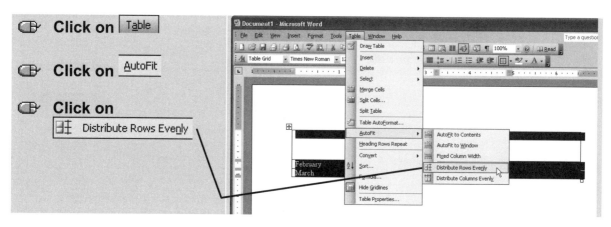

🖱 **Click on** Table

🖱 **Click on** AutoFit

🖱 **Click on**
Distribute Rows Evenly

Now all the rows are exactly the same height.

Borders

Word 2003 automatically places a thin border around the cells. You can change this border for each cell, column, or row. You can make the borders thicker or give them a different color, for example. But first you have to select the part of the table you want to adjust.

 Please note:

First select ... then specify the border.

You can change the border for just the top row, for example. First, you have to select this row. Here's how you do that:

Click somewhere in the top row

Click on Table

Click on Select

Click on Row

The top row is now selected and you can change its border:

Click on

You see a separate dialog box where you can specify the borders:

First, make the different kinds of lines visible.

Click beside

on

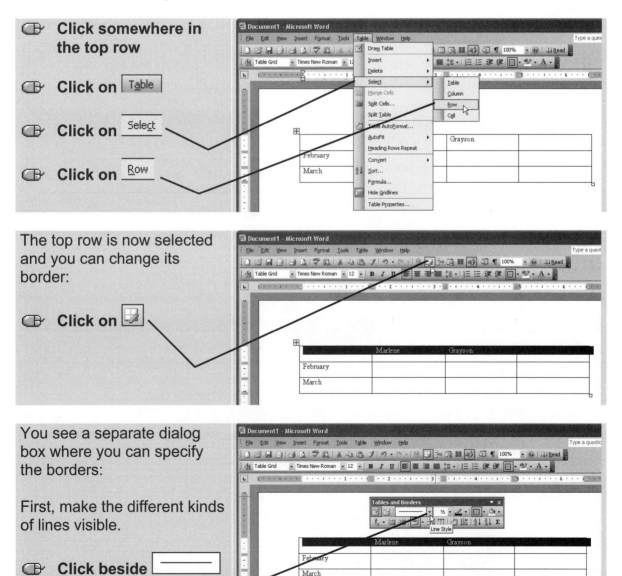

Now you can select a line, for example, a double line.

Click on ═══════

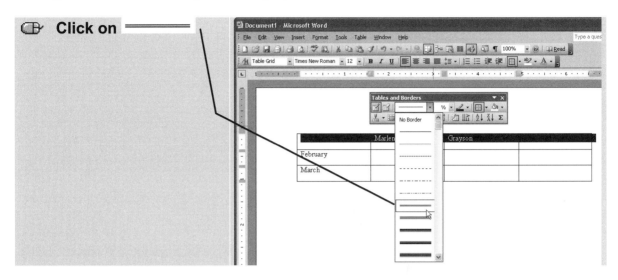

Then you specify where this line should appear. You can add it to the top, the bottom, or all the way around the selected rows, for example.

Click on ⏷ **beside** ⊞ ⏷

Now you can specify where the line should run, for example, around the row like a frame:

Click on the frame ⊞

Now the top row is framed by a double line:

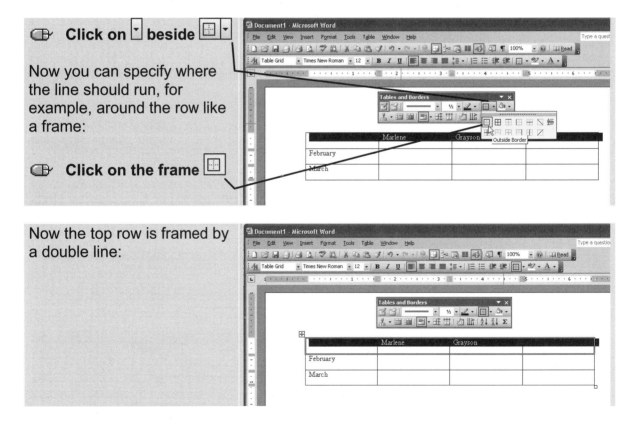

Tip

> **Lines Above, Below, or Diagonal**
> Using this window, you can determine how the lines will be placed:
>
>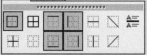
>
> Your choice will be applied to the selected part of the table, such as a single cell, several cells, a row or a column, or the whole table. You can add one thick line under one single cell, for example.

Shading

You can add a background color (shading) to a cell, a row, or a column. First you have to select the desired part of the table.

 Please note:

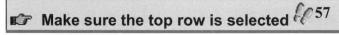

☞ **Make sure the top row is selected** 🖑 57

You can give this row a gray background, for example. You use the same dialog box to do that.

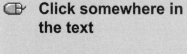 **Click on** ⊡ **beside** 🎨▾

Now you see a color chart:

☞ **Click on light gray**

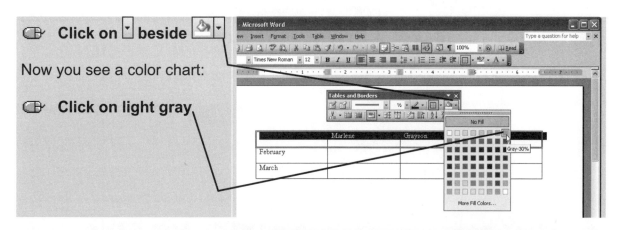

☞ **Click somewhere in the text**

The top row now has a gray background:

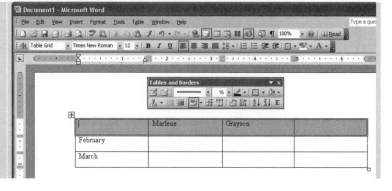

Ready-made Borders and Shading

Word 2003 has an extensive gallery of table style templates from which you can choose. This formatting applies to the whole table.

☞ **Click on**

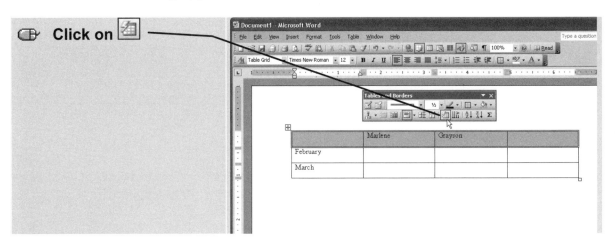

HELP!

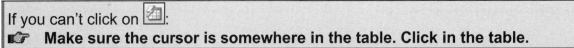

If you can't click on :

☞ **Make sure the cursor is somewhere in the table. Click in the table.**

You can see the different styles you can use in the *Table AutoFormat* dialog box:

☞ **Click on** Table Classic 2

☞ **Click on** Apply

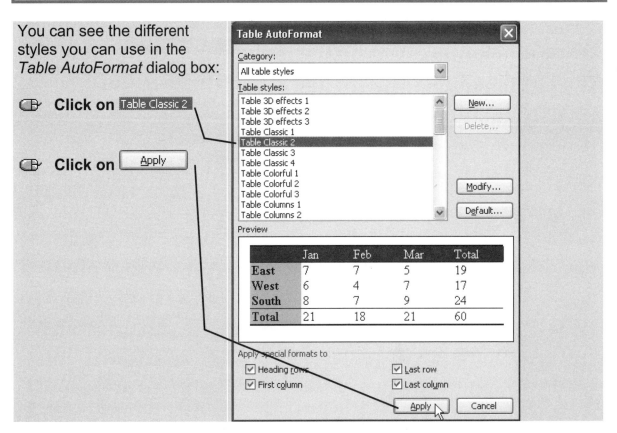

You see that the table now looks very different:

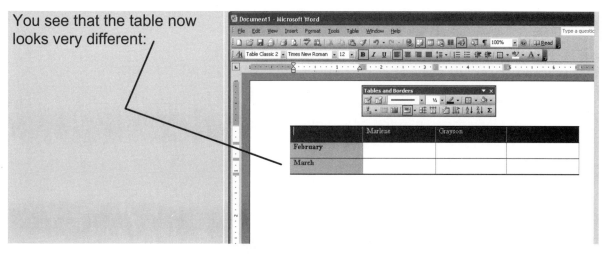

You can easily remove this formatting:

☞ **Click on** 🔙

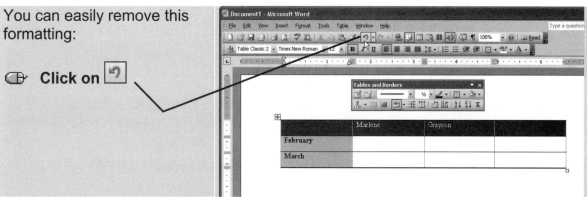

Now the table has its old style back:

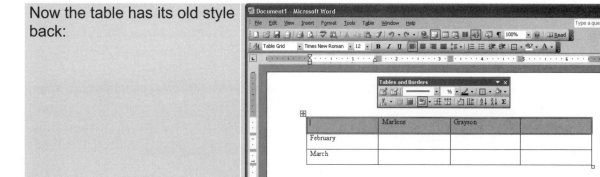

Placing Text in a Cell

You can format text in a cell in various ways. You can make the letters bold, italic, or colored.

You can also place the text in the cell in different ways:

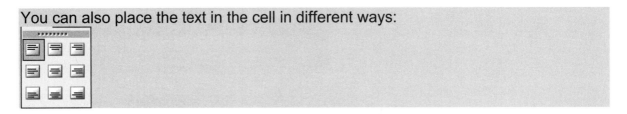

By default, the text is placed at the top left of the cell.

☞ **Please note:**

☞ **Make sure the top row is selected** ✍⁵⁷

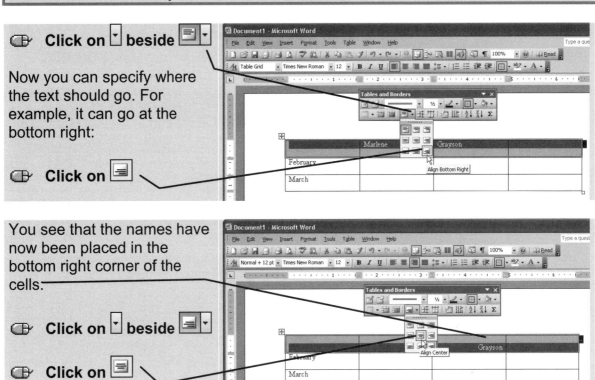

☞ **Click on** ⬚ **beside** ▤▾

Now you can specify where the text should go. For example, it can go at the bottom right:

☞ **Click on** ▤

You see that the names have now been placed in the bottom right corner of the cells:

☞ **Click on** ⬚ **beside** ▤▾

☞ **Click on** ▤

You see that the names have now been placed in the center of the cells:

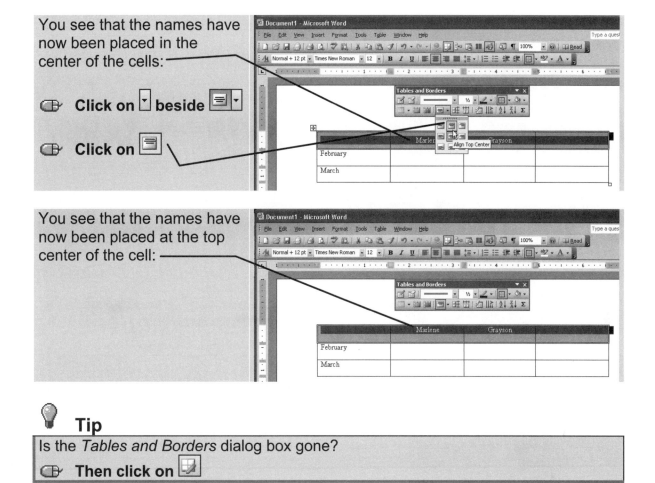

Click on ⬚ beside ☰▾

Click on ▣

You see that the names have now been placed at the top center of the cell:

Tip

Is the *Tables and Borders* dialog box gone?

Then click on ▣

The Text Direction

You can also change the direction of the text. Give it a try:

Click on ▥

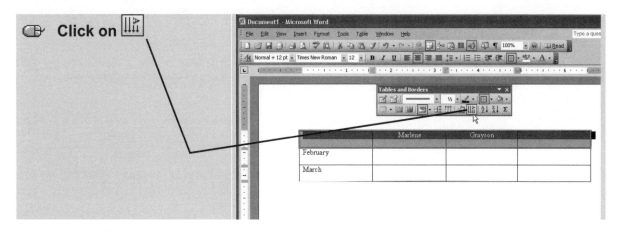

You see that the names have been rotated: ──

☞ **Click on** 🔲

You see that the names have been rotated again: ──

☞ **Click on** 🔲

You see that the names run in the normal direction again:

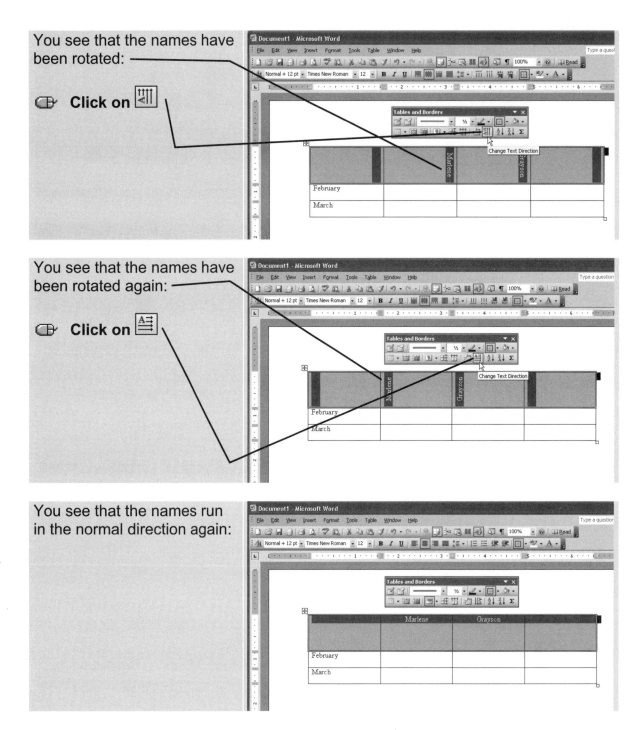

Note that the row is taller after performing these actions.

Table Calculations

You can have *Word 2003* carry out simple calculations, such as adding up numbers. Give it a try:

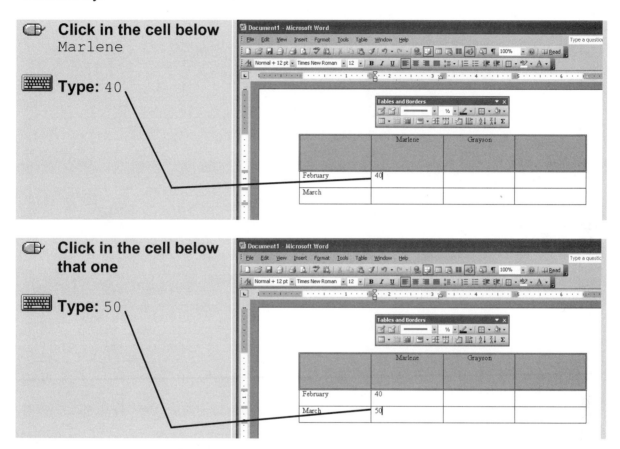

Click in the cell below Marlene

Type: 40

Click in the cell below that one

Type: 50

Under that row, you want to add a row containing the sum of the two numbers. You can add a row at the bottom like this:

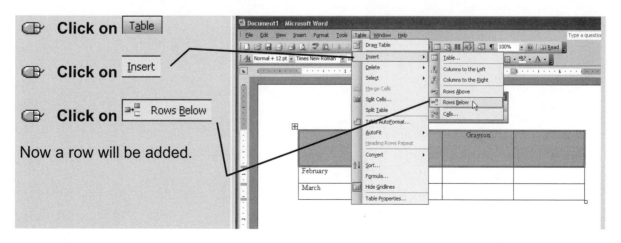

Click on Table

Click on Insert

Click on Rows Below

Now a row will be added.

🖱 **Click in the leftmost cell of the new row**

⌨ **Type:** Total

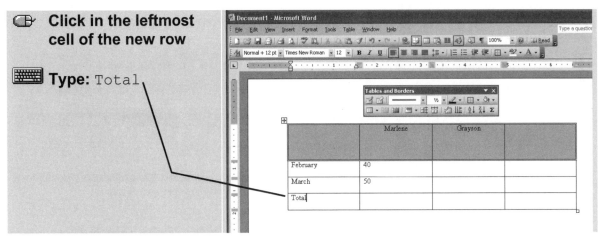

🖱 **Click in the cell beside that one**

Now you can add the two numbers.

🖱 **Click on** Σ

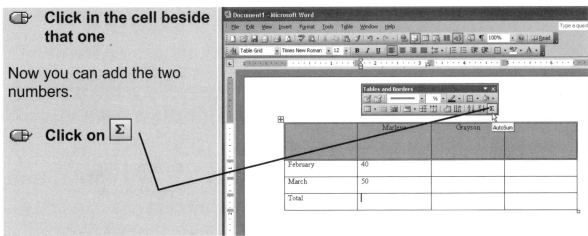

You see that the total (90) has been calculated:

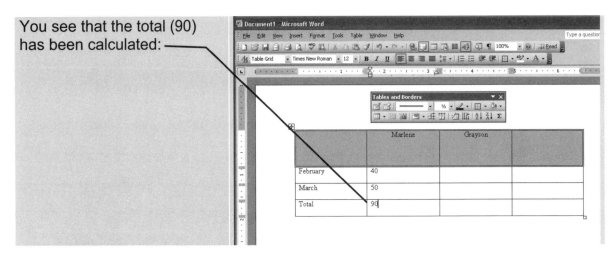

Lining Up Numbers

You can also place amounts precisely under each other in a column. You do that with a **decimal tab**. Here's how you select that:

 Click in the cell below *Grayson*

⌨ **Type:** 300.40

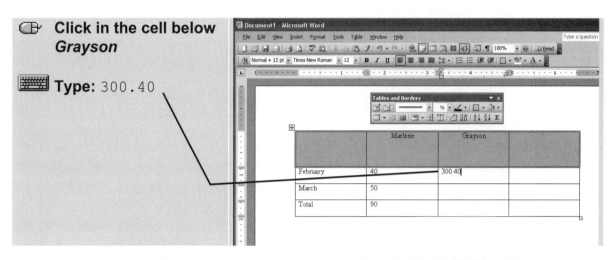

 Click in the cell below that one

⌨ **Type:** 50.50

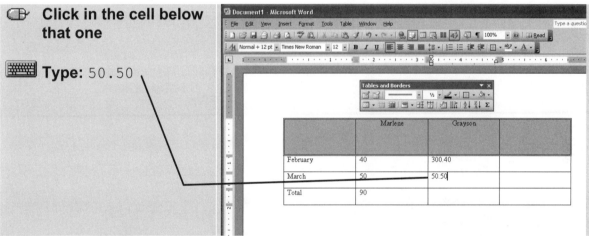

You see that the decimal points for the two amounts are not lined up. You can change that by adding a decimal tab to the column.

➡ **Please note:**

First select ... then place the tab.

Click on Table

Click on Select

Click on Column

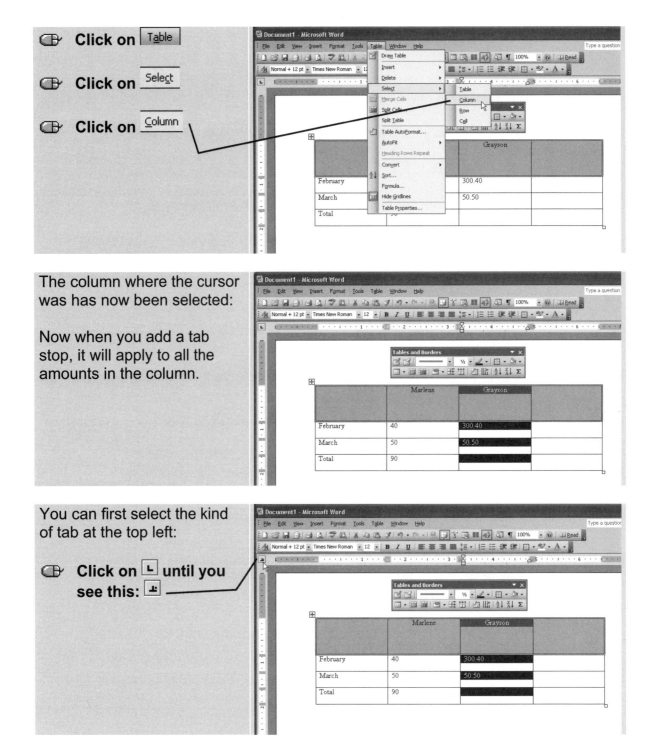

The column where the cursor was has now been selected:

Now when you add a tab stop, it will apply to all the amounts in the column.

You can first select the kind of tab at the top left:

Click on L until you see this:

Now you can place the tab stop by clicking on the ruler.

🖰 **Click at** ⌐ 4 ⌐

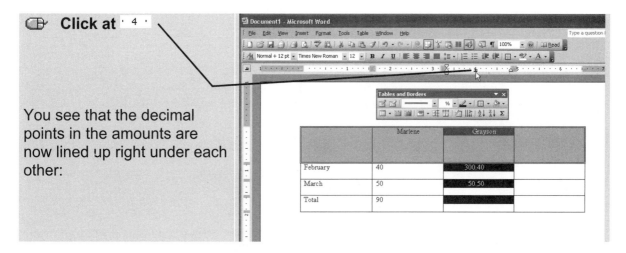

You see that the decimal points in the amounts are now lined up right under each other:

You can add up the amounts now.

🖰 **Click in the bottom cell in the column**

🖰 **Click on** Σ

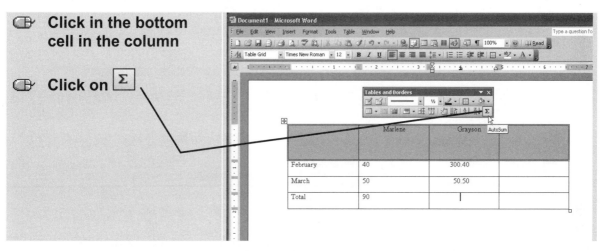

You see that the decimal point in the sum is lined up properly, but the second zero has been left off.

Word 2003 sees these digits as a number, not as an amount.

⌨ **Type:** 0 (number zero)

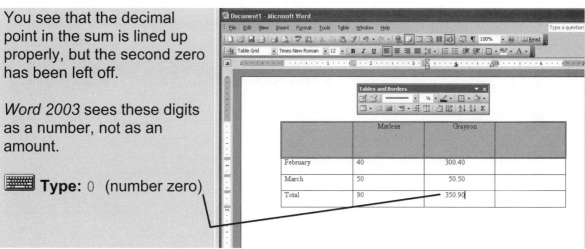

Merging Cells

You can merge cells in a table, or split a cell into multiple cells. Give it a try:

 Please note:

First select the cells ... then merge.

☞ **Select the bottom row**
*⌇⌇*57

🖱 **Click on** ⊞

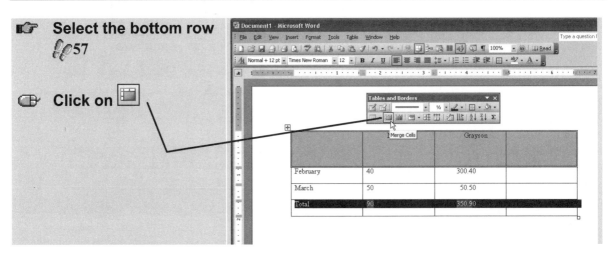

You see that the bottom row
consists of just one cell:

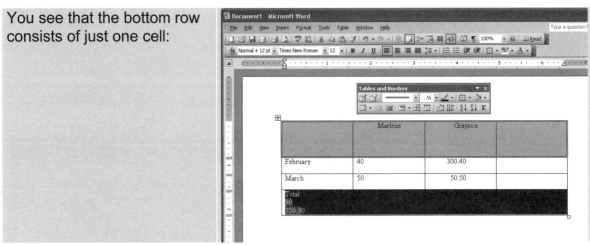

Splitting a Cell

You can also split a cell into multiple cells. Give it a try:

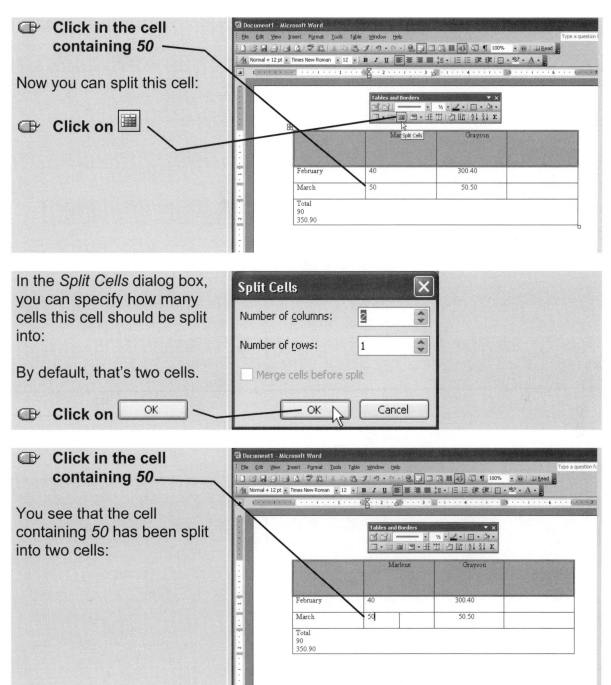

☞ **Click in the cell containing *50***

Now you can split this cell:

☞ **Click on** ⊞

In the *Split Cells* dialog box, you can specify how many cells this cell should be split into:

By default, that's two cells.

☞ **Click on** ⟨ OK ⟩

☞ **Click in the cell containing *50***

You see that the cell containing *50* has been split into two cells:

Deleting a Table

You can't delete a table or part of a table using the Delete key. Take a look:

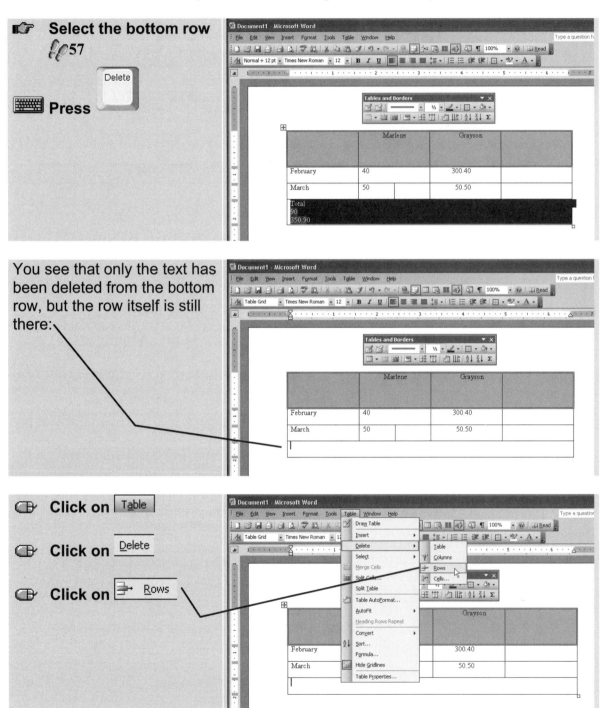

☞ **Select the bottom row**
🐾57

⌨ **Press** [Delete]

You see that only the text has been deleted from the bottom row, but the row itself is still there:

🖱 **Click on** [Table]

🖱 **Click on** [Delete]

🖱 **Click on** [➡ Rows]

Now the bottom row has been deleted:

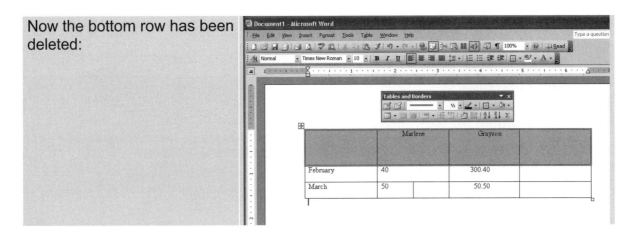

 Tip

You can delete columns or even the whole table this way. Instead of <kbd>➜ Rows</kbd>, select <kbd>↓ Columns</kbd> or <kbd>Table</kbd>.

⇨ **Please note:**

In order to use the options in the <kbd>Table</kbd> menu, the cursor has to be somewhere in the table. If the options are grayed out, then click first in the table.

☞ **Close the document and don't save the changes** 🐾14

Drawing a Table

You can also "draw" a new table yourself. Here's how you do that:

☞ **Begin a new document** 🐾53

🖰 **Click on** ✎

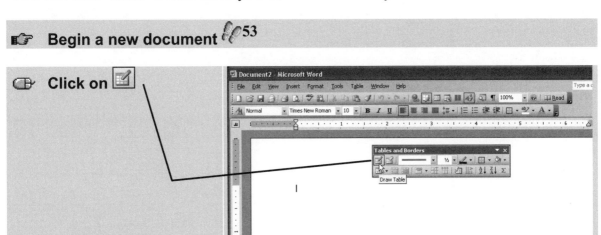

The mouse pointer changes into 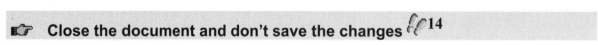. Now you can draw the table by holding down the mouse button and dragging with the mouse.

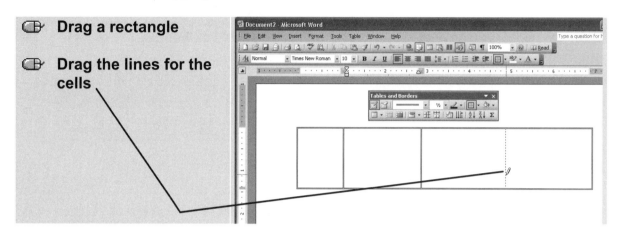

- 🖰 **Drag a rectangle**

- 🖰 **Drag the lines for the cells**

💡 **Tip**

Removing the Lines

You can use the eraser to remove the lines:

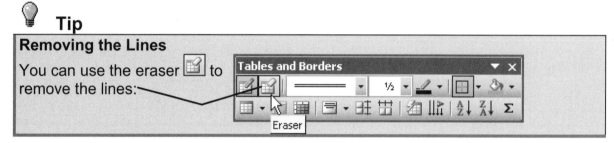

☞ **Close the document and don't save the changes** 14

You can practice what you've learned in the following exercise.

Exercises

Have you forgotten how to perform a particular action? Use the number beside the footsteps to look it up in the appendix *How Do I Do That Again?*

Exercise: Creating a Table

In this exercise, you'll practice working with tables.

- ✓ Start *Word 2003*. 6

- ✓ Close the *Getting Started* Task Pane. 69

- ✓ Select the font *Times New Roman*. 21

- ✓ Set the font size to *12*. 22

- ✓ Create a table two cells wide and three cells high. 58

- ✓ Type *January* into column one, row two. 59

- ✓ Type *February* into column one, row three. 59

- ✓ Type *20* into the cell next to *January* and *30* into the cell next to *February*. 59

- ✓ Add a row. 60

- ✓ Type *Total* into column one, row four. 59

- ✓ Place the cursor in column two, row four.

- ✓ Activate the *Tables and Borders* dialog box. 61

- ✓ Have *Word 2003* calculate the total in the cell next to *Total*. 62

- ✓ Delete the row containing *Total*. 63

- ✓ Close *Word 2003* without saving the changes. 13

Tips

 Tip

Tab Types
Word 2003 has different kinds of tabs. The most important ones are:

⌊	*Left Tab* Align the left side of the text with the tab.
⊥	*Center Tab* Align the midpoint of the text with the tab.
⌟	*Right Tab* Align the right side of the text with the tab.
⊥	*Decimal Tab* Align the decimal point in the number with the tab.

 Tip

Sorting
You can sort a column containing names or numbers, for example. Here's how you do that:

☞ **Select the column**

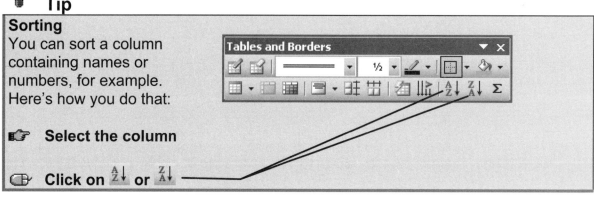

👆 **Click on** A↓ **or** Z↓

10. Letters, Templates, and Wizards

Word 2003 contains many helpful tools. For example, you can quickly and easily create letters and other common texts with the help of templates and *Wizards*.
A template is a sample document in which some things have already been filled in, such as styles, text and images. A letter template may contain the address and the salutation, for example. You can make changes to the template, and that's a lot less work than having to create the whole document from scratch.
Wizards are even simpler. A *Wizard* is a small program that leads you through document creation step by step. The entire document is built up in a series of steps. As an extra feature, *Word 2003* offers the option to use addresses you've previously stored in a table to print address labels, for example. That way you don't have to type them in over and over again.

In this chapter, you'll learn how to:

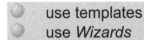

- use templates
- use *Wizards*
- create envelopes and labels

Starting a New Document

Every new document in *Word 2003* has a template as its basis. This model contains preset values for font, font size, paragraph formatting, and so on. A template can also contain text, pictures, or entry fields.
In *Word 2003* you can choose among various templates for letters, memos, faxes, and many more document types.

☞ **Start *Word 2003*** 6

☞ **For your document display, select the *Print Layout* view** 10

☞ **Close the *Getting Started* Task Pane** 69

☞ **Close the *Tables and Borders* dialog box** 71

Here's how you select a template:

🖰 **Click on** File

🖰 **Click on** Close

This prevents *Word* from opening a new window for the template.

🖰 **Click on** File

🖰 **Click on** New...

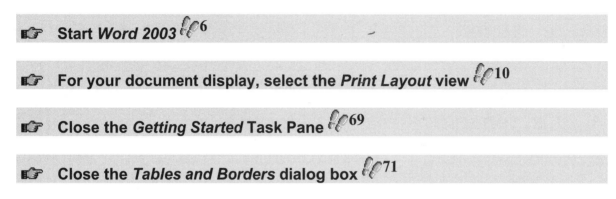

🖰 **Click on** On my computer...

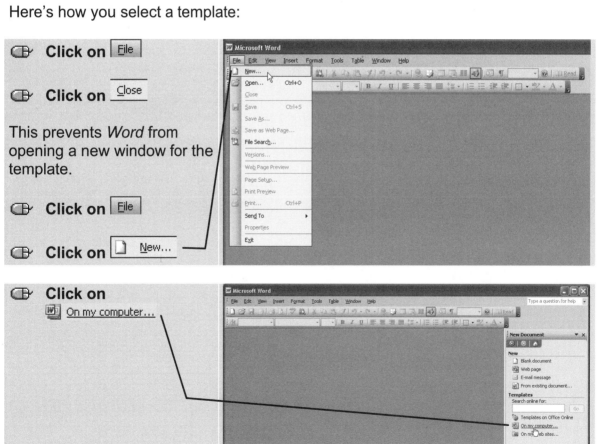

Please note:

The available templates may vary from computer to computer. It depends on the way *Word 2003* was installed. You may therefore see more or fewer templates on your computer.

Now you see the *Templates* dialog box:

In the category *General*, you probably see several templates, such as a *Blank Document*, a *Web Page* and an *E-mail Message*:

By default, *Blank Document* is selected.
New documents are usually based on this template.

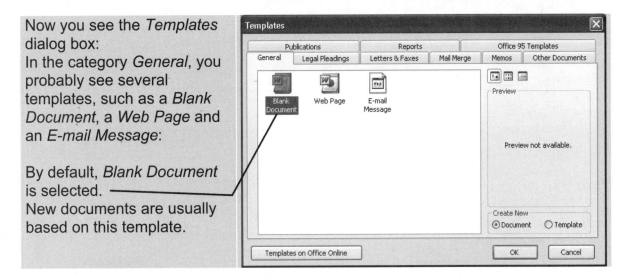

You can also select a different template, for example, a letter. You see that the other tabs offer different choices.

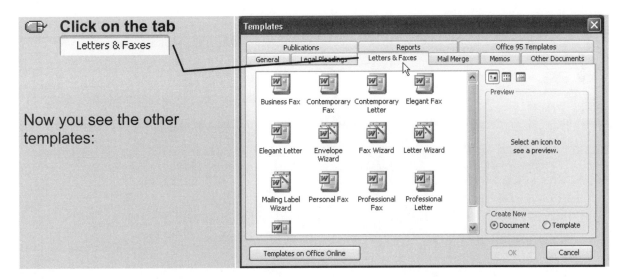

Now you see the other templates:

Click on the tab

Letters & Faxes

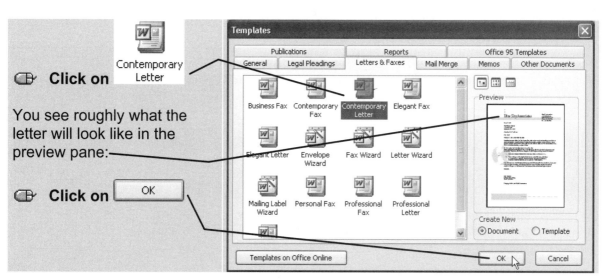

Click on Contemporary Letter

You see roughly what the letter will look like in the preview pane:

Click on OK

Now you see this letter:

In the text, you see entry fields between square brackets [ ]:

You type in your specific data in fields like these.

Click on

[Click here and type return address]

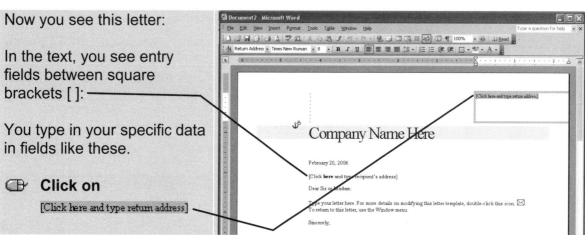

Type:
122 Wisteria Lane

You can click on every field [ ] and fill in the appropriate text this way.

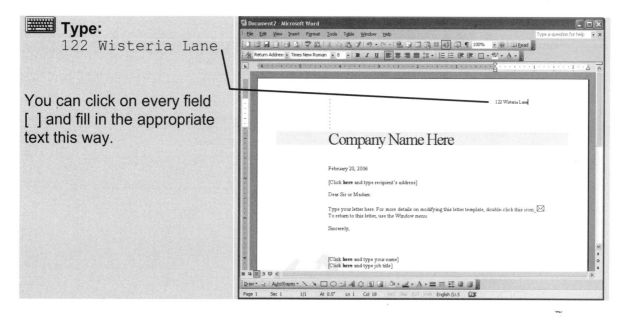

You can change all the text in this sample letter. For example, you can change the company name.

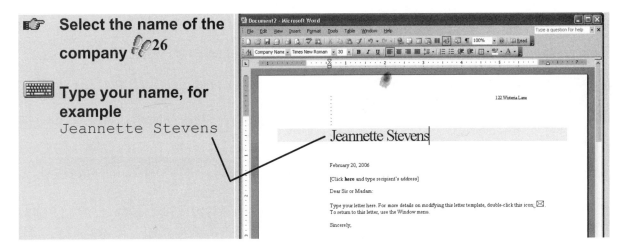

The text is replaced. You can close this document now.

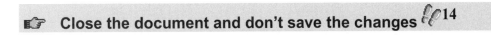

Starting the Letter Wizard

Word 2003 also has *Wizards*. These are small programs that produce ready-made documents for you. To do that, they ask you several questions and gather a variety of information from you. *Wizard* is a pretty impressive word, but the term is a little exaggerated. They're more helpful tools than all-powerful magicians.

Word has several different *Wizards*. The most commonly used *Wizard* is probably the one for creating letters. Here's how you start this *Wizard*:

Click on

    On my computer...

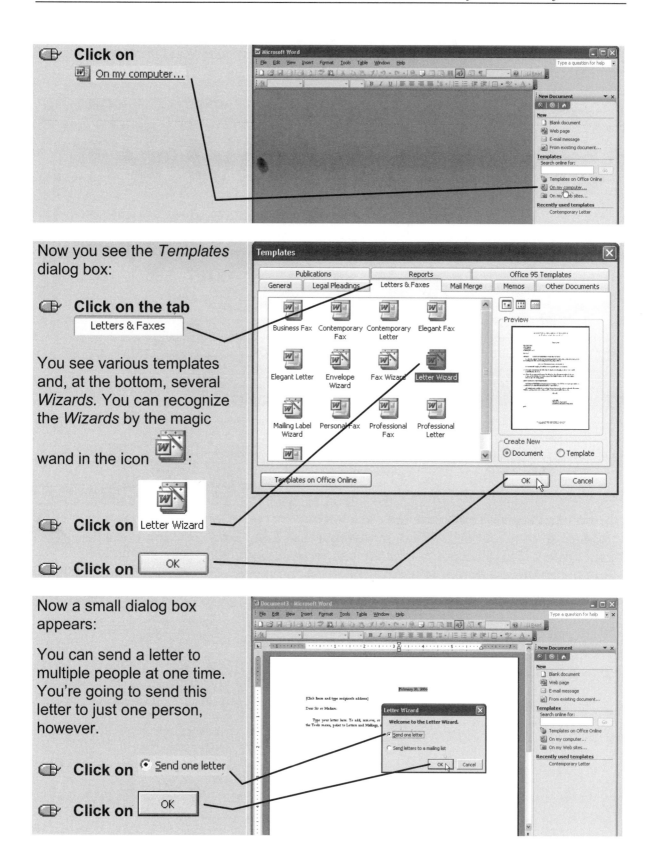

Now you see the *Templates* dialog box:

Click on the tab

    Letters & Faxes

You see various templates and, at the bottom, several *Wizards.* You can recognize the *Wizards* by the magic

wand in the icon:

Click on Letter Wizard

Click on OK

Now a small dialog box appears:

You can send a letter to multiple people at one time. You're going to send this letter to just one person, however.

Click on Send one letter

Click on OK

Then the *Letter Wizard* dialog box appears:

You can select the format for the letter here. You can leave this unchanged for this letter.

☞ **Click on** Next>

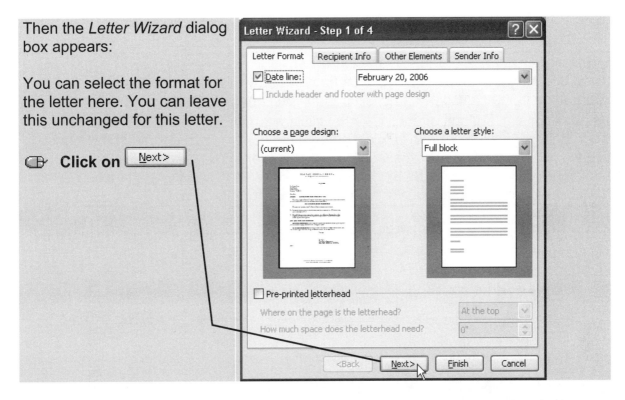

In the next window, you can fill in the name, address, and salutation to use in the letter.

Type the name
Suzanne Shipley

Type the address 1432 Eddingford Place Clayton, NC 27520

You can choose from several different salutations.
Of course, you can also just type in your own text:

Type Dear Sue,

☞ **Click on** Next>

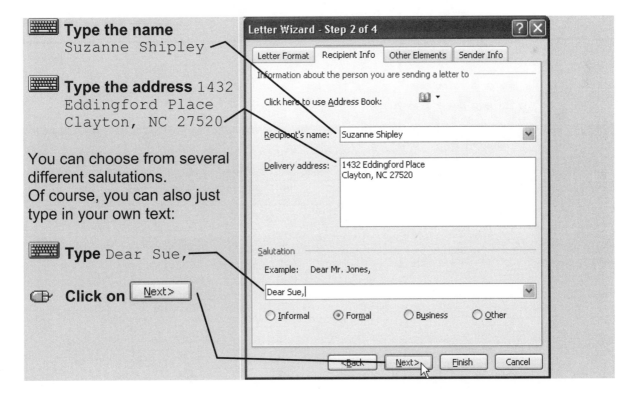

Tip

Word and Outlook Contacts Work Together
If you use *Microsoft Outlook* on your computer, and you've saved address
information in the *Outlook Contacts* list, then you can use this list in the *Letter
Wizard*. You can search for addresses by clicking on the 📖 ▾ icon. *Word* doesn't
work together with the *Outlook Express* address book. If you use that address book,
you won't be able to use addresses directly from *Word*. You can use this address
book in *Word* with a little extra work, however. To do that, see the explanation in the
PDF file **Address Book and Word** on the website for this book.

In the next window, you can fill in various elements, such as that the letter should be
sent certified mail.

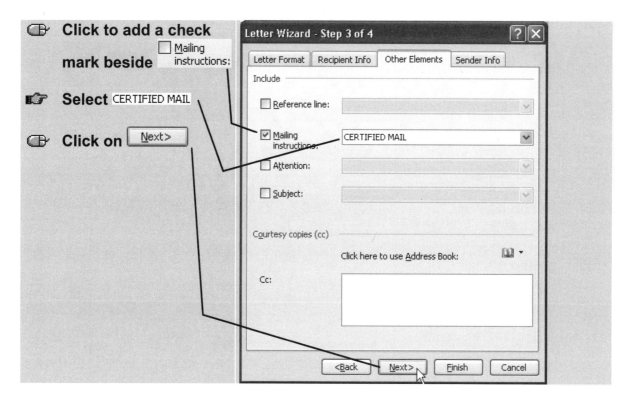

☞ **Click to add a check**

mark beside

☞ **Select** CERTIFIED MAIL

☞ **Click on** Next>

In the last window, you can type in your own information and the closing.

⌨ Type your name

⌨ Type your address

You can select from various closings. You can also type in the exact text you want.

☞ Select for example

Best wishes,

Is everything filled in correctly?

🖱 Then click on Finish

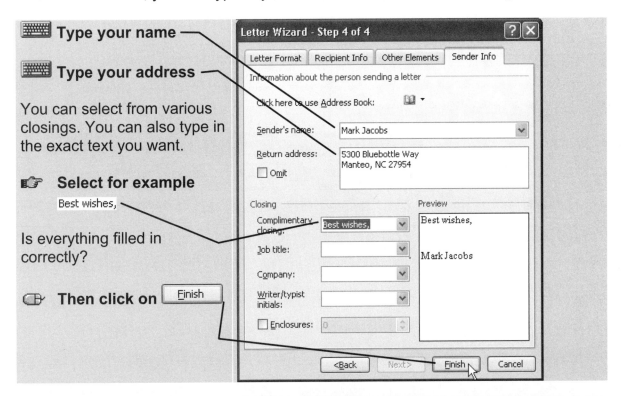

The *Letter Wizard* is now finished.
You can now alter the letter text as you desire.

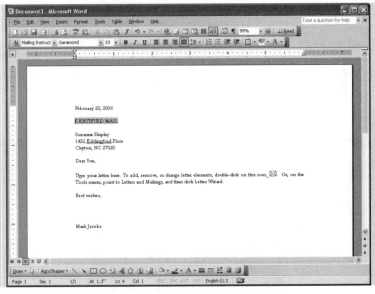

You'll read how to create envelopes later in this chapter.

☞ Close the letter and don't save the changes ✍14

Storing Your Own Name and Address in Word

You can store your own name and address data in *Word 2003*. You can then use this information as the return address on an envelope, for example.

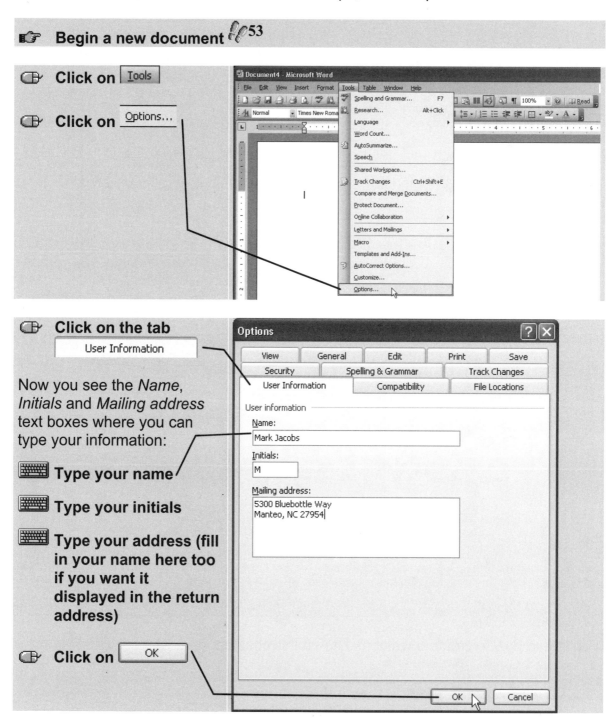

Now you can insert your own address in all kinds of situations, such as creating an envelope.

Printing Envelopes

You can also print an envelope for your letter. Here's how you do that:

👆 **Click on** Tools

👆 **Click on** Letters and Mailings

👆 **Click on** 🗐 Envelopes and Labels...

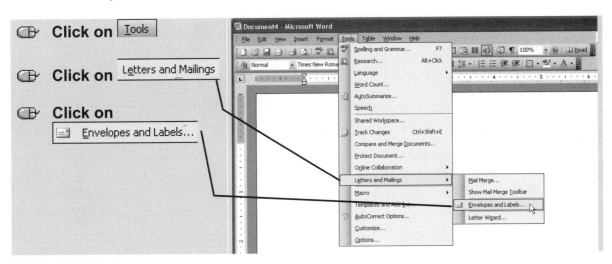

Now you see the *Envelopes and Labels* dialog box:

👆 **Click on the tab** Envelopes

Your return address is already filled in:

You can add to this if you want; for example, you could add your name.

⌨ **Type the name and address of the recipient**

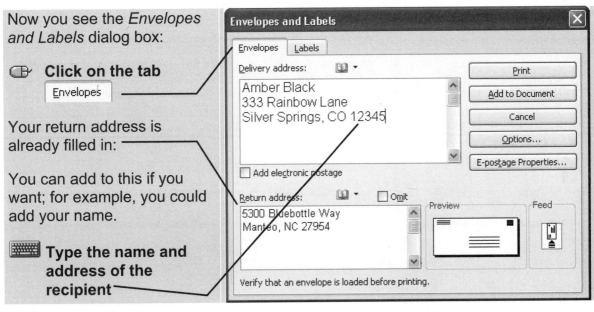

Tip

Do you use the *Contacts* list in *Outlook* on your PC? Then you can click on the icon
 beside Delivery address:
Then you'll see your list of
contacts:

☞ **Click on the recipient,
for example**

☞ **Click on** OK

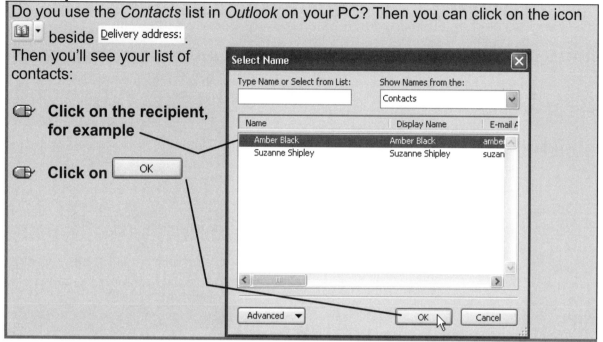

The recipient's name and
address are now filled in:

Once all the information is
filled in, you can select the
envelope type:

☞ **Click on**
Options...

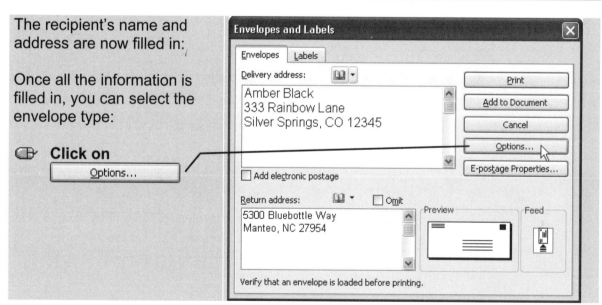

Envelopes come in all shapes and sizes. To print one, you need to know the proper
size.

☞ **Measure the length and width of the envelope you use**

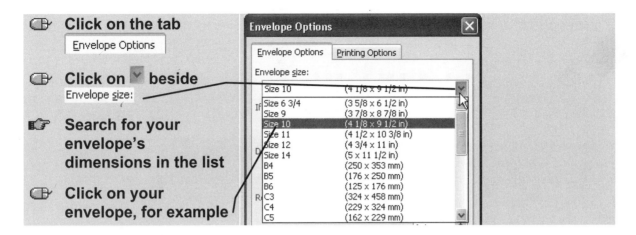

👆 **Click on the tab**
   Envelope Options

👆 **Click on ⌄ beside**
   Envelope size:

👉 **Search for your envelope's dimensions in the list**

👆 **Click on your envelope, for example**

The second important setting is the way the envelope should be inserted in the printer.

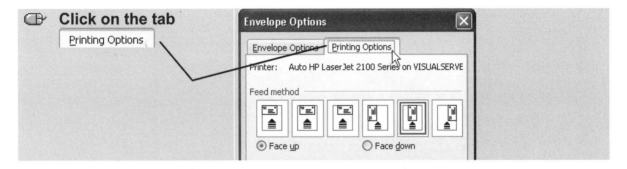

👆 **Click on the tab**
   Printing Options

Printers differ in the way they can print envelopes.

- the side of the envelope to print on should face up
- the side of the envelope to print on should face down

👉 **Look in your printer's manual to see which side will be printed**

 Tip

If you can't find this information, then you can test it yourself by printing a marked piece of paper. See whether the top side or the bottom side gets printed.

Printers also differ in the way the envelope should be placed in the paper tray.

- whether the envelope should be placed lengthwise or widthwise
- whether the envelope should be placed in the middle, at the left, or at the right in the paper tray

👉 **Look in your printer's manual to see how the envelope should be placed in the paper tray**

You see the different ways the envelope can be placed in the printer:

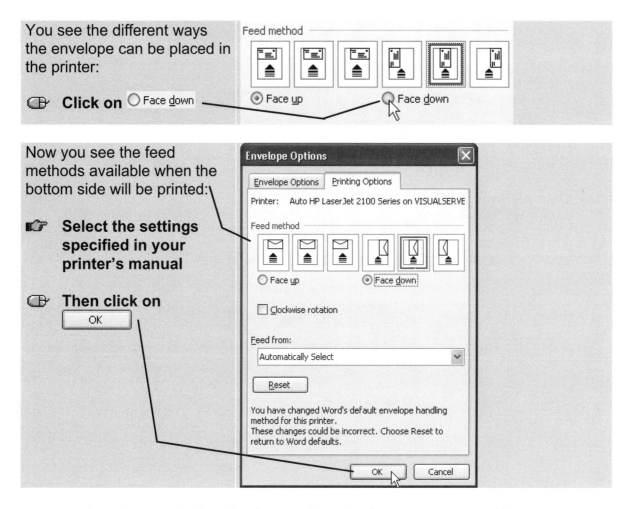

☞ **Click on** ○ Face down

Now you see the feed methods available when the bottom side will be printed:

☞ **Select the settings specified in your printer's manual**

☞ **Then click on**
    OK

Now you have the option to print the envelope right away, or to add it to the document.

Choose to add it to the document now:

☞ **Click on**
    Add to Document

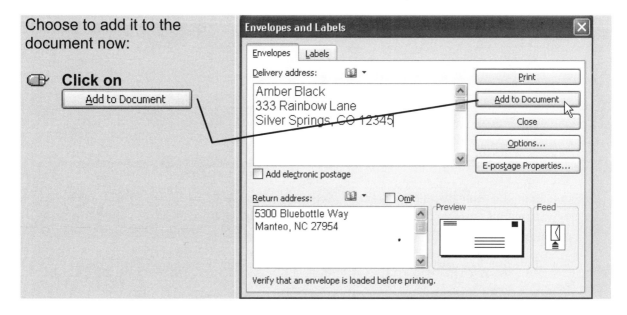

You now see the envelope as it will be printed:

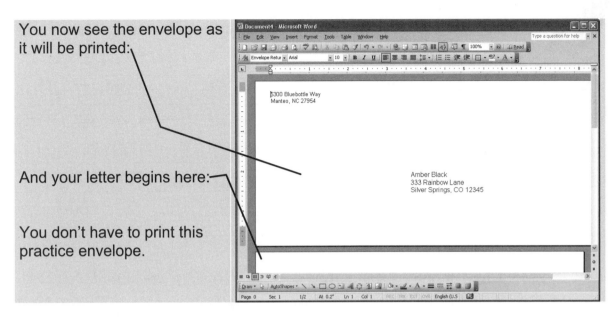

And your letter begins here:

You don't have to print this practice envelope.

 Close this document and don't save the changes 🦶¹⁴

💡 Tip

Word 2003 "remembers" the way envelopes should be placed in your printer. Nevertheless, it's a good idea to write your settings down on paper. You can do that by making a simple drawing.

Creating Labels with the Mail Merge Wizard

The *Mail Merge Wizard* is a useful tool in *Word*. It lets you use an existing address list as the source for creating mailing labels, for example. An address list created as a *Word* table is an appropriate form for the *Wizard*. You learned how to create a table in chapter 9. Now you can apply this knowledge.

Open a new document 🦶⁵³ **and use *Landscape* orientation** 🦶⁷³

Create a table with 8 columns and 11 rows 🦶⁵⁸

Type the following headings into row 1 in bold: *Title, First Name, Initial, Last Name, Address, City, State, Zip Code* 🦶⁵⁹

Fill all the rows with names and addresses 🦶⁵⁹

You can use real people and addresses, or you can just make them up.

The completed table now looks like this:

Title	First Name	Initial	Last Name	Address	City	State	Zip Code
Mr.	Addo	B.	Stuur	1 Computer Lane	Mountain View	CA	91919
Ms.	Marlene	D.	Meyer	3 Diskette Street	San Francisco	CA	92929
Mr.	Patrick	L.	Blair	4 CD-ROM Circle	Hollywood	CA	93130
Dr.	Rita	S.	Benson	2 Monitor Street	New York	NY	12345
Mr.	Hank	F.	Moller	5 DVD Way	Durham	NC	27272
Mrs.	Yvette	G.	Hellman	3 Hard Drive	Orlando	FL	33333
Dr.	Alex	K.	White	78 Icon Alley	Miami	FL	43435
Ms.	Lydia	L.	Dillsworth	23 Text Avenue	Mountain View	CA	91919
Mr.	Peter	A.	Bitter	82 Revision Circle	Kansas City	MO	65432
Mrs.	Chris	T.	Hollingsworth	8 Website Way	Anchorage	AK	53795

☞ **Save the table under the name *Address List* in the *My Documents* folder** 𝓁𝓁20

☞ **Close the document** 𝓁𝓁14

💡 **Tip**

Don't want to do all that typing? You can download the file **Address List.doc** from the website for this book **www.visualsteps.com/word2003**. Downloading instructions are listed on the website.

Now you're going to create labels from this address list.

☞ **Begin a new document** 𝓁𝓁53

🖰 **Click on** Tools

🖰 **Click on** Letters and Mailings

🖰 **Click on** Mail Merge...

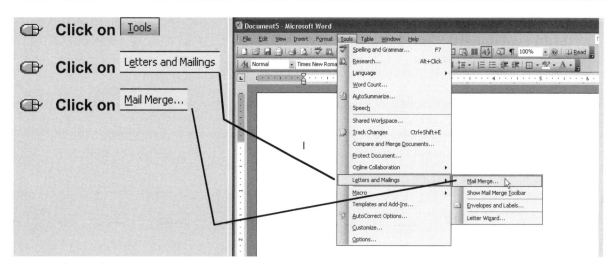

On the right-hand side of the window, you see the *Mail Merge* Task Pane:

You're going to create labels:

👆 **Click on** ○ Labels

The option ⦿ Labels is now selected:

👆 **Click on**
➡️ Next: Starting document

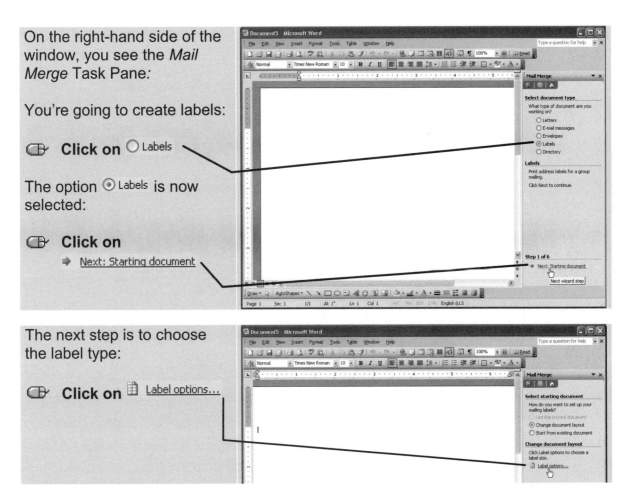

The next step is to choose the label type:

👆 **Click on** 📄 Label options...

Word contains label information for several well-known brands. In this example, you'll select an *Avery* label.

☞ **Select** Avery standard **beside** Label products:

☞ **Select product number** 8160 - Address

👆 **Click on** OK

Of course, you can select a different brand or type. You can even define your own label by clicking on New Label...

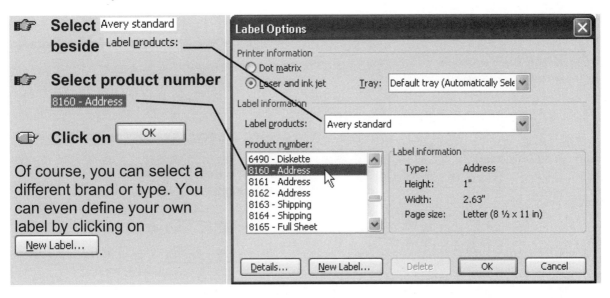

Now you see the sample labels:

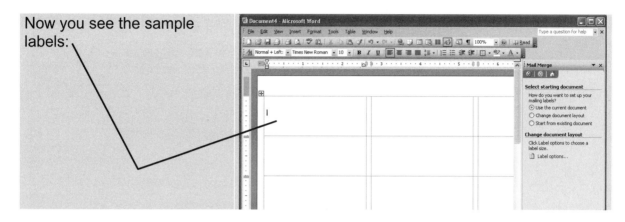

 HELP! I don't see any sample labels in the window.

If you don't see the sample labels, then the option *Show Gridlines* is not active. You can easily change that:

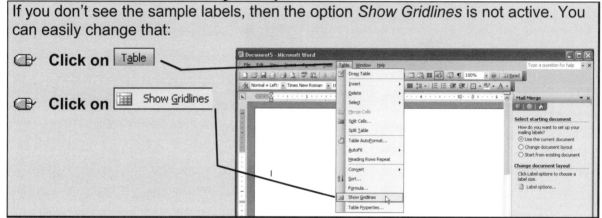

Click on Table

Click on Show Gridlines

The next step in the *Wizard* is to select the addresses to use:

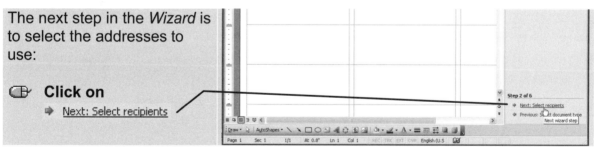

Click on
➡ Next: Select recipients

In this case, you're going to use an existing list:

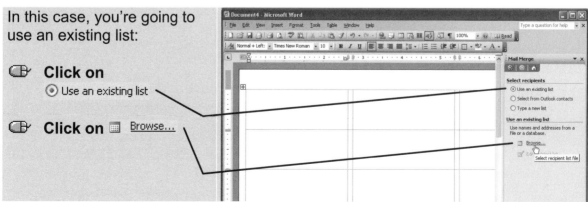

Click on
⊙ Use an existing list

Click on Browse...

You saved the address list in the *My Documents* folder on the hard drive.

You see the *Select Data Source* dialog box:

☞ **Click on** My Documents

You see the contents of the *My Documents* folder:
Of course, the contents of your folder will be different. The file **Address List** will be there somewhere.

☞ **Click on** Address List.doc

☞ **Click on** Open

You see the data you typed into *Address List* in the *Mail Merge Recipients* dialog box:
The lines with a check mark will be used for the labels.
If you don't want to use certain lines, click to remove the check mark.

☞ **Click on** OK

You see the window containing labels again. Every label now contains the text «Next Record».

☞ **Click on**
→ Next: Arrange your labels

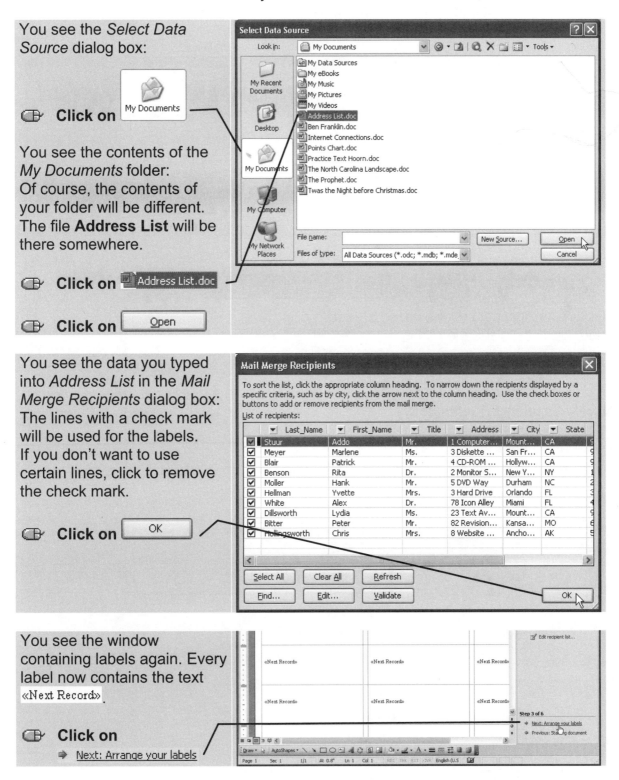

The next step is to specify exactly what you want to print on your label. That might be just the name and address, for example. Or you might want to add Mr. or Mrs. to the name. Here's how you do that:

Click in the first label

Click on More items...

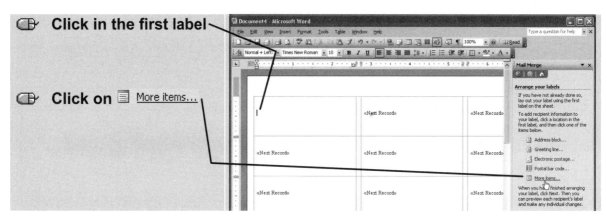

In the *Insert Merge Field* dialog box, you see which fields are present in your own address list. To see them, the option ⊙ Database Fields should be selected:

Every heading in your table is a field. You can add a selected field.
Start with the Title field:

Click on Title

Click on Insert

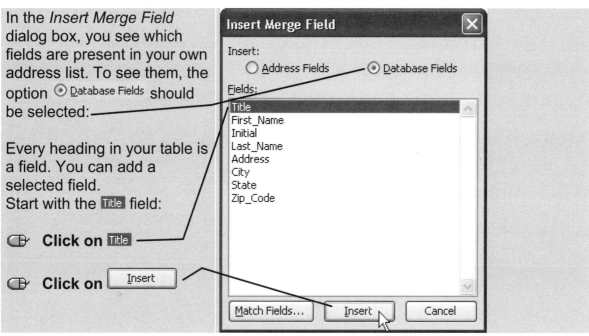

Now you see «Title» in the first label:

Now you can add in the other fields in the same way. You can decide whether you want to use the middle initial in the name on the label.

☞ **Add all the desired fields**

When you're finished with that:

🖰 **Click on** ☐ Close

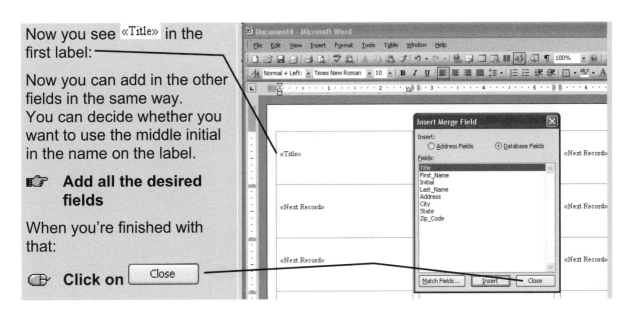

All the fields you've inserted are now shown in label 1. You still need to add spaces to them. For example, you need to add spaces between the fields «Title», «First_Name», and «Last_Name». Also, the «Address» field needs to move to the next line. «City», «State», and «Zip_Code» also need to move to a separate line, and there should be spaces between these fields. Here's how you type in a space between the fields:

🖰 **Click between** «Title» **and** «First_Name»

⌨ **Type a space**

🖰 **Click between** «First_Name» **and** «Initial»

⌨ **Type a space**

🖰 **Click between** «Initial» **and** «Last_Name»

⌨ **Type a space**

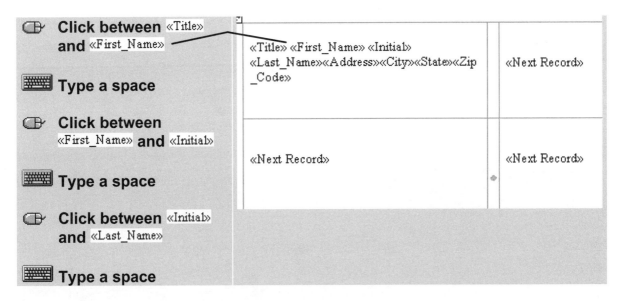

In this example, it looks like the «Last_Name» field jumps to the next line. For small labels, you can't yet see at this stage what will be printed on which line in the final printing. You'll see shortly that this all works out when you add spaces and new lines at the right locations.

You're going to move the «Address» field to the next line by pressing the *Enter* key.

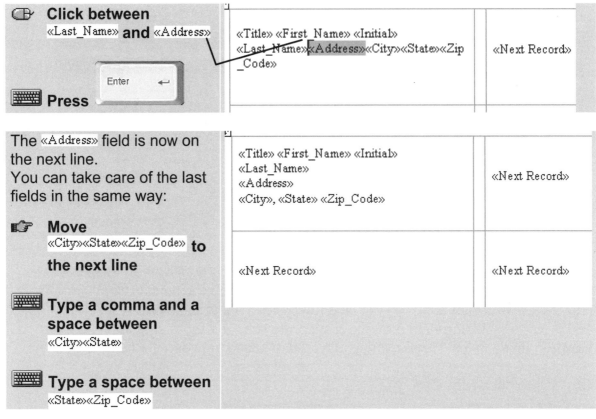

☞ **Click between**
«Last_Name» **and** «Address»

⌨ **Press**

The «Address» field is now on the next line.
You can take care of the last fields in the same way:

☞ **Move**
«City»«State»«Zip_Code» **to the next line**

⌨ **Type a comma and a space between**
«City»«State»

⌨ **Type a space between**
«State»«Zip_Code»

Label 1 is now perfect.
You're going to apply this label formatting to all the labels:

☞ **Click on** Update all labels

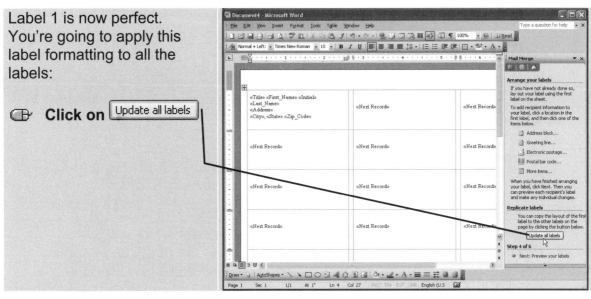

Now every label has the same structure.
Now you can go to the next step:

☞ **Click on**

➡ Next: Preview your labels

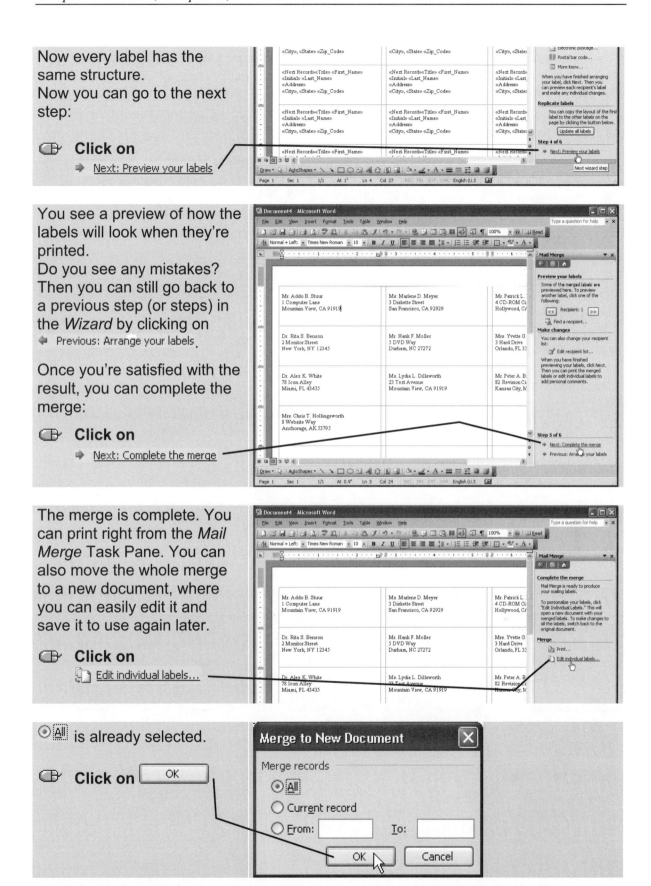

You see a preview of how the labels will look when they're printed.
Do you see any mistakes? Then you can still go back to a previous step (or steps) in the *Wizard* by clicking on

⬅ Previous: Arrange your labels

Once you're satisfied with the result, you can complete the merge:

☞ **Click on**

➡ Next: Complete the merge

The merge is complete. You can print right from the *Mail Merge* Task Pane. You can also move the whole merge to a new document, where you can easily edit it and save it to use again later.

☞ **Click on**

Edit individual labels...

⊙ All is already selected.

☞ **Click on** OK

Merge to New Document

Merge records
⊙ All
○ Current record
○ From: ___ To: ___

OK   Cancel

The *Mail Merge* Task Pane closes. You now see the labels in a new *Word* document. You can still edit the text and formatting on the labels. For example, you can change the font, font size, and style (bold or italic). Or you can center the text on the label. Or you can insert an image into one or more labels. Then you can print the labels the same way you always print a document.

☞ Print the labels, if desired 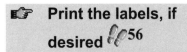**56**

You can save this document if you'd like to use it again later:

☞ Save the document, if desired **20**

If you include the label type number in the file name, it will be easier to select the associated label sheet later.

☞ Close the document

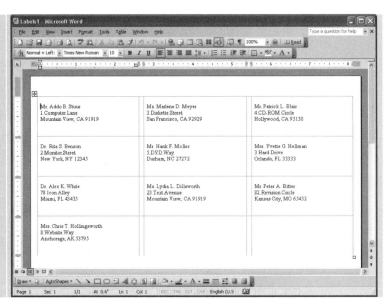

Now you see the merge document again. You can close it, too.

☞ Close the merge document and don't save the changes **14**

You can practice what you've learned in the following exercises.

💡 **Tip**

Inserting an Image
You can add an image by clicking on a label. That works the same way as inserting a picture in a regular *Word* document. You can shrink the image until it fits onto the label. Then select it and use copy and paste to quickly and easily add it to the other labels.

💡 **Tip**

Test Print
Print page 1 on regular paper first. You can use this test print to check whether the text will fit onto the label sheet properly. That will also show you right away how you should place your label sheets in the printer.

Exercises

Have you forgotten how to perform a particular action? Use the number beside the footsteps to look it up in the appendix *How Do I Do That Again?*

Exercise: Letter Wizard

In this exercise, you'll practice using the *Letter Wizard*.

☑ Start *Word 2003.* 🐾⁶

☑ Close the *Getting Started* Task Pane. 🐾⁶⁹

☑ Close the empty document (if any). 🐾¹⁴

☑ Start the *Letter Wizard.* 🐾⁶⁶

☑ Select *Send one letter.*

☑ On the *Recipient Info* tab, fill in the name and address of the recipient.

☑ Make it a certified letter on the *Other Elements* tab. 🐾⁶⁷

☑ Fill in your name and address and select a closing on the *Sender Info* tab.

☑ Complete the *Letter Wizard.* 🐾⁶⁸

☑ Close *Word 2003* without saving your changes. 🐾¹³

Tips

 Tip

Printing Envelopes

Keep a good eye on your printer when you print an envelope. The printer waits for you to manually insert the envelope.

That often means that a little light will blink, and the printer will wait until you give the command to print.

You do that by pressing a button on the printer.

☞ **Look in your printer's manual to see how to get the printer to print using manual paper feeding**

 Tip

Letter Formatting

You can have the *Letter Wizard* format letters in a particular style:

Include the date:

Select the template for the letter:

Specify how the text should be distributed over the page:

If you need to leave space for a preprinted letterhead:

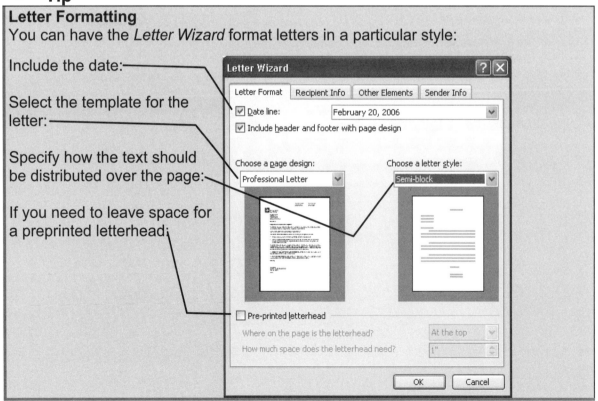

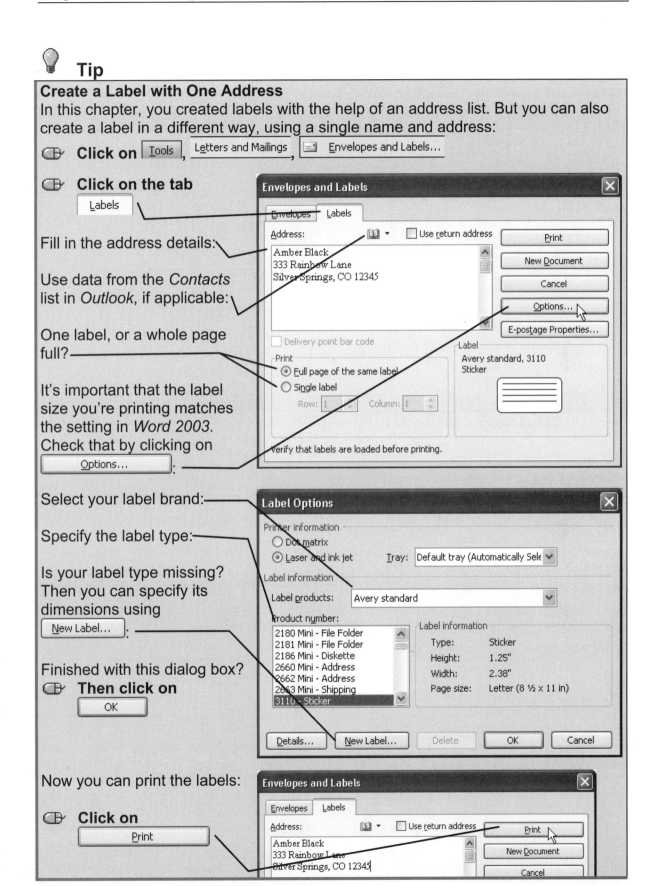

Tip

Create a Label with One Address

In this chapter, you created labels with the help of an address list. But you can also create a label in a different way, using a single name and address:

☞ **Click on** Tools , Letters and Mailings , Envelopes and Labels...

☞ **Click on the tab** Labels

Fill in the address details:

Use data from the *Contacts* list in *Outlook*, if applicable:

One label, or a whole page full?

It's important that the label size you're printing matches the setting in *Word 2003*. Check that by clicking on Options... :

Select your label brand:

Specify the label type:

Is your label type missing? Then you can specify its dimensions using New Label... :

Finished with this dialog box?

☞ **Then click on** OK

Now you can print the labels:

☞ **Click on** Print

Envelopes and Labels

Envelopes | Labels

Address: ☐ Use return address

Amber Black
333 Rainbow Lane
Silver Springs, CO 12345

☐ Delivery point bar code

Print
⦿ Full page of the same label
◯ Single label
Row: 1 Column: 1

Verify that labels are loaded before printing.

Print
New Document
Cancel
Options...
E-postage Properties...

Label
Avery standard, 3110
Sticker

Label Options

Printer information
◯ Dot matrix
⦿ Laser and ink jet   Tray: Default tray (Automatically Sele ▼

Label information
Label products: Avery standard ▼

Product number:
2180 Mini - File Folder
2181 Mini - File Folder
2186 Mini - Diskette
2660 Mini - Address
2662 Mini - Address
2663 Mini - Shipping
3110 - Sticker

Label information
Type: Sticker
Height: 1.25"
Width: 2.38"
Page size: Letter (8 ½ x 11 in)

Details... New Label... Delete OK Cancel

Envelopes and Labels

Envelopes | Labels

Address: ☐ Use return address

Amber Black
333 Rainbow Lane
Silver Springs, CO 12345

Print
New Document
Cancel

Tip

Here's another way to start the *Letter Wizard*:

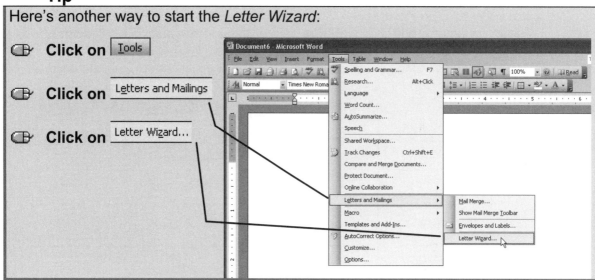

 Tip

Suitable Data Sources for the Mail Merge Wizard
The following data sources, among others, are suitable for use with the *Mail Merge Wizard*:
- an address list created in *Word* (in the form of a table, for example)
- an address list created in *Excel*
- the *Contacts* list in *Outlook*
- text files formatted a particular way (CSV files)

The Outlook Express Address Book
You can't directly use the *Outlook Express* address book in *Word*. You can, however, use the data in this address book by turning it into a text file formatted a certain way (a CSV file). You can find more information about this method in the PDF file **Address Book and Word** on the website for this book.

 Tip

If you use the program *Outlook* and you've saved addresses in the *Contacts* list, you can select the option ○ Select from Outlook contacts in step 3 in the *Mail Merge Wizard*. Then the *Contacts* list will be used as the data source for the merge.

💡 Tip

Specify the Dimensions of the Label Sheet Yourself

If your brand or type of label isn't in the list, you can specify the right dimensions yourself:

👈 **Click on** New Label...

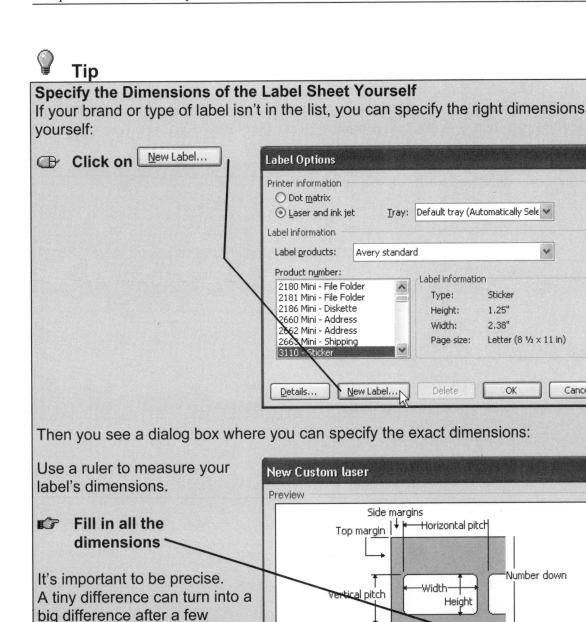

Then you see a dialog box where you can specify the exact dimensions:

Use a ruler to measure your label's dimensions.

👉 **Fill in all the dimensions**

It's important to be precise. A tiny difference can turn into a big difference after a few pages.

👉 **Give the label a name**

The label will now be displayed in the list. You can use it again in the future.

👈 **Click on** OK

Tip

Changing Data during the Mail Merge Process
You can still change information or delete people from your address file during the mail merge procedure. You can do that when you see the *Mail Merge Recipients* dialog box:

☞ **Click on** `Edit...`

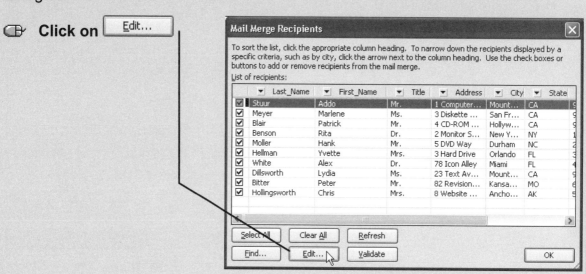

Now you see the *Data Form* dialog box, where you can alter or add data. You can also delete a person from the list, or add a new person:

You browse through the list by clicking on the buttons

Record: `|◄` `◄` 1 `►` `►|` :

You can add a person by clicking on `Add New`, or delete someone by clicking on `Delete`.

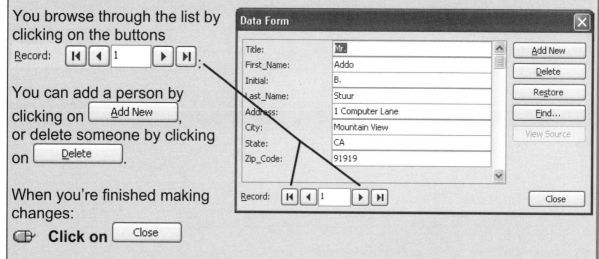

When you're finished making changes:

☞ **Click on** `Close`

If you've changed the data file, *Word* will ask you at some point if you want to save the changes.

Appendices

A. Downloading the Practice Files

This appendix describes step by step how you can download the practice files.

☞ **Start** 🅴 *Internet Explorer* 👣¹

Click in the box beside

Address

⌨ **Type:**
www.visualsteps.com/word2003

⌨ **Press** `Enter ←`

Now you see the website for this book:

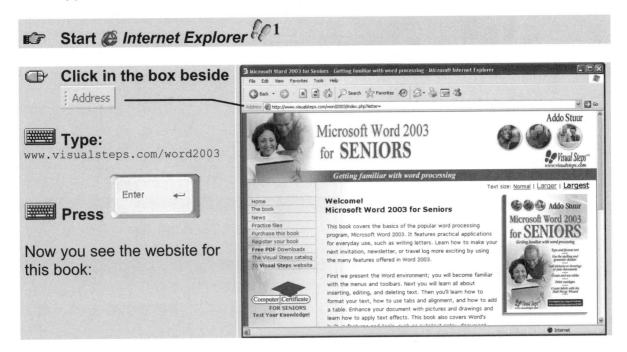

You can download the practice files from the page *Practice files*.

Click on Practice files

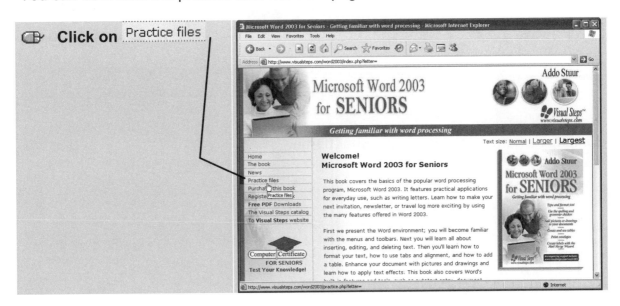

On the web page, you see a
list of several files:

☞ **Click with the right
mouse button on**
Ben Franklin.doc

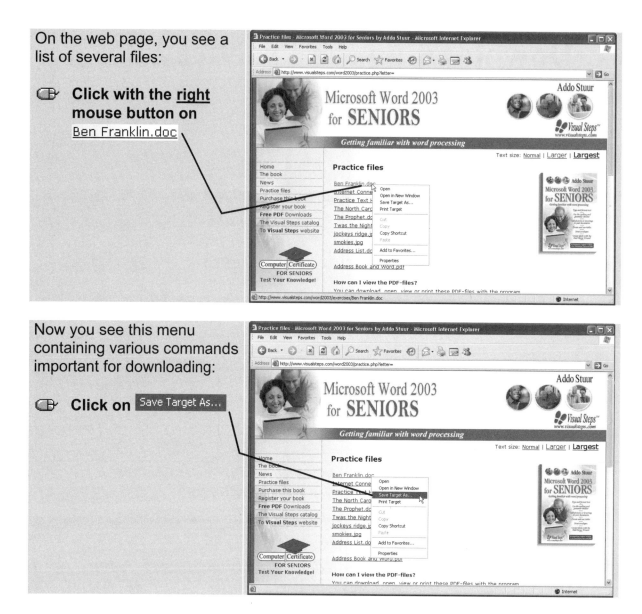

Now you see this menu
containing various commands
important for downloading:

☞ **Click on** Save Target As...

In the next window, you'll be asked **where** you want to save the file on your
computer's hard drive, and under **what name**.

You see the *Save As* dialog box:

Click on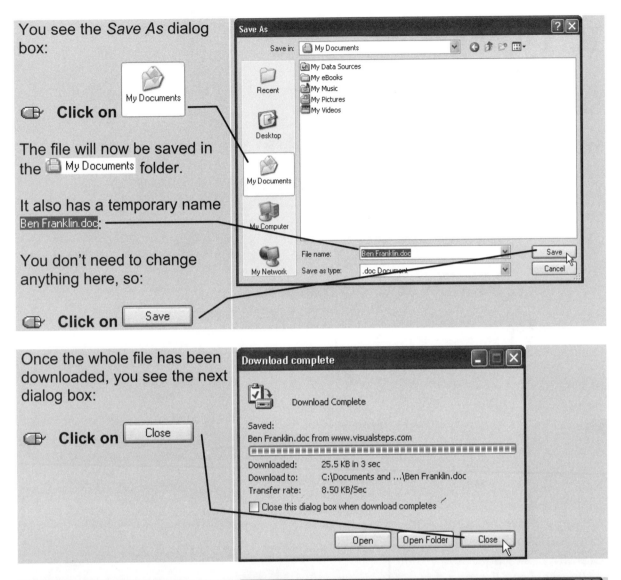

The file will now be saved in the 🗎 My Documents folder.

It also has a temporary name Ben Franklin.doc:

You don't need to change anything here, so:

Click on Save

Once the whole file has been downloaded, you see the next dialog box:

Click on Close

Now you see the *Practice Materials* page again:

Now you can download another file if you wish.

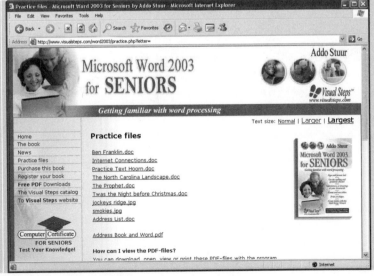

B. Typing Text

Starting Word 2003

You can start *Word 2003* using the *Start button*:

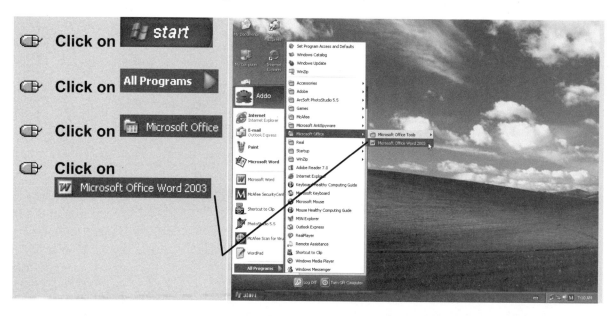

Now you see the *Word 2003* window with an empty document. On the right-hand side you see the *Getting Started* Task Pane. You won't need this Task Pane in this book.

☞ **Click on ⊠ to close the *Getting Started* Task Pane**

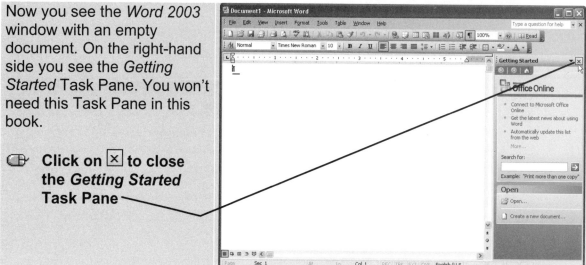

The Keyboard

A computer keyboard has over a hundred keys. That's many more than the old-fashioned typewriter had. If you look at the keyboard, you'll see all kinds of other keys in addition to the keys for the letters and numbers. You'll learn how to use several of these keys in this book.

The placement of the letters, numbers, and punctuation marks has remained exactly the same as on the typewriter:

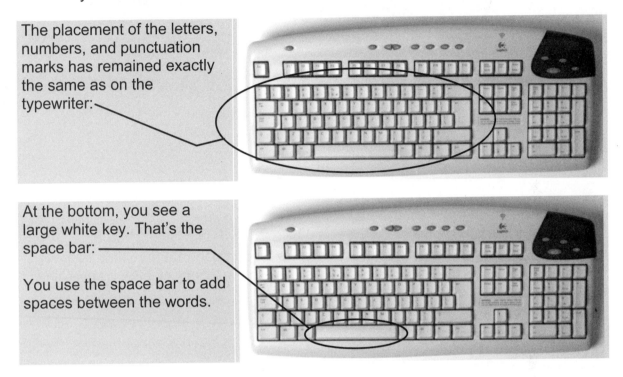

At the bottom, you see a large white key. That's the space bar:

You use the space bar to add spaces between the words.

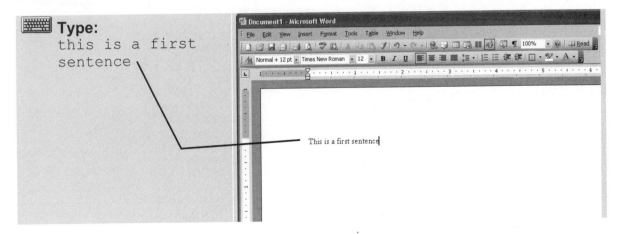

Now you can start typing. The letters appear at the location of the cursor.

Type:
this is a first sentence

This is a first sentence

Repeating Keys

Computer keys are repeating keys. That means that when you hold down a key, it automatically places multiple letters on the screen. Give it a try:

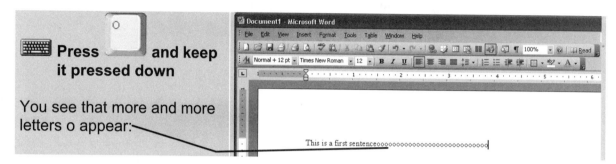

Press [o] and keep it pressed down

You see that more and more letters o appear:

Fortunately, you can easily remove those excess letters.

A Typo?

In this case, you typed the unnecessary letters o on purpose, but from time to time you'll press a wrong key by accident. You can delete the incorrect letter by pressing the Backspace key.

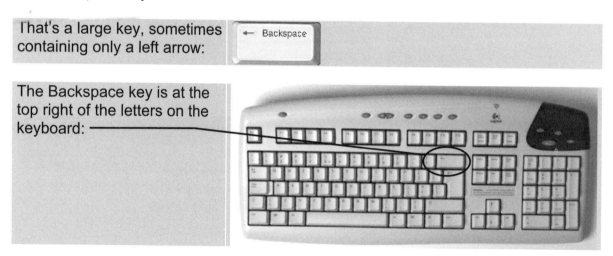

That's a large key, sometimes containing only a left arrow:

The Backspace key is at the top right of the letters on the keyboard:

The Backspace key erases characters to the left of the cursor. You can remove the excess letters o this way, for example.

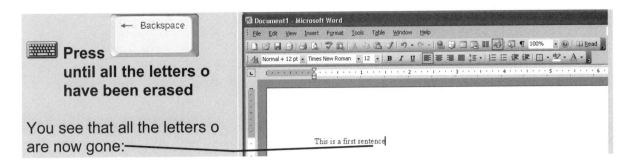

 Press until all the letters o have been erased

You see that all the letters o are now gone:

⇨ Please note:

The Backspace key is also a repeating key. Don't hold it down too long, or you'll have to type your text again.

Capital Letters

Up to this point, you've only typed lowercase letters. You can also type uppercase letters.

To do that, you use a large key with **Shift** written on it:

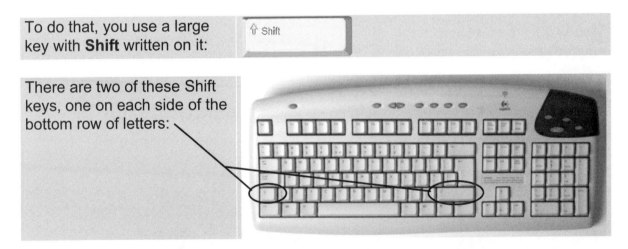

There are two of these Shift keys, one on each side of the bottom row of letters:

You always use the Shift key in combination with a letter, a number, or a punctuation mark.

- press the Shift key and keep it pressed down
- type the letter
- release the Shift key

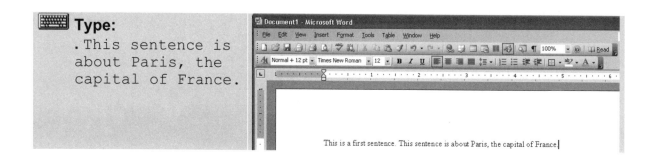

Type:
.This sentence is about Paris, the capital of France.

Words on the Next Line

Word processing programs automatically take care of the distribution of text over the page. If you type multiple sentences, the text will automatically continue on the next line. This is called text wrapping. Take a look:

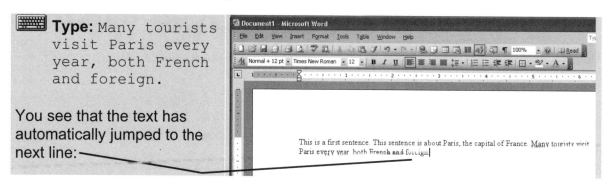

Type: Many tourists visit Paris every year, both French and foreign.

You see that the text has automatically jumped to the next line:

The computer always makes sure that long sentences fit nicely onto the paper. This happens automatically.

A New Line

If you want to start a new sentence at the left margin, you'll have to start a new line yourself.

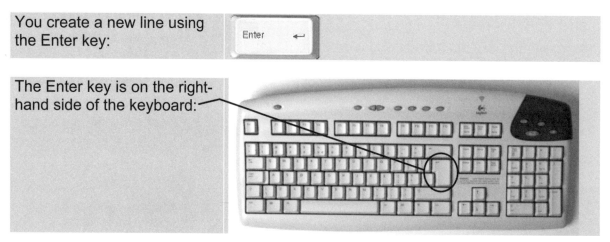

You create a new line using the Enter key:

The Enter key is on the right-hand side of the keyboard:

When you press the Enter key, the cursor (the blinking line) will move down one line.

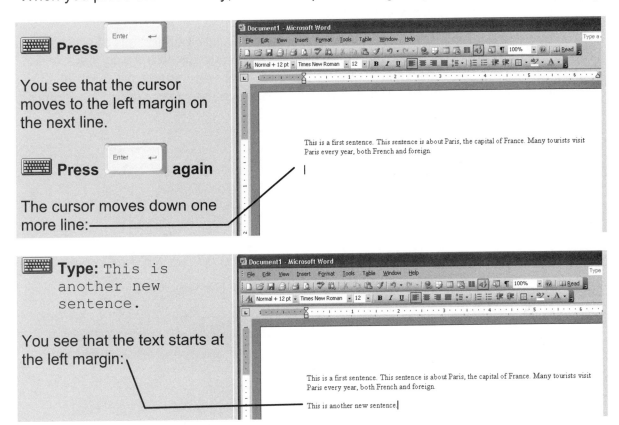

Press

You see that the cursor moves to the left margin on the next line.

Press **again**

The cursor moves down one more line:

Type: This is another new sentence.

You see that the text starts at the left margin:

Special Characters

You use the Shift key to type various other symbols or special characters too, such as these: : ? @ * % $ + | } < ! ~ & ^

Many of these symbols are shown at the top of a key:

You use the Shift key to type the top character on a key like this, just as for capital letters.

Type: ! ? : @ +

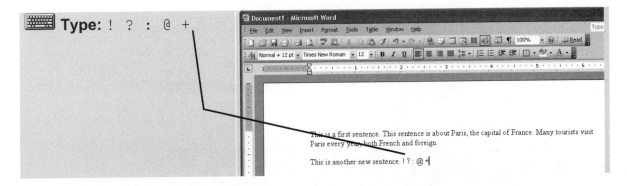

The Cursor Keys

Everyone makes a typo now and then. You may not realize it until later, after you have typed more text. To erase that mistake, you'd have to go all the way back to the beginning with the Backspace key. Of course, that's not convenient, because all the other letters will be erased too. It's a better idea to move the cursor to the location of the mistake.

You can move the cursor using the four special cursor keys. These are the keys with the arrows. They're grouped together:

Using these keys, you can move the cursor left, right, up, and down through the text.

The cursor is blinking after the +:

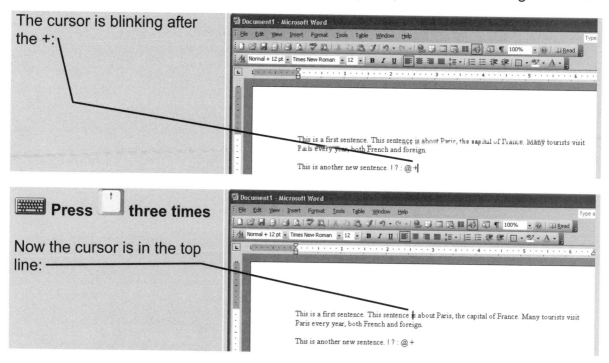

Press ↑ three times

Now the cursor is in the top line:

If you move left or right, the cursor will follow the text.

Press → until the cursor is in the second line

You see that the cursor moves to the right through the text and jumps to the next line automatically.

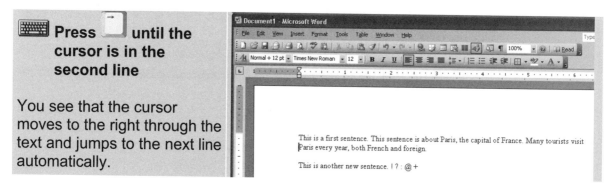

The Beginning and the End of the Text

You can use the cursor keys to move the cursor to any location in the text. You can't move the cursor over the entire piece of paper, however. There is a beginning and an end to the text. Give it a try:

Press ⬅ **and keep it pressed down until the cursor is in front of the top line**

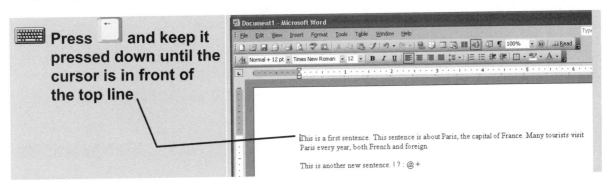

The cursor won't go any farther than the beginning of the text. On some computers, the program will even warn you about this with a sound.

Press ⬇ **and keep it pressed down until the cursor is on the bottom line**

The cursor won't go any farther.

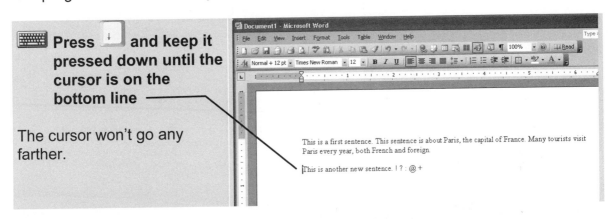

You can't move the cursor beyond the last letter or punctuation mark, either.

Press ➡ **and keep it pressed down until the cursor is after the last symbol**

Again, the cursor won't go any farther.

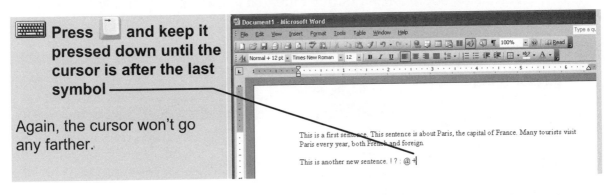

You can not move the cursor beyond the last place of insertion. This could be text, spaces, shift-enters or full enters. You can, of course, enter new text there.

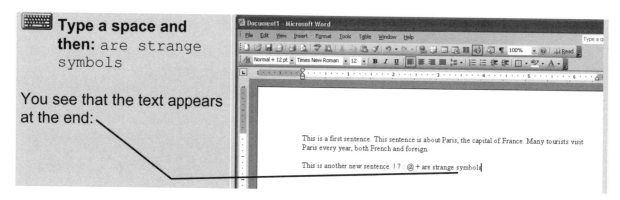

Type a space and then: `are strange symbols`

You see that the text appears at the end:

And of course you can also add empty lines to the text. The end of the text then falls on the last (blank) line.

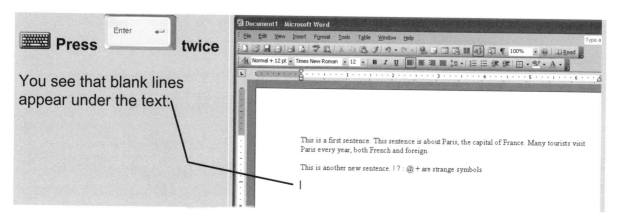

Press `Enter ←` **twice**

You see that blank lines appear under the text:

You now know how to move the cursor through the text. This will come in handy when you need to correct mistakes or change the text.

Correcting Mistakes

You can move the cursor to the left through the text to the place where you want to make your changes. For example:

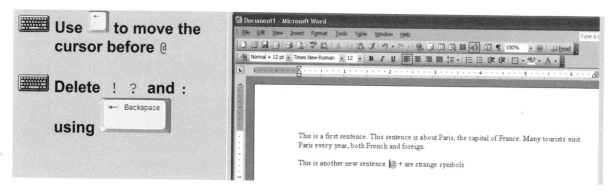

Use ⬆ **to move the cursor before** @

Delete `!` `?` **and** `:` **using** `← Backspace`

You can also replace a word with a different word now.

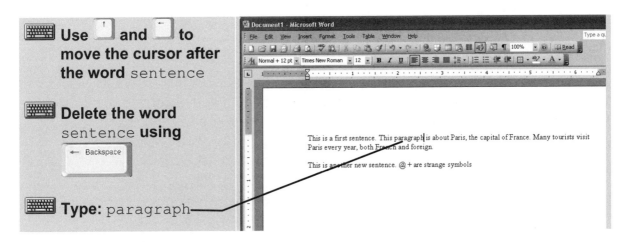

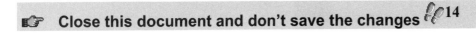

You don't have to save the practice text; you can just close the window containing the text now.

☞ **Close this document and don't save the changes** 🐾14

Now you can quit *Word 2003*.

☞ **Close *Word 2003*** 🐾13

C. Keyboard Settings

In order to type international characters such as umlauts and accents, your keyboard needs to use the right settings. You can specify these in the *Control Panel*.

You set up a QWERTY keyboard like this:

⊕ **Click on** start

⊕ **Click on** Control Panel

⊕ **Click on**
Date, Time, Language, and Regional Options

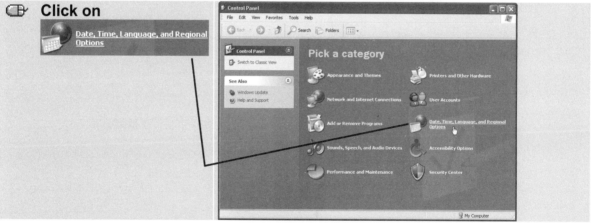

⊕ **Click on**
Regional and Language Options

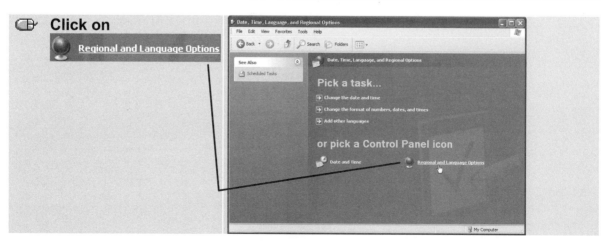

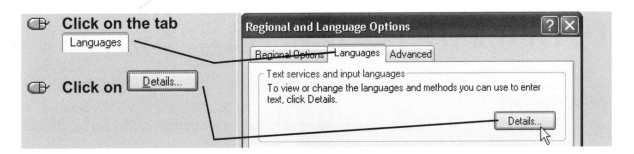

Now you can see various language settings in the *Text Services and Input Languages* dialog box.

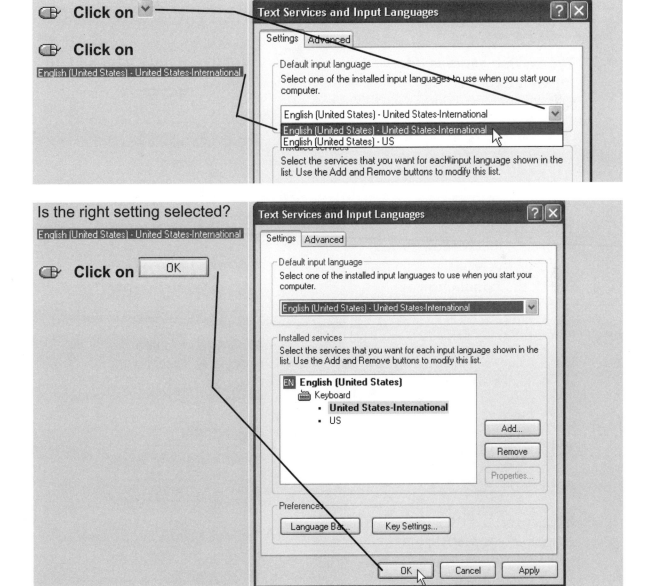

Now you can type umlauts, accents, and other special characters as described in this book.

D. How Do I Do That Again?

In this book, many tasks and exercises are followed by footsteps: 👣ˣ You can use the number beside the footsteps to look up how to do these things in this appendix.

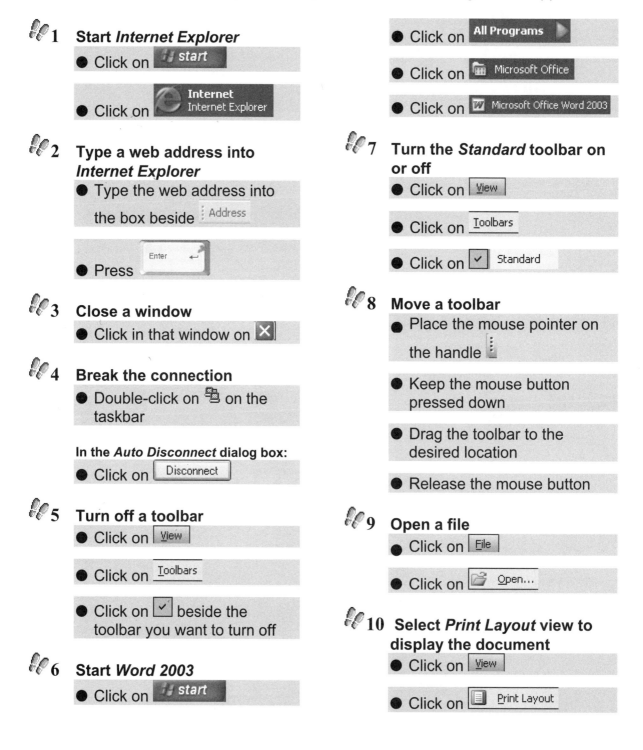

1   Start *Internet Explorer*
- Click on `start`
- Click on `Internet Internet Explorer`

2   Type a web address into *Internet Explorer*
- Type the web address into the box beside `Address`
- Press `Enter`

3   Close a window
- Click in that window on `X`

4   Break the connection
- Double-click on 🖳 on the taskbar

In the *Auto Disconnect* dialog box:
- Click on `Disconnect`

5   Turn off a toolbar
- Click on `View`
- Click on `Toolbars`
- Click on `✔` beside the toolbar you want to turn off

6   Start *Word 2003*
- Click on `start`

- Click on `All Programs`
- Click on `Microsoft Office`
- Click on `Microsoft Office Word 2003`

7   Turn the *Standard* toolbar on or off
- Click on `View`
- Click on `Toolbars`
- Click on `✔ Standard`

8   Move a toolbar
- Place the mouse pointer on the handle `⋮`
- Keep the mouse button pressed down
- Drag the toolbar to the desired location
- Release the mouse button

9   Open a file
- Click on `File`
- Click on `Open...`

10   Select *Print Layout* view to display the document
- Click on `View`
- Click on `Print Layout`

11 Hide or display hidden formatting marks
- Click on `Tools`, `Options...`
- Click on the tab `View`
- Click on `☐ All`, `OK`

12 Select *Normal* view to display the document
- Click on `View`
- Click on `☰ Normal`

13 Close *Word 2003*
- Click on `File`
- Click on `Exit`

  Question: Save Changes?
- Click on `No`

14 Close a document and <u>don't</u> save the changes
- Click on `File`
- Click on `Close`
- Click on `No`

15 Insert a symbol
- Click on `Insert`
- Click on `Symbol...`
- Click on the symbol you want to insert
- Click on `Insert`

16 Start *Manual Hyphenation*
- Click on `Tools`

- Click on `Language`
- Click on `Hyphenation...`
- Click on `Manual...`

17 Insert a hyphen
- Click on `Yes` in the *Manual Hyphenation* dialog box

18 Don't insert a hyphen
- Click on `No` in the *Manual Hyphenation* dialog box

19 Stop hyphenating
- Click on `Cancel` in the *Manual Hyphenation* dialog box

20 Save a new file in the *My Documents* folder
- Click on `File`
- Click on `💾 Save`
- Next to `File name:`, type the name for your file:
  File name: `Test`
- Next to `Save in:`, select the 📁 *My Documents* folder:
  Save in: `📖 My Documents`
- Click on `Save`

21 Change the font
- Select the text
- Click on `▾` beside
  `Times New Roman` `▾`
- Click on the font

22 Change the font size
- Select the text
- Click on ▾ beside 10 ▾
- Click on the desired size

23 Make text *bold*
- Select the text
- Click on **B**

24 Make text *italic*
- Select the text
- Click on *I*

25 *Underline* text
- Select the text
- Click on U

26 Select lines
- Place the mouse pointer in the left margin in front of the first line
- Press the mouse button
- Drag the mouse pointer down until all the lines have been selected

27 Center a paragraph
- Select the paragraph(s)
- Click on ▤

28 Right align a paragraph
- Select the paragraph(s)
- Click on ▤

29 Move around in a document
- Click on ⌃ or ⌄ on the scrollbar

30 Add a page break
- Place the cursor at the start of the paragraph
- Click on Insert
- Click on Break...
- Click to add a green dot beside ⊙ Page break
- Click on OK

31 Hide or display *Text boundaries*
- Click on Tools
- Click on Options...
- Click on the tab View
- Click to place or remove a check mark beside ☐ Text boundaries
- Click on OK

32 Change margins
- Click on File
- Click on Page Setup...
- Click on the tab Margins
- Click on ⬍ until the desired margin is reached
- Click on OK

33 Remove a page break
- Select *Normal* view to display the document
- Place the cursor on the *Page Break* line
- Press [Delete]

34 Add a header
- Click on [View]
- Click on [Header and Footer]
- Type the text to use there
- Click on [Close]

35 Add a footer
- Click on [View]
- Click on [Header and Footer]
- Click on [icon]
- Type the text to use there
- Click on [Close]

36 Magnify or shrink a picture
- Click on the picture
- Place the mouse pointer on a corner handle
- Keep the mouse button pressed down and drag up or down
- Release the mouse button

37 Insert a photo
- Click in the text at the place where the photo should go
- Click on [Insert]
- Click on [Picture]
- Click on [From File...]
- Click on the photo file
- Click on [Insert]

38 Display the *Picture* toolbar
- Click on the photo
- Click on [View]
- Click on [Toolbars]
- Click on [Picture]

39 Make text wrap square around a picture
- Double-click on the photo or picture
- Click on the tab [Layout]
- Click on [Square]
- Click on [OK]

40 Move an image
- Click on the image
- Place the mouse pointer on the picture and press the mouse button

- Drag the figure to the desired location and release the mouse button

41 Make text flow down the right side only
- Double-click on the photo or picture

- Click on the tab | Layout |

- Click on | Advanced... |

- Click on the tab | Text Wrapping |

- Click on ○ Right only

- Click on | OK |

- Click on | OK |

42 Return an image to its original size
- Double-click on the image

- Click on | Size |

- Click on | Reset |

- Click on | OK |

43 Crop an image
- Click on the picture

- Click on [⌗] on the toolbar

- Place the mouse pointer on one of the handles

- Press the mouse button and drag the handle

- Release the mouse button

44 Change the brightness
- Click on the photo

- Click on [⊡↑] or [⊡↓] a few times

45 Change the contrast
- Click on the photo

- Click on [◑↑] or [◐↓] a few times

46 Make a photo black and white
- Click on the photo

- Click on [▥]

- Click on Grayscale

47 Turn a photo into a watermark
- Click on the photo

- Click on [▥]

- Click on Washout

48 Delete an image
- Click on the image

- Press [Delete]

49 Insert Clip Art
- Click on | Insert |

- Click on Picture

- Click on [🖼] Clip Art...

- Choose a category if desired

- Click on a clip art

- Click on [×]

50 Have text wrap tightly around an image
- Double-click on the image
- Click on the tab Layout
- Click on Tight
- Click on OK

51 Move the cursor into a paragraph
- Click in the paragraph or move the cursor using the cursor keys

52 Deselect text
- Click somewhere outside the selected text

53 Begin a new, blank document
- Click on File
- Click on New...
- Click on Blank document

54 Save changes to a document
- Click on File
- Click on Save

55 Adjust tab stops
- Select the whole document
- Drag the tab stops ⌐ on the ruler to the right place:

56 Print a text
- Click on File
- Click on Print...

57 Select a row
- Click on Table
- Click on Select
- Click on Row

58 Create a table
- Click on ▦
- Click on one of the cells in the little window that appears

59 Add text to a table
- Click in one of the cells
- Type in the text
- Press Tab to go to the next cell

60 Add a row to a table
- Click on Table
- Click on Insert
- Click on Rows Above or Rows Below

61 Display the *Tables and Borders* dialog box
- Click on ▧ on the toolbar

62 Have *Word 2003* calculate the total
- Place the cursor in an empty cell, beside or under the cells containing the numbers to be added
- Click on Σ in the *Tables and Borders* dialog box

63 Delete a row
- Select the row
- Click on `Table`
- Click on `Delete`
- Click on `Rows`

64 Minimize a window
- Click in that window on `▬`

65 Maximize a window
- Click in that window on `▢`

66 Start the *Letter Wizard*
- Click on `File`
- Click on `New...`
- Click on `On my computer...`
- Click on the tab `Letters & Faxes`
- Click on `Letter Wizard`
- Click on `OK`

67 Make a letter certified mail
- Click to add a check mark beside `☐ Mailing instructions:` in the third window of the *Letter Wizard*

- Select `CERTIFIED MAIL`
- Click on `Next>`

68 Complete the *Letter Wizard*
- Click on `Finish` in the final window of the *Letter Wizard*

69 Close the *Getting Started* Task Pane
- Click on `✕`

70 Select a whole table
- Click in the table
- Click on `Table`
- Click on `Select`
- Click on `Table`

71 Close the *Tables and Borders* dialog box
- Click on `✕`

72 Open *Outlook Express*
- Click on `start`
- Click on `E-mail Outlook Express`

73 Use *Landscape* page orientation
- Click on `File`
- Click on `Page Setup...`
- Click on the tab `Margins`
- Click on `Landscape`
- Click on `OK`

E. Index